Mary O'Brien
Women's Research and Resource Centre
Ontario Institute for Studies in Education

The politics of reproduction

D1124856

Routledge & Kegan Paul
Boston, London and Henley

First published in 1981
by Routledge & Kegan Paul Ltd
39 Store Street, London WC1E 7DD,
9 Park Street, Boston, Mass. 02108, USA and
Broadway House, Newtown Road,
Henley-on-Thames, Oxon RG9 1EN

First published as a paperback 1983
Reprinted 1983
Printed in the United States of America

British Library Cataloguing in Publication Data

O'Brien, Mary
The politics of reproduction.
1. Women — Political aspects
2. Political science
I. Title
320'.01'1   JAY1

ISBN 0 7100 9498 1

The politics of reproduction

To my aunts – Bertie, Eleanor, May –
who taught me that women are strong

Contents

Acknowledgments

The possibility of this book emerged at its most fundamental level from feminist political practice, and my debts to hundreds of women are incalculable. Most directly, Cath McNaughton is number one midwife to the ideas expressed here, and has nurtured both them and me with patience, generosity and lived sisterhood. To Frieda Forman, who unifies theory and practice with vision, energy and endless grace, I owe not only criticism and ideas, but the great satisfaction of feminist working relations. To all the women struggling to found the Feminist Party of Canada I owe the crucial experience of realized feminist politics and the excitements of making history hour by hour.

My second debt is to students, at York University and most particularly in Atkinson College, where I was fortunate enough to be able to try out the analysis of reproduction presented here on bright and caring minds quite a few years ago. I also want to thank students in Integrated Studies at the University of Waterloo and, currently, in the Department of Sociology in Education at the Ontario Institute for Studies in Education. To OISE, too, I owe the rare blessing of a feminist working environment, and the stimulation of having departmental colleagues like Margrit Eichler and Dorothy Smith, whose work is exciting, ovarian feminist scholarship. I also owe much to male colleagues who transcend stereotypes in a respect and support for feminist studies which is as genuine as it is rare.

For those who taught me and were prepared to walk out on some quite fragile limbs for a doctoral dissertation which was hardly conventional I have lasting regard. My debts to Christian Lenhardt, a scholar and a gentleman who guided me through the pitfalls of nineteenth-century political theory and brought Marx and Hegel into my life, my thanks. To Virginia Macdonald, Hector Massey, David Bell, Milly Bakan, Ross Rudolph, all of York University, I owe much, as I do to Professor Lorenne Clark of the University of Toronto and Professor Elizabeth Douvan of the University of Michigan.

To Dale Spender in London, who edits the *International Women's Studies Quarterly* in a way which combines a care for the integrity of feminist scholarship with a passionate concern for women's lives, and to Philippa Brewster, my thanks.

And of course, like so many of the things which happen in the world, there would be nothing at all were it not for members of that huge, unsung regiment of women who type. When shall we acknowledge that secretaries make everything that works, work? When, do you suppose, we shall start paying them with something other than polite thanks? To Carole Trussler and Marie Scott, who can face my messy manuscripts without flinching, I offer deep respect and thanks.

Introduction

This book is about theory, but it is not a book intended only for theorists. It is about and for women. I acknowledge at once that this creates difficulties. Theory is an off-putting kind of word, for a number of people. Any university teacher will admit that to put the word theory in a course title is automatically to ensure a small enrolment in the course. What then happens is that theory appears in disguise, for the truth is that the acquisition of any body of systematic knowledge depends on the espoused conceptions of theory and method. This is widely regarded as a drag, and the inseparability of theory and method itself is not at all well understood. In the 1960s, the great decade of relevance, much theoretical activity was labelled irrelevant, and, indeed, many of the arid academic fantasies which claimed the title of theory were irrelevant.

Theory can be and often is perceived as a playing about with a bunch of abstractions which have no relation to the lives we lead and are no help in realizing the things which are dear to our hearts. In political theory, which is the sort of theory with which I am mainly concerned here, we have, as an example, dozens of theories on the nature and desirability of human freedom. We do not, however, actually have human freedom, and we are not even very sure what freedom is or ought to be like. So what is the use of theories of freedom which, over many centuries, have had no discernible impact on the creation of freedom? Better, perhaps – and this is a notion which appeals especially to women, for whom freedom, if it exists at all, appears to be a male prerogative – better, perhaps, to work for freedom than to waste time thinking about it. Or, maybe more sensibly, let's acknowledge that there is no such thing and make the best of what we have.

It is not, though, only the perceptions of university students and impatient activitists, nor the failures of theorizing in the past, which have made theory unpopular. We live in the Scientific Age, and scientific theory is, on the surface, different from what we might call traditional theory. Scientific theory is a way of organizing what actually is in such a manner that we can not only understand it better, but can apply this understanding in practical ways: we can predict, for example, what will actually happen if a certain series of events occur. This can be quite simple or enormously sophisticated. We can predict that if water is heated to a certain temperature it will begin to bubble, and we don't have to stop and think that the *idea* of temperature is a theoretical notion. This is obviously different in degree from predicting that a great parcel of electronic hardware shot off from the mainland of the United States of America will start orbiting around Mars at a particular time. Yet in both cases a theoretical perception and organization of physical events make these outcomes possible.

The success story of science in the modern era has been important in forming our idea of what theory is and ought to be. Scientific values, often lurking as objective facts, passed into the social sciences as they developed in the nineteenth century, and there was great optimism that social science would be able to do for the social world what natural science had done for the physical world. We should surely be able to gain enough understanding of how the social world worked to be able to predict how events would turn out under clearly defined sets of circumstances, just as we had done in the case of the natural world. This early optimism has abated a little, but it is not the question of positivism versus speculation which is our main concern here. What is of concern to us is the fate of traditional theorizing under the onslaught of triumphant scientism. For traditional theory took quite a shellacking. It was argued that theory of this kind did not relate to anything real, but was largely high-class daydreaming with little or no practical application. It was argued that science is objective and describes what is, whereas traditional theory is subjective and describes what ought to be, and why should any one person's theory of what ought to be be any better than any other person's? Theory is not only inexact, but elitist, favouring intellectualism over common sense.

These considerations are of interest here only in so far as they contribute to the low status of theorizing in our own times. People have in fact never stopped theorizing, and a lot of critical theorizing is now done about some of the more vulgar assumptions about scientific thought which I have just summarized. None the less, the aversion to theory is, from the perspective which I want to develop here, an important social reality. This is because of its significance in relation to contemporary feminism. Women have fought and clawed their way into the citadels of male intellectualism, only to find that the cupboards in the ivory towers are on the bare side. Tolerated in token numbers in the world of the disciplined mind, women have been told that there are 2,000 years or so of intellectual history which men have created and are now prepared to let women share, thoughtfully saving us the bother of doing it all over again. Included in this package is the contemporary view of the poverty of traditional thought. True, there are pockets of this world which retain commitments to theorizing on a somewhat grander scale; Marxism is one and existentialism another. However, and in North America particularly, social science has largely decided that what counts is what can be counted, preferably by a computer, and women may, in decently limited numbers, join in the great descriptive exercise of totting up the sum of human experience and activity and running it through computers.

The trouble is, none of this tells us women much about ourselves. Over and over again, we can describe and quantify the effects, institutions and excesses of male supremacy. We cannot say why it exists, and, more importantly, we have made little progress in changing it. It is not enough to shrug off the why question as irrelevant. I want to argue that we never will liberate ourselves as women until we develop a systematic theoretical analysis of the roots and grounds and development of male history and male philosophy. For theory is not entirely abstract; it is not the absurdity of attempting to give phoney substance to a nothing excised from a nothing. Nor is it only poetic vision. Theory at its best is fundamentally a mode of analysing human experience which is at the same time a method of organizing that experience. Yet this has clearly been *male* experience. So we must ask: What is it about male experience which has engaged the masculine mind in the business of theorizing? Why have women not done so, and why should we get into this esoteric business in any case? If the answer to these questions lies in prehistory, we do not shrug and give up the question. We investigate the evidence we have, imperfect though it may be. I hope to demonstrate that there is important evidence to be found, for example, in the work of the philosophical interpreters of the Greek polis.

This procedure needs to be defended only because of the climate created by vulgar scientism and capitalism's resistance to the revolutionary implications of dialectical analysis. It was Lenin who converted Karl Marx's important notion of praxis into a slogan – no practice without theory. Neither Lenin nor Marx was the first to understand that social change can only be brought about by unifying knowing and doing, thinking and acting, the unity which the word 'praxis' attempts to catch and hold. Plato and Aristotle and the whole line of political thinkers have understood the relation of praxis and social change in varying degrees and in brilliantly diverse ways. One thing, however, which is a constant in all this huge body of intellectual effort, is of prime interest to us here. Social thought, social action and political change are the prerogatives of the male of the species. Politics is a man's world.

In fact, the need to develop a theoretical basis for a feminism which can transform the world is an increasingly recognized need in the women's movement. The difficulty is knowing where to start. We cannot philosophize out of thin air, without becoming the merely normative speculators which theorists are so often accused of being. Somehow, the tradition of intellectual activity which history lays on us must be dealt with. It must also be transcended, a transcendence for which a feminine standpoint is a necessary but not a sufficient condition. One way of starting is, of course, an examination of the way men have gone about the business of unifying their historical activities with the actions which have, in a concrete sense, 'made history'. Feminist praxis has as its aim the making of a future, which is the making of a history. The way in which men have done this would be of little interest if it were disconnected, bizarre, contingent and quite irrational. It is none of these things. At its best, it has unified the thinker with the problems of his times, and the fact that his interpretation of these problems may be prejudiced by ideological presuppositions does not mean that they are therefore to be dismissed. Theorists, like all of us, come from somewhere, and where they come from is a significant factor in their theorizing, even where the theory claims to be metaphysical or universal, either above and beyond the mundane realities of lived lives, or common to all lives. The shortcut way to say this is to say that theory is culturally determined. Neat though this is, it begs the larger questions of what culture is, and how the relations between person and culture work. Traditional theory may not have provided satisfactory answers to these questions, but it did not sweep them under the rug, either. The relation of the individual to cultures and to collectivities has always been a central concern of political theory. It is now a central concern of women, but women find this problem even more complex, because the culture which must provide us with the experiences, the questions and the theories and methods which we use as tools of understanding is a male dominant culture. What women need to do, to put it in the simplest way, is to be able to demonstrate that male dominant culture and the male-stream thought which buttresses and justifies it are both, in some sense, prejudiced by the very fact that they are masculine.

One way of doing this, or at least of starting to do it, is to consider male philosophy as an ideology of male supremacy. This is not simply pejorative. I use ideology as a concept, a tool for comprehending certain aspects of theorizing as an activity. One aspect is clearly the specific historical and social situation of the theorists. Perhaps more important than this, however, is the aspect concerning the nature of thought itself. The difficult question of whether thoughts are 'real' is an old one. What is at stake, and what is so confusing, is the difficulty of being certain as to how thought about anything is related to what is being thought about. The most complex case is maybe that of thought which thinks about thought, which was Socrates' notion of what philosophy was about. On a more concrete level, we have to recognize that thought, however imaginative and speculative, is somehow related to what is thought about, but also in some sense separated from what is thought about. It is this separation which is the key to understanding what is meant here by ideological thought. Thought need not represent what is thought about in a totally accurate reflection. The mind is not a make-up mirror. As in all reflections, physical as well as mental, there exists the possibility of distortion as well as the possibility of new and creative perception. The ideological aspect of thought is that aspect in which distortion can occur. It should be stressed that this need not be a wilful or deliberate distortion. In the process of separating itself from what is thought about, thought frees itself, as it were, from the fetters of brute fact. This process may enhance the objects of thought, bringing out the shades and nuances of the less obvious properties of such objects. In this sense, it can be a constructive and creative activity. Yet the separation is illusory, in that the thinker cannot separate herself from her lived situation, and reality disturbs the purity of the relation of mind to the object of thought. Again, this may be a process which is not wholly conscious or deliberate. We can say that ideological thought is the presentation of error in a sincere and convincing way, an error which emerges from the particular position in time and space of the thinker and of the structure of thought itself. The presentation is sincere and convincing because it is 'real': that is to say, the distortions are not dreamt up, but emerge from the situation and intention of the theorist, situations shared by those who have received this work most sympathetically. The distortions represent something real in the place where the thinker is coming from. Rousseau, to take a well known example, visualizes the polity in terms of the city-state of Geneva, where he was born, and thus proclaims as general realities certain limited assumptions about political process which cannot be realistically extended from Geneva to France.

When I say, then, that male-stream thought is ideological thought, what I am saying is that it misrepresents one level of reality in the need to give expression to another level of reality. Whatever men are looking at, and whatever else they may be, they are male. The taken-for-granted reality, which we are interested in here because we must examine it critically, is the perceived reality of being male. If we know how the process of ideological thought has worked with men's efforts to give expression to masculine experience, we are in a better position to subject male-stream thought to a critical analysis: What exactly is it about masculine experience that colours conceptions of reality? We are also in a better position to understand how we might go about developing feminist theory, and to explore the reality of being female. It is the first of these considerations which have led me to write this book, and it is the second which I hope to be able to carry forward into some clearer notion of what a feminist theory would be like.

These considerations grow out of where I come from, and what I have been talking about so far is my experience as a student of political theory. The female student of this tradition has to come to terms with the fact that this huge and impressive human achievement mixes its wisdom with male-supremacist assumption, that it takes for granted certain propositions 'about the relationship of men and women, and that it does this consistently. Political theory justifies male supremacy: the problem is to winkle out those aspects which may be called ideological in the sense which I have described, and to enquire into those realities of masculine experience which have been represented in a way which not only distorts and reinterprets reality, but which, on occasion, turns reality completely upside down.

However, the study of political theory is not the only experience which has convinced me of the need for strenuous theoretical efforts on the part of feminists. A second important factor is the experience within the women's movement. In the west, the excitements and enthusiasms of the earlier days of the movement are settling down into more sombre appraisals, or heating up into factional and disruptive argumentation. Recent economic dislocation has exposed the fragility of women's hard-won gains, and it has seemed to some serious observers that International Women's Year (1975) might have marked the end of yet another public outcry around 'the woman question', now ready to creep back into its million kitchens grey. This, I believe, is far too pessimistic a view. What I want to argue is that the movement is alive and well, but a little uncertain and indeterminate as to the direction now to be travelled and the strategies to be employed. I want further to argue that one important reason for this hiatus is our failure to develop a theoretical component for a feminist praxis, a unity of our thinking about what we must do with our methods of doing it. At the same time, I want to transcend the limitations of Marxist preoccupation with class struggle as the only operative field of praxis. Not, of course, that I deny the reality of class struggle, but it is quite clear that Marxist notions, or pseudo-Marxist notions, have proved divisive in the feminist movement. The battle as to whether sex struggle is a part of or separate from class struggle is a continuing motif of feminist deliberation. It is easy to answer that it is both, but more difficult to demonstrate how and why it can be part of but separate from the historical movement of class struggle. What I try to do in this book is provide a theoretical framework in which this kind of assertion can be made in a cogent way.

The other great source of factionalism in the women's movement relates to the vexed question of sexuality, and the opposition of oppressive heterosexuality to an idyllic dream of Lesbian women excising personal power relations from a swinish world. I believe that the confusion of sexual freedom with freedom in general has not only damaged the solidarity of women, but is based on an inadequate conceptualization of the nature of sexuality. Having said this, I can no longer withhold the information that this book is really about motherhood: despised, derided and neglected motherhood. To the question: Where does feminist theory start? I answer: Within the process of human reproduction. Of that process, sexuality is but a part. I intend to argue that it is not within sexual relations but within *the total process of human reproduction* that the ideology of male supremacy finds its roots and its rationales. More controversially, I argue that it is from an adequate understanding of the process of reproduction, nature's traditional and bitter trap for the suppression of women, that women can begin to understand their possibilities and their freedom.

This argument, too, derives from my own experience, but not, paradoxically, from the experience of motherhood, for I have no children. It is not, perhaps, common or even thought to be proper to inject these kind of subjective considerations into treatises on political theory, but women must begin making their own rules of rational discourse, and I happen to think this is important. Long before I decided to become a student of political philosophy at the advanced age of forty-one, I had spent my working life in hospital nursing, and a great deal of my personal life in grassroots political activity. Both of these experiences contributed to my decision to study political theory. Let me speak first of political practice, which is perhaps not quite so significant in the present context as my experience as a practising midwife.

I spent my childhood in Glasgow, Scotland, during the severe economic depression of the 1930s. This is clearly not enough to make one a socialist, for the phenomenon of the working-class Tory is a persistent feature of British politics. However, I came across the Fabian Society and its works at quite an early age, and was an uncritical fan of Beatrice Webb. This is a bit ironic, given Webb's impatience with the woman's movement and outright contempt for the suffragettes who were her contemporaries. However, democratic socialism was, for me, an attractive political position, and I joined the Labour Party in my teens and worked very hard for its fortunes in the decade immediately following the Second World War. Like many of my generation of starry-eyed idealists, I was shattered by the events of 1956, the year of Suez and the Soviet invasion of Hungary. It seemed to many of us that the promise of a rational and equitable society brought about by commitment and the hard work of ordinary people had collapsed in a real maelstrom, generated by the evidently essential violence embedded in the exercise of political power. The major political systems of the world had seen themselves threatened, and responded in the only way which they seemed to understand: the exercise of military might. Britain, France and the USSR stood in the nakedness of their imperialist skins on the banks of the Nile and the Danube, while Americans leapt to protect their capitalist investments in a sickening show of phoney 'democratic' concern. Suez and Hungary were devastating to humanist illusion, and these plagues on both houses took me out of the political process for years. None the less, I could hardly help being aware of my own naiveté, and the fact that I really had only the haziest of notions as to why these things happened. When feminism rekindled my interest in politics, it was a very cynical interest which I brought to yet another notion of liberation. I was acutely aware of the fact that this cause, too, might be brittle and ephemeral unless one was able to bring to the struggle some systematic knowledge, not only of the practical content of these aspirations, but of the form of political process. In other words, I needed theoretical understanding. As I have already indicated, I could not find it in the theoretical tradition, but I did find that this tradition was an obscurely promising place to start.

The fact that I was a practising midwife in the industrial maze of Clydeside society was much more significant, for this experience was the root of a profound scepticism which I have brought to bear on the radical polemics of such liberationists as Shulamith Firestone, who believes childbirth to be barbaric, or of such female male-supremacists as Hannah Arendt, who perceives childbirth as animal. To be sure, childbirth is hard and often painful labour, a strenuous task peculiarly unsuited to being performed under a halo, but, equally clearly, it is a social and cultural affair. It is true that the conditions surrounding childbirth may indeed be barbaric. On Clydeside in the 1950s it was not at all uncommon to find poor housing, overcrowding, husbands weakened by industrial disease or drunkeness, and mothers whose own infancy in the Great Depression, with its legacy of malnutrition, had left them with a bone structure very different to that designed by nature to facilitate the passage of the newborn child. Despite such conditions, childbirth was not privative. It was something of a celebration among neighbour women and the two grandmothers, priestesses of custom who dispensed superstition, wisdom, strong tea and sisterhood with impressive impartiality. Childbirth was essentially a social, indeed a public affair, a celebration and a rite. This sociability has largely been lost, and was perhaps never as strong in North America as it was in Europe.

Midwifery as an art is disappearing, though many feminists see a need to revive it, a view which I share. Childbirth in the circumstances under which I practised midwifery was still a celebration of femininity. One of the current problems of the affirmation of sisterhood is precisely a lack of the social ceremonies and unifying public occasions which the brotherhood of man has always valued. One can watch strong men cry as the national anthem is played at the beginning of a sporting occasion, and the unifying myths of militarism have survived even the cauldron of Vietnam. Lesser cultic activities thrive in masonic brotherhoods, trade unions and various occupational and interest clubs. For women, there are few social structures of this nature, and it is simply not enough to meet in earnest groups. We have to celebrate our femininity, and that is exactly what these proletarian women in the dingy streets of industrial Glasgow were doing. The midwife was a privileged participant in a quintessentially social celebration of the strength of being female. Its basis was the maligned function of reproduction.

Now, of course, childbirth has become a responsibility of the 'health industry', a hospital occasion presided over by obstetrical entrepreneurs, usually male, in conditions of depersonalized asepsis which transforms woman, in every sense the agent, into a patient. Medical developments have no doubt reduced the life-risking dangers of parturition, but they have done so at the price of concealing and reducing the unifying female sociability attendant on the birth of a new life. One can exaggerate this effect, but there is a sense in which reproduction has become commodity production, just as the social relations of reproduction have become property relations. This raises again the question of class analysis, for clearly these developments are related significantly to general effects common to social forms in capitalist society and to aspects of bourgeois culture and ideology. The desocialization of childbirth is part of a general trend towards the isolation of individuals and the efficient 'rationalizing' of human events, which are part of the prevailing notion of society as a giant marketplace. The question is: Is this *all* that it is? The answer clearly is no. We must not romanticize earlier and simpler forms of childbirth. The sociability in question clearly could not challenge the reality of a dominant male-supremacist culture, and the anthropological identifications of rites of parturition in non-capitalist societies by no means indicates that the condition of women vis-à-vis men in such societies is necessarily different or somehow better. What this means, of course, is that male supremacy is a phenomenon which, in capitalist societies, takes particular and identifiable forms. I intend to argue that, while the cultural forms of the social relations of reproduction do indeed vary in ways which are discernibly related to the economic realm, class analysis cannot wholly comprehend the genesis and actuality of male dominance. I can argue in this way because my early experience as a midwife to the working class has given me an alternative perception of reproduction.

The sensibilities of a woman and a midwife make the study of political theory an adventurous affair. One tends to read the bits which are usually regarded as of less interest than the major body of the work of any theorists, for the truth is that most of the big names in the tradition have been far more interested in reproductive realities than are those exegetes who have set themselves up to explain the tradition to those who like their theory predigested, if at all. In this book we shall be much concerned with extracted notions of selected theorists, and our interest will be a critical one. The family appears in political theory, as it does in history, in a number of ways: it has been perceived as the 'basic unit' of political society, as the economic unity of society, as the repository of tradition, custom and morality, as a mode of safely siphoning off the disorderly dangers of sexual passion. It has also been perceived as the most practical mode of rearing children and replacing those lost in battle, or of replacing the labour power of the industrial proletariat. This wide variety of views of the family, together with the marvellous variation in family forms which have appeared in history, all have two properties in common. One is the conviction that the family is necessary. The second is that the family is the proper sphere of women. Only in the contemporary industrialized world have these propositions begun to be challenged.

This preoccupation with family is reflected by political theorists: there are clearly relationships between actual political forms, political theory and the social relations of reproduction. It is this relationship which is to be analysed. In subsequent chapters, I hope to develop a theory and a method of analysis and a conceptual vocabulary by which social and political theory can be subjected to feminist critique. This will be a constructive critique, in that out of it may grow not only some understanding of the origins and development of the fact and ideology of male supremacy, but also the rudiments of a feminist theory which will have some descriptive and strategic value. It is not to be argued that the defence of male supremacy is really all that political theory is: it is argued that whatever else it is, political theory has also been a standard bearer for a specifically political ideology of male supremacy. This is the particular aspect of political theory which is to be examined, and the effect is a pronounced onesidedness, which will no doubt offend students of the discipline. No apology, however, is offered for the onesidedness: it might be called a corrective bias. The conventional concerns of political philosophy are well able to look to their own laurels, and there is a huge tradition of primary and secondary sources in which the handful of visionaries and geniuses march with a great army of special pleaders and intellectual journeymen. Those who want to study, for example, Plato's theory of forms or Locke's notion of individual property ownership can find plenty of material. Those who want to know how philosophical opinion reflected on the simple biological facts of masculinity will find no handy text. These are the enquiries which are addressed here. Feminist theory has to be biased because it is anti-bias. We have to correct a profound and long-sustained imbalance, and this cannot be done without jumping rather brutally and without invitation on the end of the philosophical seesaw which has lingered too long in the rarefied heights of the complacent taken-for-grantedness of male conceptions of the nature of man. Perhaps more important than these considerations, however, is the presupposition which informs the whole exercise: it is posited that there is such a thing as a 'feminist perspective'. It is also assumed that this perspective must carve out its own subject matter, and in so doing can provide new and illuminating reappraisals of the more encrusted tenets of male-stream thought. Meantime, we may quite cheerfully borrow from that tradition any contributions in terms of theory and methodology which are needed for the development of feminist theory. In this way, we avoid slavish and ultimately inappropriate devotion to any particular set of theoretical beliefs. We do not say that the tradition must be rejected in a wholesale way. Indeed, we argue that most of it is part of a heritage of human achievement of which the race can quite properly be proud. What we do, therefore, is work in a dialectical way. We seek to uncover contradictions in traditional thought: to root these contradictions in the realities of male experience; to point out that they have been valid in specific historical circumstances; to say why they are no longer valid; to conserve what is valuable and to transcend what is not; to create something new which is none the less continuous with history and creative of a future. If one wants a metaphor for this process, women do not have very far to look. We are labouring to give birth to a new philosophy of birth. This contribution to feminist theory will be like traditional theoretical activity in so far as it culls from that tradition the conceptual and analytical tools which can transform the tradition. It will be unlike the tradition in that the generic perspective brought to bear is one which has historically been excluded from the tradition. The unifying thread in all this is human history, but human history perceived as a social process which has as an absolutely and inescapably necessary substructure the process of human reproduction.

The use of this word 'generic' raises the question of an appropriate vocabulary. The word 'sex' is avoided simply because it has too many levels of meaning. Sex can be instinct, drive, an act in response to that drive, a gender, a role, an emotional bomb or a causal variable. For purposes of analytical clarity, I have confined the use of 'sex' and 'sexuality' to the description of copulatory activity. This is clearly unsatisfactory in that human sexuality is a great deal more than copulation. None the less, sexuality is perceived here as affecting but one moment in the biological process of reproduction, which, unlike the human participants, is quite indifferent to orgasmic and conjugal delights.

For the social relations between men and women and for the differentiation of male and female the word 'gender' is preferred. While a sustained attempt has been made to use this terminology consistently, it is in many instances cumbersome and contrary to ordinary usage, and the desire for consistency sometimes yields to the compulsions of custom.

I have also used 'it' as the preferred pronoun to describe infants when it is not necessary to make a generic differentation and is tedious to write he/she. I should like to assure all infants that I do not regard them as things, even when I callously describe them as products. The difficulty with the analysis of process as such is partly that it tends to rob process of its fundamental property of movement: process does not stand still, yet we must attempt to isolate its moments. In addition to this, it is necessary to strip off the accretions and residues of history, culture and ideology, not in a subjective search for some elusive 'essence', but in an attempt to 'abstract' the objective and material base of the social relations of reproduction. In this process of analysing process, a vocabulary of abstraction is necessary, and my 'it' infant is in the first instance an abstraction.

With regard to adults as a collectivity not requiring generic differentiation, the English language offers no satisfactory word. 'People' does not always fit, and our ideologically pierced ears would not thrill had Shakespeare declared: 'Oh, what a wond'rous work of God is a person'. Likewise, the word 'human' is now regarded in feminist circles with some suspicion, on the grounds that it is just as spurious in its claim to generic inclusiveness as the ubiquitous 'man'. Despite this caveat, I have used human in all cases in a fully generic sense. In general the word 'men' is used to describe the masculine portion of the species, while 'man' is used to describe conceptualizations about men in general. Pronouns are simply incorrigible, and have been avoided as far as possible where no adult generic differentiation is being made. All of this does nothing at all towards an elegant syntax.

The discussion of vocabulary must include some reference to the use of the word 'labour'. The same word in English refers to both productive and reproductive labour. Both types of labour are important to this analysis, but the insistence on this importance does not rest on either the exploitation or misunderstanding of a semantic ambiguity. Productive and reproductive labour differ in scope, a differentiation inseparable from gender. Productive labour is universal: all people can work, even although class society permits a few not to do so. Only women perform reproductive labour. Further, the ability to avoid productive labour is not 'natural': drones must eat, and someone else must therefore labour for their subsistence, an obvious basis for power relations. However, in a way severely limited by social circumstances, productive labour has had, historically, elements of choice and free will embedded in its fundamental process, which is the process of adapting the natural world to the conditions of human survival. Even in the capitalist mode of production, the labour market is a 'free' market, and there are options available, however limited, in the modes of labour, even though there is no option for the worker to do anything other than sell labour power. Once pregnant, women have no choice at all but to labour to bring forth the fruit of their wombs and for much of history have had only circumscribed choices in whether or not to become pregnant. Men are biologically free from the necessity to labour reproductively. Productive labour is also versatile, in the sense that historically people have constantly created new products which in turn have created new needs. There are clear differences, too, in the nature of the value which reproductive labour creates. All of these differentiations must be examined in more detail. However, as the analysis of reproductive labour process which I intend to offer is derived in significant ways from Marx's analysis of the productive labour process, it is important to state the vital characteristics which the processes have in common, and which permit this kind of methodological adaptation. In fact, these shared characteristics constitute the presuppositions of analysis. They are:

1 Both forms of labour are activities which *mediate* the separation between people and nature.

2 Both forms of labour are also mediations of contradictions *within* the fundamental processes of which labour is a necessary component. I will attempt to demonstrate what these oppositions are with regard to the process of reproduction. In general, Marx's analysis of the dialectics of productive labour process is accepted as essentially correct, with some reservations in terms of the level of Hegelian abstraction to which he occasionally flies.

3 Both processes, production and reproduction, emerging as they do from *necessity*, contribute to the dialectical structure of human consciousness. There is a reproductive, generic aspect of consciousness, just as there is a productive, class aspect of consciousness. Again, Marx's analysis of the latter is accepted as basically correct.

4 Both forms of labour produce values and create new needs. The values and needs created are not, however, commensurable. In its abstract form, the productive process creates values and needs for the producer: in any form, reproductive labour creates another and needy human. Production in its historic development becomes socially necessary labour: reproduction is primordially *necessarily social labour*.

There are further ambiguities related to the word 'reproduction'. Marx, for example, talks of men 'reproducing' themselves daily, stoking the organism with the fuels of physical and social survival. We shall be using the word to refer to the biological instauration of the species and the analysis of the process which is an essential and material base of human history. The preliminary analysis of this process can be found in the next chapter, but in the meantime let me make it quite clear what I posit as the scope of the process of reproduction: it begins with ovulation and ends when the 'product', the child, is no longer dependent on others for the necessities of survival. This is an abstraction, of course, from the continuity of the species, but it is a necessary abstraction if we are to understand that the social relations of reproduction and historical, as opposed to genetic, continuity are as inseparable from reproductive process as the social relations of production are inseparable from labour process.

The problems of linguistic and conceptual vocabulary are much wider than these particular instances. It is an axiom of feminist understanding that the dogmas of male supremacy invade all human institutions and pervade all modes of discourse. This situation is of significance in the present work in two ways: in terms of intention and in terms of scope.

In terms of intention, I have hoped to make a move from the passive polemics against an engulfing chauvinism to a real demonstration of the internal consistencies of male supremacy, working from the versions of male-supremacist ideology to be found in traditional political theory. For this reason I have not coined new terms to describe those aspects of politics which it is claimed are specifically coloured by male reproductive consciousness. Such concepts as second nature, the public and private realms and the notion of fraternity, for example, are hardly novel in the annals of political understanding. Likewise, the notions of organic and self-perpetuating political and legal entities are very old indeed, and the notion of 'the body politic' has always carried reproductive connotations in terms of the establishment of continuity over time and the need for regeneration. This is true of such apparently diverse concepts as Burkean constitutionalism and Mao's continuing revolution. What I hope to show is that such theories are not merely analogues of generational continuity and procreation, but take social forms which meet in a quite practical way the problems of the integrity of male reproductive consciousness with itself, with nature and with time, problems which are posed by the actual process of reproduction.

In terms of scope, the pervasiveness of masculine perspective makes it difficult to confine the discussion within self-evident parameters of a particular academic discipline, even a quite versatile one like political theory, which has tended to resist mainstream concentration on parametrical restriction. I have had recourse to history, anthropology and literature, but I am neither historian, anthropologist nor littératrice. Likewise, I am much concerned with the Greek polis as a developed case of politics as a man's world, but I am not a classicist. In these areas, I have not hesitated to use secondary source material, and the governing factor in the selection of such material has been a sensitivity on the part of the writer in question for the significance of genderic relationships. There is thus a quite frank preference for such historians as Ehrenburg and Bonnard, and the Marxist economist Ernest Mandel, who recognize the question of women's place in history as a proper area of historical enquiry. In any case, a current tendency in western scholarship and its more depressingly trivial surrogates, which seeks to compartmentalize knowledge in a tidy division of intellectual labour, is not very useful to male-stream thought. It is particularly useless to women confronting the holistic ideology of male supremacy. Feminist scholarship does not lean towards an interdisciplinary approach by accident: it does so because male supremacy penetrates every human activity.

It remains to indicate in an introductory way the course to be followed in the formulation of what is in effect a feminist theory about theory.

The first chapter is in itself the product of the ensuing chapters as well as an introduction to them: in my beginning is my end. It is concerned with the analysis of the process of reproduction and in elaborating the human significance of the dialectics of that biological process. From this analysis, a selection of the conceptual concerns of feminist theory is elaborated. There is some discussion of Hegel, Marx and Freud, all of whom have contributed to the analytical framework employed or have had something relevant to say in terms of the concepts which are being elaborated.

Chapter 2 moves to a critical examination of the theoretical framework employed in several of the more influential works which have appeared in the area of feminist studies, in particular the work of de Beauvoir, Millett, Firestone and Reed. The reliance of these women on existing theories, however selective the approach, is perceived as a weakness which perpetuates elements of male-stream thought which are inimical to women, most notably in the denial of creativity, historicity and intellectual significance to human reproduction.

Chapters 3 and 4 are concerned with the relation of creation to procreation as a determinant of the social forms of the separation of the public realm and politics from the private realm and family. It is argued that men's historically demonstrable need for a 'second nature' arises from this division, and the operations of these concepts in the work of Arendt, Machiavelli and Plato are discussed. It is argued that Plato, and we deal specifically with *The Symposium*, consciously annexes reproductive dynamic from generic relation and relocates it arbitrarily in creative intellectual intercourse between men. This is the idealist ideology of male supremacy.

Chapter 5 turns to Marxist interpretation of the polis life, whose real and imagined virtues frame the idealist political vision. Of especial interest is the work of George Thomson, which demonstrates the limitations of economism in either describing or understanding the historical move from family to polity. This leads to a critical analysis of the conflation of production and reproduction in Marx's own work, in which Marx pre-empts reproductive dynamic and awards it arbitrarily to the process of production. This is the materialist ideology of male supremacy.

A short conclusion attempts to indicate some of the dimensions of the theoretical task which history now presents to women, and the problems of unifying feminist theory with feminist practice.

I The dialectics of reproduction

When we ask questions about the suppression of women and its causes, the answers which are given usually relate the social condition of women to female reproductive function. The trap in this correlation is, of course, that it suggests that male dominance is in some sense 'natural', as natural as motherhood. Biological reproduction, the argument goes, is a natural process with which human reason can only deal from the standpoint of natural science. If we want clearer understanding of the process, we should turn to biology, anatomy and physiology or, increasingly, to the problematic wonders of genetics. What these sciences show us is that mammalian reproduction is but one class of animal reproduction. Anything specifically human in the process apparently must await the appearance of the product of the process, the child, as a separate but dependent creature. The actual business of fertilization, parturition and birth, the anatomy and physiology of reproduction, we are told does not differ significantly between human females and, say, baboons. The sexual instinct, naturally strong and irresistible as it is, ensures that the species will continue, and women are in an understandable sense the handmaidens of biological continuity. To be sure, this non-differentiation between the human and other animals is superseded in terms of human inventiveness with regard to the social relations which are developed to deal with the questions of the helplessness of the newborn, the socialization and education of the child and the sexual relations of men and women. The human family in all its varied forms is quite different from the animal pack, herd or whatever. The family is a historical development with its roots in a natural necessity. The necessity itself is invariant, and women's place in the social relations of reproduction is therefore circumscribed by her childbearing function. While this view has been a staple of masculine thought, it has also been shared by important feminist writers, including de Beauvoir and Shulamith Firestone.[1] Feminist versions retain the premise of the argument but alter the conclusion. Traditional wisdom says: Women are naturally trapped in the childbearing function / Women therefore cannot participate in social life on equal terms with men. In place of this, a new syllogism is coined: Women are naturally trapped in the childbearing function / Therefore the liberation of women depends on their being freed from this trap.

Perhaps it is not the conclusion which is wrong, but the premise. What does it mean to be trapped in a natural function? Clearly, reproduction has been regarded as quite different from other natural functions which, on the surface, seem to be equally imbued with necessity; eating, sexuality and dying, for example, share with birth the status of biological necessities. Yet it has never been suggested that these topics can be understood only in terms of natural science. They have all become the subject matters of rather impressive bodies of philosophical thought; in fact, we have great modern theoretical systems firmly based upon just these biological necessities. Dialectical materialism takes as its fundamental postulate the need to eat: Marx has transformed this very simple fact of biological necessity into the breeding ground of a theoretical system of enormous vitality and explanatory utility, in which productive labour remakes our consciousness, our needs and our world. The simple sex-act has been transformed by the clinical genius of Freud into a theoretical *a priori* of a system in which libido shapes our consciousness and our world. Death has haunted the male philosophical imagination since Man the Thinker first glimmered into action, and in our own time has become the stark reality which preoccupies existentialism, an untidy and passionately pessimistic body of thought in which lonely and heroic man attempts to defy the absurdity of the void which houses his consciousness and his world. The inevitability and necessity of these biological events has quite clearly not exempted them from historical force and theoretical significance.

We have no comparable philosophies of birth. Birth was at one time important in a symbolic way to theological visions, mostly with a view to depreciating women's part, and rendering it passive and even virginal, while paternity took on divine trappings. Reproductive process is not a process which male-stream thought finds either ontologically or epistemologically interesting on the biological level. The human family is philosophically interesting, but its biological base is simply given.

Women cannot be so dense nor so perverse. This male theoretical attitude towards birth is neither natural, accidental nor conspiratorial. It has a material base, and that base lies in the philosophically neglected and generically differentiated process of human reproduction itself. The general thesis which is to be proffered here is that reproductive process is not only the material base of the historical forms of the social relations of reproduction, but that it is also a dialectical process, which changes historically. There are a couple of essential preconditions which need to be posited before a dialectical, historical and material analysis of reproductive process can make sound theoretical sense. The first of these arises from the claim that the process changes historically. This contentious proposition rests upon the neglected consideration that human reproduction is inseparable from human consciousness. This seems self-evident, but the strong historical tendency which we have just discussed to see reproduction as 'pure' biological process carries the implication that reproduction is all body and without mind; irrational or at least prerational. The presupposition of an inseparability of experienced process and human consciousness of process is central to the theory of the dialectics of reproduction to be developed here. This unity of event and consciousness of event is the base of the attribution of historicity to reproductive process: it will be argued that the first and significant historical change in the process was not a biological mutation of some kind, but a transformation in male reproductive consciousness, which was triggered by the historical discovery of physiological paternity. The second and much more recent change in reproductive praxis is brought about by technology. Technology, we may note, has been the historical process which has accelerated changes in modes of production, but contraceptive technology is qualitatively different from all other technologies. Its impact on the economic realm is not especially striking, except that the profits are obscenely large and little interest is shown in utilizing them for the development of a safer and better technology. Yet this technology, even in its imperfect form, brings about a fundamental historical change of the kind which Hegel called a world historical event. This is not simply because of the effects on demographic patterns and family relations, which are already obvious. Beneath these changes and, indeed, essential to the growth of the women's movement, is a change in the underlying dialectics of reproductive consciousness. The freedom for women to choose parenthood is a historical development as significant as the discovery of physiological paternity. Both create a transformation in human consciousness of human relations with the natural world which must, as it were, be re-negotiated or, to use the language of dialectical analysis, be mediated.

It is precisely because of this world historical event that we are able now to begin to look at the process of reproduction in a different way. Women have been in a similar position to that which Karl Marx diagnosed as that of utopian socialists in the early nineteenth century.[2] Marx and Engels described the activities of these earlier prophets as the work of those who sensed that something was fundamentally out of kilter in the society in which they lived, and who saw that the progressive promise of human control over the natural and social environment was being sadly eroded by the brutality of industrial production and the exploitation of the working class. Unable to articulate the grounds of this process in correct theoretical terms, utopians advocated a total destruction and rebuilding of society, a breaking up of all values and a rejection of all conventional morality. This would bring about the arrival of a world which they had spun in the humane and indignant web of their own outraged sensibilities. Utopians were so innocent of the true nature of class struggle that they even called on the ruling class for help in destroying itself.

The failure to develop a correct theoretical understanding of their own historical situation did not emerge from defective understanding or a paucity of intellectual gifts on the part of the utopian socialists, Marx and Engels argue. The pace of history does not flag while the process of history waits for a good idea to come along and give it a push. Ideas are, as Marx famously argued, the product of history, and history is not the product of ideas. In the lived lives of early socialists, the development of the capitalist mode of production and the forms of class struggle which it was creating were still at a primitive stage. It could be seen that there were indeed antagonistic classes, but the significance of class struggle in human history could not be understood until the struggle itself had been developed and uncovered in the clear opposition of bourgeoisie and proletariat. This required a high level of generality in the capitalist mode of production and a critique of the developed theory and ideology of political economy, the bourgeois mode of production and the bourgeois philosophy. Only then could a new and higher form of social theory even begin to be developed. Marx was never a foolishly modest man, and he considered that his own theoretical activity was a significant stage in this development, but he recognized his own historical specificity in a clear-headed way which his more orthodox and ahistorical followers would do well to cultivate. What we now call Marxism was the theoretical interpretation of a set of particular historical conditions in relation to a universal process of history, the history of class struggle. Until this struggle reached an advanced stage of polarity, which development depended in turn upon a particular stage of technological and ideological sophistication and a simplification of class division, the substructure of historical process remained obscure.

This short analysis of utopian socialism in *The Communist Manifesto* is a very useful one. It provides a method for analysing the subsequent impact of technology on the social relations of reproduction, an event quite obscure to Marx in his own epoch. We are presently emerging from a stage of feminist utopianism, which calls for the destruction of the world of male supremacy, and even sometimes expects the ruling sex to assist in its own funeral rites. Like the stage of utopian socialism, this feminist utopianism is an important stage, for it publicizes injustice and pinpoints problems. However, the social relations of reproduction are now increasingly displaying evidence of transformation, evidence which permits a clearer understanding of the historical forces at work. This understanding will come from women who, as the dehumanized people of this dialectical struggle, are at the same time the progressive social force in the restructuring of the social relations in question. Yet women cannot accomplish this historical mission without a clear theoretical understanding of the dimensions of the task and of the processes at work, and it is clear that the struggle in process cannot be subsumed in class struggle. We cannot analyse reproduction from the standpoint of any existing theory. The theories themselves are products of male-stream thought, and are among the objects to be explained, but embedded somewhere in the theory and practice of male supremacy are the seeds of its growth and inevitable decay. What we must therefore do is turn to the fundamental biological process in which reproductive relations are grounded and subject it to analysis from a female perspective. This cannot be done in terms of a critique of political economy, nor in terms of the canons of psychoanalysis, existentialism or any other fine flowering branch of male-stream thought. As we have observed, there is no philosophy of birth, and yet it is of birth that we must theorize. What this means is that we must not only develop a theory, but develop a *feminist perspective* and a *method of enquiry* from which such a theory can emerge.

Of these rather daunting tasks, the methodological one turns out to be the least difficult. Here we can borrow from intellectual tradition, not because dialectical analysis is groovier and ideologically more congenial than other modes of theorizing, but because reproductive process is dialectical, material and historical. Clearly, an analysis which claims to be historical, material and dialectical owes a great deal to Marx, and in fact the strategy of analysing reproductive process – 'as such', as some philosophers would say – is inspired by Marx's analysis of 'pure' productive labour in *Capital*, I,3,VII, i. 'Pure' here means abstracted from the social context. This is done for purposes of theoretical clarity, for of course neither production nor reproduction can appear in isolation from their social and historical context. What is attempted is not simply an adaptation of Marx's analysis, but an immanent critique of that analysis. Put in the simplest way, we may claim to retain what is of value in Marx's analysis while using his own method to transcend and revise his own theoretical model. This sense of the history of thought as a dialectical process is more commonly associated with the work of Hegel than with Marx's materialism, and we shall also borrow from Hegel, whose insight into the dialectical structure of reproductive process was the major stimulus to this analysis. In one sense, this is a Hegelian/Marxist analysis, but no claim at all is made on the authority of these luminous thinkers, nor any apology to their orthodox disciples. This is a feminist analysis, and the two gentlemen in question were immersed in the tradition of male-stream thought, Hegel in particular being an unrepentant and often bitter misogynist. None the less, the debt to both of these men is acknowledged without reservation, while we proceed quite buoyantly and without embarrassment to ignore, with a calculated naiveté, the major propositions of their respective systems, concentrating on the social relations of reproduction which both seriously misunderstood.

It was Hegel, the objective idealist, and not Marx, the materialist, who noticed that the process of reproduction was dialectically structured.[3] The further consideration that it is also capable of significant transformation in historical terms, however, eluded the highly refined historical understanding of the old wizard of dialectics. The effect of this combination of perspicacity and opacity in Hegel's own work was an odd one, for Hegel placed vital aspects of reproductive relations outside of history proper, history being understood to start only when the human rational faculty had clearly separated the human world from the rest of the animal world in the development of self-consciousness and historical consciousness. For Hegel, the patriarchy was not a historical institution but a 'prehistorical', natural arrangement.[4] Likewise, the restriction of women to activities related to the care of individual lives in the limited area of family and domestic life was also prehistorical. Hegel was irritated by the fact that women, because they are defective in the exercise of reason, don't always appear to appreciate the limitations of their organic and ancestral preoccupations. For Hegel, the household was the arena of death.[5] He understood, of course, that the forms of family do change historically, and indeed saw the process by which the self-sufficiency of the family in both economic and moral terms was progressively eroded as a significant part of historical dialectics. In his bourgeois understanding of paterfamilias, which was a strong factor in Hegel's own self-understanding, he was a little nostalgic about this. As the plotter of the progress of reason in history, however, he recognized the inevitability of the contraction of the family over time, for reason's most complete appearance in history was realized for Hegel in the modern state. The contraction of the family and the expansion of civil society, political rule and inventive economics were the inevitable manifestations of the rationalization of human affairs.

The family in Hegel's scheme gives us a clearer idea of dialectical process. Though each particular family dies out, the universal family form is never abolished; it is transcended and transformed while it is at the same time preserved. Nothing is ever lost in Hegel's view of history, yet nothing is static either. The family remains for the very good reason that it is necessary, but less necessary, because less rational, than other wholly man-made institutions, such as the economic, legal and religious institutions in which reason systematically hitches a ride from the abstract realm of metaphysics to the concrete realities of collective human life. The necessity embodied in the family can never transcend its natural component, which is the biological need of each life. Thus, the reproduction of the race is a dead core in the dynamics of human history, inert, intransigent and often downright irritating. The mute genealogical continuity of the genderically differentiated human race is quite different from the continuity of the history which man creatively struggles to make for himself. None the less, the family does have one characteristic which transcends the merely organic, and this has to do with its ethical aspect. The family is, as it were, ethical by compulsion, an ethics quite different from that, for example, by which men learn the rational and noble morality of going to war, to kill and be killed in the imperative conservation of the society which they have made in unwitting compliance with cunning reason. The ethical essence of the family lies in the dependence of infants, which makes the first demand on people to think of the welfare of another rather than only on personal survival. It is because of this demand that women can add to their limited rational capacity a limited moral understanding. Women care for their children, just as they keep green the memory of ancestors. The family is the sole source and appropriate realm of female ethical being.[6] Female morality, like women themselves, remains particular, and relates only to the individuals in the family, concentrating on biological life. It is because female morality is essentially biological that Hegel sees the perfect moral male/female relationship as that of brother and sister, and Antigone appears in his work as history's only heroine. Women cannot understand the necessity to rise above the consideration of individual survival to the 'higher' appreciation of the community and its more sophisticated and rational ethics. Male morality, on the other hand, transcends particularity to become the ethics of universal man and the socio-historical realities in which this universally is expressed. Boys grow up under the eye of a particular male parent, who counteracts the limitations of maternal particularity until such time as the male child can transcend this patriarchal domination, and proceed to take his place in the larger male-dominant society which meets the young man's need to become, among other things, a patriarch himself.

Of the two needs, biological and ethical, which guarantee the survival of some form of family in history, the ethical function is clearly superior to the reproductive function, for it has a moral and human component added to the merely organic workings of biology. Male supremacy is therefore ethical and rational rather than biological, for men have this capacity to struggle for universality, to disregard particular life in the affirmation of a more rational whole. Male supremacy is therefore necessary to historical development; it is a historical constant.

We are not concerned to demonstrate in detail Hegel's male chauvinism, nor are we dismissing 'the system' in a couple of pages.[7] What is unique and significant is Hegel's recognition that the process of reproduction is formally structured in a dialectical way. In fact, reproductive process, like the history of the family, serves to clarify a little further our understanding of dialectics. As a young man, Hegel was much concerned with the relation of sexuality to self-consciousness, and with the question of how this relation comes to be realized in the institution of the family. Sexual desire, which young Hegel decorously refers to as 'love', is a problematic affair, for it appears at first sight to destroy ones sense of self in a very thorough way. The lover is swept pell-mell into a unity with another which negates his sense of individuality and annuls his consciousness of self: 'the individual cannot bear to think of himself in this nullity ... nothing carries the root of its own being in itself ... true union consists only between living things which are alike in power.'[8]

When Hegel claims that self-consciousness 'cannot bear' negation and separation from itself, or, to put this another way, that human consciousness resists alienation and negation of the self, he is making a claim about the structure of consciousness which is vital to the theory of reproductive consciousness developed here. Hegel sees this lack of distinction as emerging from an identity of power in the lovers, as each contributes a seed. This is an elementary instance of the synthesis of oppositions. The uniting seeds of the lovers, young Hegel says, constitute a unity which annuls the distinction between the particular seed of each individual donor. As donors of seed, therefore, male and female are alike in power. Yet this power is problematic: not only does the new and unified seed annul the distinction between the separate seeds, but the individuals themselves, in the grip of sexual passion, suffer a loss of self-distinction. Sexuality annuls the distinction between the lover as human lover and the lover as mere physical organism. Lovers are stripped first of their identity, which is submerged in the other, and secondly of their general humanity. The seed itself cannot unify these separations, because, at this stage, it is still only what Hegel calls an 'undifferentiated unity'.[9] Yet it has the potential for the restoration of a new and restored unity in that it is 'a seed of immortality, of the eternal and self-generating race'.[10] The process of reproduction is therefore a process of 'unity, separated opposites, re-union,'[11] for the child breaks free from the original unity to constitute a new potential self-consciousness which affirms the continuity of the species.

It is, I think, important to struggle with Hegel's difficult analysis for a number of reasons. The first of these applies to many of the philosophical fathers of patriarchy whose views of reproduction and the family we shall be analysing. This is not simply an academic exercise. What underlies these notions is not simply prejudice, but clues as to the lived experience which informs male reproductive consciousness. The process by which this experience is transformed into an ideology of male supremacy is crucial to our analysis of reproductive consciousness. The feminist critique of male-stream thought in general must, however, proceed from something more dynamic than mere standpoint; it must have a theory and a method. Hegel is extraordinarily illuminating in that he gives us not only large hints as to what to look for, but a great deal of help in knowing how to go about our search in a systematic and methodical way. Most great thinkers have aspired in some sense to give an account of the whole of human experience, or at least to define the limits of holistic possibility. Hegel is particularly ambitious in his passionate pursuit of absolute knowledge. Yet any account of human experience which has been taken seriously has had to deal with ancient and vexed questions relating to the contradictions within human experience of individuality and sociability and, in many instances, the extension of this problem to questions about the origins of individual and social reality and the forms of individual and social consciousness. Clearly, there is enormous historical variation in the way in which these kinds of questions are asked and answered, yet there is a guiding thread of assumptions of male superiority emerging from the process of history, whether perceived as evolutionary, spiritual, factual or romantic, whether unilinear, cyclical or dialectical. In Hegel's work, and, as we shall see, in the work of Marx too, there exists side by side a powerful statement of important human realities, and a powerful and immanent mode of critique of the limitations built into the work in question.

Thus we may accept Hegel's insight that the process of reproduction is dialectically structured. We also accept the proposition that human consciousness resists alienation. We can then proceed to show that Hegel's analysis of the process is, in important respects, simply wrong.

Let us take the important questions separately, and apply the perspective of female reproductive consciousness to the male reproductive experience instead of the other way round. First of all, there are questions relating to the 'unity' of the seeds and the nature of the successive separations which Hegel posits. Second, there is a problem with the notion of the child 'breaking free' into the world. Third, there are unresolved ambiguities in Hegel's notion of the relation of the continuity of the race, which I shall call 'genetic continuity', and the actual course of human history.

In terms of the separation and reunification by which human reproduction proceeds, Hegel's errors stem from his failure to give proper consideration to the generic differentiation in consciousness of reproductive process, and to a misrepresentation – and whether this is deliberate or merely misguided is really not very important – to a misrepresentation of what actually happens. The 'unity' which Hegel posits, the unity of the previously differentiated seeds, is an abstract unity. Hegel would not be upset by this charge, because for Hegel that which is biological and uncoloured by reason is by definition abstract. Nature, pre-rational old lady that she is, is, in historical terms, both impotent and abstract. However it is not by virtue of the nature of Nature that Hegel posits the unity of the male and female seeds as abstract. It is because, from the male perspective, the unity of the seeds is actually an abstract affair. Hegel simply fails to recognize that it is not as lover that man is negated, and that it is not in terms of sexuality that he is annulled. Man is negated not as lover but as *parent*, and this negation rests squarely on the alienation of the male seed in the copulative act. The unity of the seeds is quite objective, not abstract at all, but it is a unity and development which is experientially present in an immediate way only to female reproductive consciousness. It is hard to grasp, given the immense and visible parcel in which man-made history has packaged the idea of paternity, that paternity is in fact an abstract idea. It rests very specifically on theory, not unified immediately with practice. Paternity is the conceptualization of a cause and effect relationship, the relationship between copulation and childbirth, and even the idea of paternity must await the development of a certain level of human intellectual development before it can be discovered. Hegel appears to have been at least uneasy about his too facile analysis of the unities and oppositions within the dialectics of reproduction. His original manuscript states that the child is the embodied unity of the separated parents. Later, he added the words, 'The child is the parents themselves,' but then scored them out and let the original formulation stand.[12] He may have seen that the too total identification of child with parents rather spoilt the argument for the creation of a new tool of reason in the world which would develop autonomously, but be differentiated generically by something other than mere anatomy. We shall never know. What we do know is that Hegel did see the need to objectify paternity, to make particular fatherhood real rather than abstract, to transform the child as the product only of man in general, which *some man* has fathered, to a living and less ambiguous unity with one particular man which makes sense of patriarchy. The reality he actually chooses to transform the spirituality of sexual love to the reality of the lived marriage is not, finally, the child who is the transcendent but uncertain carrier of the paternal seed, but the more reliable bourgeois standby of family property.[13] To be sure, the child cannot embody the unity of the parents for ever, for it must grow and in turn become a parent and create a new family. Property passes from generation to generation, it is a principle of genetic continuity rendered in a tangible way. Yet, from a feminist standpoint, Hegel does rather seem to have abandoned, or 'transcended', biological continuity on inadequate grounds. Why, we may ask, is this 'embodied unity', represented by the child, not sufficiently concrete to realize the relationship of love between the man and the woman in the ordinary world? The answer, which Hegel does not clarify, is that the alienation of the seed cannot be cancelled in the act of love, but is a much more complex affair. 'Between the conception and the creation', T. S. Eliot writes, 'Falls the shadow.' Male-stream thought has not analysed its shadows, perhaps, with sufficient rigour. Clearly, the alienation of the seed is a masculine experience, but there is a female form of alienation, too. The male alienates the individual seed in copulation, but the woman alienates the unified and transformed form of the originally opposing seeds in the act of giving birth.

This leads us to the second difficulty with Hegel's analysis, the assertion that the child 'breaks free' from impotent biology to arrive in the world clothed in dependence and the potential, if he is male, to partake of the universality of man. This notion of children falling from eternity into time, and from infinity into space, by virtue of some dynamic essence donated by the male seed is one of the most venerable of chauvinist chestnuts. From Aristotle's attribution of soul to the sperm to the melancholy 'thrownness' which precipitates the Heideggerian existent into the world, children evidently arrive without any theoretically important assistance from their mothers, so that the mediative nature of labour and the formation of female reproductive consciousness remain unanalysed. In fact, of course, children are the products of labour. It is particularly interesting to find Hegel totally neglecting this consideration. It was Hegel, after all, who offered the profound and brilliant insight that labour is an active force in the mediation of man and the natural world, a mediation in which the labourer and the world are transformed in significant ways.[14] In labouring, man in a real sense creates a world of his own and a history for himself and his species. As far as this labour is productive labour, or the creative labours of the legislators, philosophers, theologians and poets, it is not in fact exclusively male activity, though it is mostly male activity which finds its way into the written records and ideologies of male supremacy. Hegel not only neglects women's participation in productive labour, but does not even recognize reproductive labour as a category of labour in general, requiring analysis and understanding. He evidently does not consider that reproductive labour has the creative and mediative powers which he finds even in slave labour. Hegel held the remarkable view that the only thing comparable to work in the reproductive process is copulation, for it is in 'love' that the race is reproduced.[15] Historically, of course, the idea of copulation as work is one with which women have had, bitterly, to learn to live; but in prostitution it is the body which is the commodity. For Hegel, the product of the 'work' of copulation is the child, and the real work, reproductive labour, finds no place in the analysis.

There is more here than mere neglect. Reproductive labour has a function which transcends the production of the infant, and is significant in understanding the generic differentiation of reproductive consciousness. The birth of the child is women's alienation of that unity to which men have no experiential access, but women's alienation from their seed is *mediated in labour*. Women do not, like men, have to take further action to annul their alienation from the race, for their labour confirms their integration. Not only does this fact differentiate male and female reproductive consciousness, it differentiates male and female temporal consciousness. The philosophers of history have shown little interest in this opposition of temporal modes of being, which is, after all, rather significant in any understanding of historical process. Female temporal consciousness is continuous, whereas male temporal consciousness is discontinuous. A central problem, and one to which we shall come back again and again, is the problem of continuity. History, even where it is perceived dialectically as struggle and change and eternal restlessness, is continuous, yet Hegel feels able to make the extraordinary claim in his later work that history has been completed. Hegel believed that his own achievement in comprehending the unity of reason and history had somehow signalled this completion of history. Despite this claim, however, history is indubitably a continuous process.

The nature of this continuity is for Hegel a complex relation of two opposing things: ideas on the one hand, and man's historical creations on the other, including the creation and control of property. Property is not recognized by Hegel as a symbol of continuity which men need and women do not, but simply as an instance of reason at work. Hegel was annoyed at the Romans for permitting women to hold property, for this sullied the purity of women's true work in the world, which has to do with individual survival and the mindless continuity of the generations. What all this means is that the family has among its functions the care for biological and emotional life via the activities of women, on the one hand; on the other hand, it protects the family's material wealth via the proprietorial activities of men. This latter task of conserving property cannot be done, however, by the family alone, and the scope of family responsibility is continually contracted. Property needs a civil society to make the laws of inheritance and proprietorship binding on all patriarchs. Men are forced out of the family situation into community, co-operation and friction with other men, for if the only relationship to an object which is possible is the relationship of control, there is clearly room for a lot of masculine struggle over property.

Hegel does not retreat to myths of primitive contracts to explain how this struggle is regulated. He transcends the limitations of contract theory by attempting to unify reason with history, rather than simply imposing reason on a not obviously rational reality. Here, he advances significantly from the limitations of the notion of process as progress which had been popular in the Enlightenment. Yet despite this, the elaboration of principles of continuity divorced from genetic continuity is important to Hegel, as it is to male-stream thought in general. Men have always sought principles of continuity outside of natural continuity. Historically there have been all kinds of such principles, some of which have attempted to subsume both biological continuity and political society, such as hereditary monarchy and primogeniture. There have been theories of continuity which have nothing to do with human reality at all, but cleave to a notion of eternity expressed in contemplative or religious terms. Politics has been a prime candidate as a principle of continuity in male historical praxis in the western tradition, ever since Plato and Aristotle defined the political community as the stabilizer of human relations. The political community is here when we are born and remains when we die. Certainly, it may change its spots once in a while, but the perceived need for stability over time and for regulation of both property relations and the social relations of reproduction all require a political-legal context which mere genetic continuity evidently could not provide.

Hegel's great achievement is to attempt to spell out the actual relation between opposing ideal and real aspects of continuity. History is continuity. The questions which interest us relate to men's need for principles of continuity, ideologies of continuity, and why they translate these principles into social realities which are shot through with the oppression of men by men and rest foursquarely on the greater and 'naturally' justified oppression of women. Marxist class analysis offers a realistic account of the first of these, but says nothing about the second. We must ask again: What is *wrong* with genetic continuity as a necessary material base of history? Hegel gives hints that he knows the answer, but these are expressed in such recondite and abstract terms that it is difficult to be sure. For the answer is really not obscure. The fact is that men make principles of continuity because they are separated from genetic continuity with the alienation of the male seed. Genetic continuity constitutes one pole of the substructure of necessity which is the material condition of human history. Unlike the other pole – the necessity to produce – the reproductive pole resists male participation and control.

Hegel's view of reproduction is very valuable to a feminist analysis, though it is hardly the easiest way into the ramifications by which male-stream thought has elaborated the ideological justification of male supremacy. Yet even in this very preliminary and limited engagement with Hegel, a number of considerations emerge. Perhaps we should try to review them in an orderly way. First, we have from Hegel the discovery that the process of reproduction is structured in a dialectical way, though Hegel's insight does not stretch to the proposition that the process changes historically. This is because, for Hegel, all historical change is made real by reason, but he does not see rationality operating within merely organic process, and he does not discuss the real-life problems created for men by their alienation from genetic continuity. Second, we have from Hegel the beginnings of a method, the method of dialectical analysis, which shows promise of usefulness to feminist critique provided that its masculine limitations and internal contradictions can be transcended. Third, we have begun this process of immanent critique of Hegel by identifying, in a still crude way, realities of reproductive process which will bear further examination. Finally, we note that some of the problems which are emerging are related in a significant way to philosophical problems which are much older than Hegel, and which his system, so magnificently ambitious, cannot finally resolve. We have tentatively identified these as problems of alienation, of separation of man from nature and from continuous time. To make a bold preliminary generalization, they are problems of the *dualism* which is the persistent motif of male philosophy. Under this general category, we find a whole series of oppositions which haunt the male philosophical imagination: mind and body, subject and object, past and present, spirit and matter, individual and social, and so forth. Hegel was confident that his philosophical system could mediate these ancient antagonisms, and we are not especially concerned here with the quarrels which have emerged in discussions of whether or not he succeeded. What we must note is that the one dualism which Hegel himself finally failed to mediate successfully was the opposition of male and female.[16] We are entitled to wonder if the two are connected, if the masculine reproductive consciousness is not a possible basis for the dualistic preoccupation of male-stream thought.

The limitations of Hegel's vision also emerge from the fact that, despite his insistence on the objective reality of history, he cannot ultimately transcend the idealist tradition. This, of course, is the nitty-gritty of Marx's immanent critique of the Hegelian dialectics. Yet Marx's own insistence on a materialist interpretation of history does not produce a materialist view of the social relations of reproduction. Uncharacteristically, Marx applies to the history and prospects of women a different idealist abstraction, and one very popular in current social science. The condition of women becomes for Marx merely a *quantitative* indicator of how well men are progressing in their struggle towards a truly human history. This notion he takes from Proudhon, whose other quantitative fallacies he treats with vigorous and quite mordant blasts of criticism. We shall be discussing the significance and limitations of Marx's work for a feminist philosophy in a later chapter. Here, we are still concerned with questions of theory and method. It is disappointing to Marxist feminists that Marx's materialist viewpoint produces a less sophisticated understanding of reproduction than that which Hegel offers. None the less, this analysis of reproductive process accepts Marx's view of a dialectical logic of necessity grounded in material process as essentially correct. What is argued is that necessity has two poles, two appetites, two processes with which to deal. Marx tells us that human consciousness develops dialectically because it reflects the primordial experience of people in their productive existence in the world, and the *process* of labour is dialectically structured. The labour process is a dialectical process.[17] This is true, but it is also true that reproductive process is formally dialectical, and it is argued that at a very primordial level the operation of these two processes determines the mode of operation of human consciousness. Yet the poles themselves are in an opposition to one another, an opposition whose mediation cannot be left to the workings of subjective consciousness, but must be worked out in terms of real live people living a conscious life in a world which they continuously transform. At a very practical level, there can be real and often devastating tension between the level of subsistence and the numbers of mouths to feed. This situation is the root of Malthusian pessimism, against which Marx argues the possibility of rational regulation of productivity. The possibility of rational control of reproductivity was not an idea which either Malthus or Marx could seriously entertain. Today, of course we can, although the notion is still new enough to present a utopian face. None the less, even the possibility of rational and harmonizing human control of both poles of necessity is a pretty mind-blowing affair. However long and difficult the route to such a state of affairs may be, it cannot be dismissed as mere romance.

The opposition of production and reproduction is not, in any case, a merely quantitative calculation, but has more complex ramifications. Productive labour is common to all people, for all individuals can produce, even though all are not identically productive. Productive labour is in this sense a universal. Antagonisms between producers are created historically by the division of labour, in which the universality of labour is obscured by the opposition between those who labour and those who do not. Marx does not think that what he calls the 'natural', generic division of labour gives rise to this kind of opposition. This is because he does not perceive the possibility of a change in the process of reproduction, which is assumed to be wholly biological and indifferent to conscious comprehension of its workings. Reproductive relations do change historically, in Marx's view, but only as reflections of a change in productive relations. The fact that as material process, biological reproduction necessarily also sets up an opposition between those who labour reproductively (women) and those who do not (men), does not command Marx's attention. None the less, the alienation of the male seed does in fact set up a series of real oppositions in social terms. Standing opposed to each other are:

1 The man and the child, who may or may not be his;
2 The woman who labours to bring forth her child and the man who does not labour;
3 The man who is separated from biological continuity, and the women whose integration with natural process and genetic time is affirmed in reproductive labour;
4 Following from 1, individual man and all other possible potencies, men in general.

Maternal reproductive consciousness is a unity of consciousness and involuntary labour which is, of course, quite different from the unity of head and hand which makes productive labour creative and permits a multiplication and diversification of products, but maternal labour does confirm for women the conception of the child as *her* child. Fathers do not labour and do not have this certainty; paternity is a unity of thought (specifically the knowledge of the relation between sexuality and childbirth) and action. The action in which men commonly annul the alienation of their seed is that action which is described here as the 'appropriation of the child'.

In his analysis of the dialectics of labour process, Marx offered his useful and celebrated parable of the architect and the bee: 'what distinguishes the worst architect from the best of bees is this, that the architect raises his structure in his imagination'.[18] What the architect is clearly doing is objectifying a concept, making real that which is currently still ideal. He is also, incidentally, drawing attention to the status of ideas in Marx's work which he does not often make quite so explicit, and which so many of his putative disciples have chosen to ignore. The architect is, himself, a historical 'product', but he is not merely a predetermined actor in a predetermined social drama. He functions by unifying the work of head and hand, though doubtless a few bricklayers will be needed before the structure opens its doors. These men too, however, will know what they are doing. Marx's metaphor helps us to understand something of the distinction between productive labour, which is the process he is describing, and reproductive process, about which he has nothing to say. The processes are similar in form, though quite different in content. In its 'pure' form, as described by Marx, productive labour is the act of an individual. To comprehend a self and a world and a task to be done, to work out the way to do it, to act upon this determination, to make something and know that one has made it, to 'reproduce' oneself daily by means of the labour process; all of this is the unity of thinking and doing, the fundamental praxis of production which is embedded in socio-historical modes of production. Reproduction is quite different. What has generally been argued or implied is that biological reproduction differs in that it is not an act of rational will. No one denies a motherly imagination, which forsees the child in a variety of ways. Women have their visions of the child to be born; visions, perhaps, of its beauty and its intellectual brilliance, its sex and its moral worth. The vision may also be less idyllic. In Scotland, there is an old phrase still used by women who are asked the usual question about whether they want a boy or a girl. 'As long as it's like the world' is the traditional answer, which reflects the dread of deformity or mental incapacity. Maternal imagination may also be fraught with anxiety about another mouth to feed, another dependence to bear. In other words, female reproductive consciousness knows that a child will be born, knows what a child is, and speculates in general terms about this child's potential. Yet mother and architect are quite different. The woman cannot realize her visions, cannot make them come true, by virtue of the reproductive labour in which she involuntarily engages, if at all. Unlike the architect, her will does not influence the shape of her product. Unlike the bee, she knows that her product, like herself, will have a history. Like the architect, she knows what she is doing; like the bee, she cannot help what she is doing.

These differentiations are real, but they are not so important as the formal similarities in the two processes. Both processes are dialectical, and the modes of understanding which grasp them are dialectically structured. Our friend Hegel went to tremendous and often obscure lengths to demonstrate that the structure of human consciousness itself, and the process of thinking, are dialectically structured. This is because mind and world are in some sense opposed, that the thinking subject stands apart from the object of perception and of thought. Hegel argues that the gap between the self and world is mediated by an objectified ideal unity of reason and action, while Marx argues for a lived, experiential unity of action and theory. The structure of consciousness is in any case dialectical because it reflects and reflects upon a being in the world which is dialectically structured. We want to extend and reinforce the theory that human consciousness is dialectical by arguing that the most primordial of human experiences are dialectically structured, but that there are two of them, the reproduction of the self and the reproduction of the race, which stand in opposition to one another.

Let us think back from the need to produce to the hunger which produced the need, and consider the process of digestion, and how it is experienced. This particular process is not usually used in an exemplary way, for as a 'product', human excrement is not regarded as a higher stage of anything, nor as a suitable object of philosophy. The honourable exception is Freud. In his theories of infant development, Freud assumed the presence of alimentary and sexual hungers in all subjects, but the great fuss over his theories of polymorphous infantile sexuality and the emotional satisfactions of defecation has obscured an important truth. From our own digestive processes, we are conscious of a basic structure of process, our own participation in the opposition of externality and internality, and of the unification and transformation of objects.

People did not perish from the earth, however, as they sat in mute contemplation of their stool, and human history has surged somehow from scatology to eschatology. All that is argued here is that human consciousness apprehends the living body primordially as a medium of the opposition of internality and externality, of mediation, of negation and of qualitative transformation. Negation is rather a fancy word for the disappearance of an apple into the alimentary tract, but none the less that is what happens to the apple. It is negated and transformed. When Marx argues that production and consumption are inseparable, he is enunciating not an economic dogma but an epistemological truth. Human consciousness *is* structured dialectically because the most basic human experiences are structured dialectically. In his analysis of labour process, however, Marx analyses the product of production and simply neglects the product of consumption. For Marx, the product of consumption is not the excretory product of mere digestion; the product of consumption is the *reproduction* of the life of the individual. We all understand in a common-sense and relatively uncritical way this relation of life and livelihood, of 'making a living', which is what Marx means by the reproductive aspect of producing. At an immediate level, however, we also understand the dialectical structure of our biological functions, but Marx does not analyse these. Whether this was a question of delicacy or not we cannot say; iconoclast though he was, Marx never freed himself entirely from the fetters of Victorian notions of respectability. Probably too, Marx, like Hegel, perceived organic functions as resistant to the operations of the free and rational human will, and therefore not true instances of human praxis. Marx and Hegel are not interested in immediate experience, but in mediated experience, though they did not consider the mediations involved in paternity. Further, though digestive metabolism is, as it were, experienced dialectics in a formal sense, it is not the creation of value, and Marx's definition of labour is that labour is the production of value. Freud, on the other hand, insists that the product of metabolism is a value for infants. Neither of them argue that a child itself is a value produced by reproductive labour.

The value created by productive labour is for Marx twofold. There is, of course, the value of the product, but there is also the value of sociability. Marx's abstract formulation of the labour process never loses sight of the social nature of labour. The need to produce sets up definable sets of social relations. This is, of course, historically true, but is not true in the pure case. If we were able to abstract any individual from the social world and dump her into the natural world, the possibility of personal survival would not automatically disappear; the individual could, like all those legendary castaways on desert islands, survive in a biological sense, could 'reproduce' her organism. Likewise, if we visualize primeval man ranging in the fecund forest, his personal survival by his own efforts is not impossible. In the most primordial and abstract sense, 'reproduction' in Marx's sense − the daily reproduction of oneself − is *not necessarily social*. It becomes social historically. Reproduction in the biological sense, however, is necessarily social from any perspective, practical or abstract. The arch wisdom of the baby congratulation card is correct: One plus one equals three. This has not, of course, stopped men making myths of self-regenerating creatures. Yet the more common male arguments as to the essential sociability of mankind are rarely grounded in the essential integrative sociability of reproductive process.[19] Men are awarded some 'essence' of sociability by idealist philosophers, usually related to human nature theories or God's will. Marx's materialism grounds sociability in the historical development of productive relations. A feminist philosophy of birth must ground sociability and the ethics of integration where they belong: in the essentially social process of reproduction.

Freud, after his impressive insight into the relation of the structure of individual consciousness and alimentary dialectics, turns his attention less successfully to the question of the childhood of the race.[20] He wants to argue that psychic structure is a response to both individual and collective experience, and he looks rather yearningly on the romantic notion of some kind of subconscious ancestral memory. Freud's primitive man is, as it were, an adult child and, being romantic, he not only disregards productive activity, but has no reproductive consciousness either.[21] He is concerned with his sexuality, a sexuality related to reproduction only in a regressive way: this man is preoccupied with his parents and his brothers, the existing kin, and thinks not one whit of his own progeny. The significance of male/female opposition is seen by Freud to rest in sexual antagonisms between men, rather than in reproductive relations. The truth is, of course, that reproductive activity is genderically differentiated, while sexuality as such is not. Sexuality, like digestion, is a biological universal. Men and women are sexual creatures, and libido is not the prerogative of the male. Freud's error in separating primitive sexuality from reproductive process is magnificent in scale, and is only possible because it has an objective base: the process of reproduction does impose a temporal gap between sexuality and parturition for men, and it also separates men from all stages of the process except copulation. It is thus from the standpoint of separated sexuality rather than integrated birth that Freud launches humanity on to the guilty tides of history. He offers us a group of primitive brothers eager to appropriate their mother as sex-object, the apparent absence of other women being not actual and historical but psychological and Oedipal. Female sexuality remains insignificant in this creation drama, as does reproduction. The brothers are constrained to kill one source of life, their father, while the mother lives on. With a sensitivity remarkable under the circumstances, the brothers are ashamed of their lust and their patricide. Freud even suggests that out of this sense of guilt they not only renounced the sexual favours which their patricide was intended to ensure, but also bestowed upon their mother, presumably as compensation, the 'mother right discovered by Bachofen.'[22] This was a temporary aberration, however. Once they had sublimated their guilt, men assumed their natural position of superiority and sexual entrepreneurship.

Freud's creation myth is wrong because he posits a primordial opposition in sexuality – passive woman versus active man – while he neglects the real generic oppositions in reproductive process. He offers us a sexual myth which is myth precisely because it separates sexuality from reproduction, It is, however, a persuasive myth in the masculine mind, because the process of reproduction actually does separate *male* sexuality from reproduction, in the alienation of the male seed. Freud's myth, like all masculine creation myths, defies the dialectical significance of the uncertainty of paternity.

Marx, on the other hand, finds at the dawn of human history a happy primitive man, guiltlessly and satisfyingly discovering his unity with people and nature in productive activity, and, in the dialectical process of need ⟷ labour ⟷ production ⟷ consumption, changing the world, himself and his social relations. This man appears to be untroubled by sexual yearnings: his problem is his species continuity.

Marx's man is related to his forefathers, not biologically, but in terms of his status as heir to the tools of his ancestors. How is this affirmed? Because, says Marx, the simplest observation of the instruments of production, of tools, shows the labour of past ages.[23] Perhaps so: but past ages are not then apprehended in action but in passive observation, and it is difficult to see how these artifacts advertise their human content immediately. Women do not apprehend the reality of past ages in a meditation on the probable history of a hammer, but in the mediation of real labour. This fact is not discussed by Marx. What he wants to do is to show that human continuity is a continuity of labour, the labour of ancestors congealed in the means of reproduction. This is important, for it abolishes the notion that the appropriation of the means of production can ever be understood as a fair and rational exchange, for there can be no rational commerce with the dead. Marx needs a continuity which is both material and historical, and his single productive individual is integrated in productive activity with a universal class of heirs and successors for whom the presence of ancestors is made manifest in tools. Living children cannot be recognized as the guarantors of the reality of the dead within this framework, for there is no dead productive labour power congealed in their living persons. The fact that there is reproductive labour power congealed in every living or dead person presumably does not count. Marx is not wrong about these tools as evidence of past generations: the question that feminist consciousness asks relates to the onesidedness of the analysis.

The task of reconciling the contributions of Marx and Freud to human understanding is a major intellectual problem of our times, and one which many feminists see as crucial. Freud tells us a great deal about the repressive conditions of the bourgeois form of family, Marx extends our knowledge of the problem of oppression in general. None the less, the theories as they are handed down to us are both onesided. Freud is insensitive to the importance of both production and reproduction, leaning heavily upon an autonomously determinant libido. Marx conflates production and reproduction, analyses productive labour only, and thus reduces the awareness of species continuity to an economist construction.

Hegel, Marx and Freud contribute to understanding of reproductive process in both negative and positive ways. Negatively, the question is largely one of omission. Hegel does not grasp the sense in which paternity is in fact an idea, precisely because he does not see that man is negated, not as lover, but as parent. This is the nullity which men clearly 'cannot bear', and history demonstrates the lengths to which men have gone to ameliorate the uncertainty of paternity, both conceptually and institutionally. Marx, prodigious though his humanity indubitably is, analyses 'value' in a way which has nothing to say about the human value which inheres in the 'product' of reproductive labour, and the value of the individual therefore tends to disappear in the collectivity of class. Freud becomes a little confused in his attempts to draw a parallel between the infancy of the individual and the infancy of the race. Having shrewdly perceived the importance of both of the biologically immediate experiences of digestion and sexuality for the infant, he analyses the childhood of the race only in terms of sexuality, not considering that adults must somewhere and at some time have comprehended both digestive and reproductive process as *discovery*. The discovery of reproductive dialectics is likely to have been historically later, in that it is neither individual nor immediate, and cannot be understood as dialectical process without the discovery of the causal relation of impregnation and birth. This requires an advanced stage of the development of human mental capacity.

The failure to take reproduction seriously in theoretical terms is not a failure only of these three particular men. Later on, we shall look at the way in which other thinkers, including some feminist ones, have tended to regard reproductive process as something prior and irrelevant to the more interesting questions of the history of the family, the ethics of parenthood or the processes of child development, to name but a few aspects of the social relations of reproduction which have been treated in serious and scholarly ways. The general neglect of reproductive process is itself a historical phenomenon of great interest. It is simply not good enough to dismiss people like Hegel, Marx, Freud and their philosophical predecessors as male supremacists whose vision was distorted by mere prejudice. As we have argued, it is only at a certain stage of development that the significance of the process of reproduction, as the grounds of specific sets of social relations, can be grasped in a theoretical way. Thus, the omissions in the work of these and other social thinkers challenge us to enquire into their roots. The development of a sophisticated technology of contraception, which transforms reproductive process, changes the historical situation in a way which demands such an enquiry from a specifically feminist perspective. This, of course, was something which male-stream thought could not and cannot do, so that the inevitability of male supremacy barely and only rarely bothered even to justify itself, and even less often turned a critical perspective on its reproductive consciousness. The few male critics of male supremacy, of whom Marx is one and John Stuart Mill another, were not able to mount their critiques on solid theoretical grounds. Marx and Engels are trapped in economic history. Mill falls back on the twin notions of superior male physical strength and defective masculine moral sense to explain and condemn the oppression of women.

Our feminist perspective is a material perspective, in that it attempts to root this long oppression in material biological process, rather than in mute, brute biology. For this reason, we have begun with some discussion of the nature and form of process as such, and have argued that the process of human understanding is indeed, as Hegel and Marx argued, dialectical. We have further argued that the dialectical structure of forms of consciousness is rooted in the dialectical structure of the primordial biological experience of our lived bodies, in that both digestive process and reproductive process are dialectically structures: they are instances of separation, unification and transformation. Likewise, the necessary human processes which these fundamental needs entail – which are the act of producing, in the case of the provision of sustenance, and the birth and care of infants, in the case of reproduction – are also dialectically structured. This dialectical form is carried into the social relations which emerge from the primal processes, social relations constituted by human praxis. The dialectics of productive experience and productive relations have been analysed and comprehended in an enlightening theoretical way in the work of Hegel and Marx. Reproductive dialectics and reproductive consciousness have not been subjected to such rigorous treatment. The dialectical model is useful for this purpose, but it must undergo considerable modification. Reproductive experience is not differentiated by the division of labour and subsequent social class formations, which is the historical form of development of production. Reproductive experience is differentiated at its most fundamental level in terms of gender: the opposition in question is the male/female opposition. This relation also becomes historically one of dominance and subordination, a relation which has developed for itself a lived reality, a powerful ideology and a determinable psychology. Male supremacy is not wholly material, wholly ideal or wholly psychological, but has aspects of all of these. This we saw even in our brief discussion of Hegel the idealist, Marx the materialist and Freud the psychoanalyst. What we must now do is to gather these partial gleanings and the immanent critique which has begun to develop into a more systematic expression. If, as is claimed, the biological process of reproduction and the human reproductive consciousness which emerge from it are dialectically structured, we must attempt a dialectical analysis of that process. As it has also been argued that the process changes historically, then we must also state which historical form of the process is under consideration. What follows is a consideration of that form of reproductive process which falls between the discovery of physiological paternity and the development of mass contraceptive technology, which is, of course, the form which has prevailed throughout most of recorded history.

The dialectics of reproduction

As a young student midwife, I learned about the stages of gestation and the stages of labour. This was a description of a unilinear process, starting at conception and finishing with the satisfactory establishment of lactation. In Canada, as in the United States, there are no midwives, and obstetrics is a branch of nursing, a development against which British midwives fought hard and unsuccessfully in the nineteenth century.[24] However, the texts available in obstetrical nursing still conform to the descriptive unilinear format.[25] They do not discuss questions of reproductive consciousness. We find discussions of the empirical signs by which pregnancy can be detected. There will usually be a chapter on the psychological stresses of pregnancy, and a chapter on the social aspects of childcare, and social support services available to mothers. There may even be a couple of sentences about fathers, but there will be no discussion at all of the formal problematic of paternity nor of the significance of patriarchy.[26] We may even find some theoretical work, theories of technique and physiological theory, but a theory of birth as such and the language of traditional philosophy will not intrude upon these practical treatises. Hegel's observation that the unity of the male and female seeds is at the same time the negation of the particularity of each seed would seem like a hopelessly obscure way of expressing a quite straightforward natural mechanism. Finally, the crucial differentiations in male and female reproductive experience are not particularly significant in terms of descriptive anatomy and physiology. What happens in textbooks, in fact, is much closer formally to what happens in male reproductive experience, despite the fact that the texts are indubitably dealing with an actual female experience and the books referred to here are intended for the predominantly female group of student nurses. What we find is that the whole process of reproduction is separated in an arbitrary way from the historical, experiential reality of generic relationships, of species continuity and of the social relations of reproduction. It becomes abstract process, just as paternity is essentially abstract process. This is not surprising. Modern obstetrics, as opposed to ancient midwifery, has been a male enterprise.[27] Men have brought to obstetrics the sense of their own alienated parental experience of reproduction, and have translated this into the forms and languages of an 'objective' science. Thus, the process appears as a neat unilinear affair going on in women's bodies in a rather mechanistic way. We do not claim that this is wrong or useless: we claim that it is not enough. We learn nothing from descriptive obstetrics which can further our knowledge of the dialectics of reproductive experience and reproductive consciousness, and we learn very little of the social relations of reproduction. We have therefore to identify the significant aspects of reproductive process in a way which can deal with the ambivalences gleaned from our preliminary meditation on masculine thought, as well as the inadequacies of the naturalistic descriptive approach to reproductive process.

Immediately, we have a problem with vocabulary. Physiological description moves from well-marked stage to well-marked stage in a unilinear time sequence: ovulation, conception, pregnancy, labour. We shall have to use a different language of process for a dialectical analysis. It is proposed that we start by referring to the identifiable and important points in reproductive process as 'moments'. Marx says sarcastically that this terminology has little value except to make things clear to the Germans, which is a crack at Hegelians.[28] However, the word is useful if its usage is explicated carefully. The moments in question are not ticks on a clock, nor are they moments in the idealist sense of abstracted instants in the flow of subjective consciousness. What we want to catch is the sense of determining, active factors which operate in a related way at both the biological and conceptual levels. We also want to capture the sense of a non-isolated *event in time*, a happening which unifies the sense of the two words 'momentous' and 'momentary'. The moments in question have nothing at all to do with stop-watches, X-rays or microscopes. The terminology is intended to evade both empirical inertia and biological determinism. This cannot be done without semantic juggling, but it cannot be rendered intelligible without language either. We can start by making a simple taxonomy of reproductive moments, but we must go on to elaborate the way in which they differ from 'stages' of reproductive process, the ways in which they interact; and we must also develop a theoretical framework for the analysis of the social relations which, it is claimed, constitute a historical superstructure in which the contradictions within and between these moments are worked out.

First, then, a simple statement of the moments of reproductive process:

The moment of menstruation
The moment of ovulation
The moment of copulation
The moment of alienation
The moment of conception
The moment of gestation
The moment of labour
The moment of birth
The moment of appropriation
The moment of nurture

Immediately, we see that there are important differences in these moments. Most, for example, are involuntary: appropriation and nurture are the only completely voluntary moments. Copulation is a halfway house: it has a strong instinctual component, but a great deal of human effort has been invested historically in demonstrating that it can or at least ought to be controlled by the human will. Alienation and appropriation are male moments: copulation and nurture are genderically shared moments; all of the others are women's moments. Yet these latter are differentiated too. Ovulation and conception are not tangible moments; they are not only involuntary, but are not immediately apprehended by consciousness. We therefore have quite a complex process going on, in terms of several factors quite outside the realm of simple biology. When we speak of voluntary and involuntary moments, we have entered the realm of the human will. When we speak of copulation and nurture, we speak of social relations. When we speak of appropriation, we speak of a relationship of dominance and control. Clearly, there is much more to reproduction than meets a narrow physiological eye.

However, not all of these moments are of equal interest to our analysis. Menstruation, for example, might be called a negative moment: it signifies its importance to reproductive process by not happening. Further, it shares with many of these moments a great big burden of accumulated symbolism and sheer superstition. Later on in our discussion we shall look at some of the bizarre ideological currents which have been introduced into the bloody flux of femininity, which seems to have fairly consistently frightened men out of their wits. Scientific understanding of the menstrual cycle was relatively late in developing, and Aristotle's deductions about the role of menstruation in reproduction are marvellous instances of the strength and weakness of formal logic; impeccably structured, they are quite untrue.[29] Aristotle appears to have believed that, as the blood disappeared with pregnancy, it must be needed for the manufacture of the child, and one can admire the ingenuity of that speculation. It may well have been commonly held in antiquity, and is perhaps part of the linguistic development which understands kin as 'blood' relations. Aristotle's further deduction that women contribute nothing to the child but this arrested menstrual flow has more to do with ideological patriarchy than it has to do with logical speculation, but this idea that women contribute only 'material' to babies while men contribute spirit or soul or some other human 'essence' must have struck chords in the masculine imagination, for it lingered for centuries. It is worth noting here to reinforce the contention that men do indeed attempt to resist the alienation of their seed, in this instance by claiming superior procreative potential for a sanctified sperm. Against this contention, it might be argued, quite persuasively, that men are quite indifferent to the uncertainty of paternity and, indeed, have very often been reluctant husbands who might well prefer to exploit that uncertainty to evade the responsibilities which male history has decreed for paternity. There can be no doubt that this sort of evasion has happened in particular cases, but far more powerful has been men's collective and concentrated attention to the problem of male separation from reproduction, both in their development of human institutions and in their articulation of ideologies of male supremacy. To suggest that men in general are indifferent to paternity is to make nonsense of centuries of strenuous masculine activity to negate the uncertainty of fatherhood, activity of which the institution of marriage is only the most obvious example.

The fact that menstruation seems to have inspired men to derogatory efforts in myth, magic and mania, despite the involuntary and wholly female nature of menstruation, is probably at least partly due to the visibility of menstruation. Such moments of reproduction as ovulation and conception are also involuntary, but being neither visible nor understood for a very long stretch of history, they have not excited quite such extravagant symbolism. As early as classical times, the notion of conception had already passed from any notion of unification, if such a notion ever did exist, to the notion of the domination of the male seed. This clearly has significant aspects for the understanding of the nature of man's perception of his role in copulation, and is part of the structure of what became known as male *potency*. However, we cannot simply say that men 'naturally' understood copulation not only as pleasurable, but as an exercise in domination and perhaps even priestly or political duty.[30] Pleasurability is an immediate property of copulation, whereas dominance and superiority are not. The notion of potency requires historical development; it is a complex concept, which goes far beyond the mere capacity to impregnate. Potency is a masculine triumph over men's natural alienation from the process of reproduction, a triumph to whose dimensions and historical manifestations we shall have to return. Potency is the name men have given to their historically wrought success in mediating experienced contradictions in their reproductive consciousness.

The involuntary mechanics, then, of ovulation and conception remain abstract in terms of male reproductive consciousness, while masculine science and speculation orders their structure according to masculine needs. The gestation period is also involuntary, although it has always been possible to terminate pregnancy with varying degrees of feminine suffering, up to and including the deaths of mothers, children or both. Pregnancy is clearly significant in terms of women's understanding of their reproductive capacity. It also has visible manifestations, a fact which can bring pride or shame to women in societies where patriarchal values prevail. The most rigorous feminist theorizing must swerve away from the path of detached analysis when it contemplates the anguish in which millions of women through the ages have concealed and terminated pregnancy. This is one reason why we must develop different modes of understanding and expression of female experience. Objectivity is a fraud if it rejects sisterhood as wishful sentiment, or spurns the understanding of the unifying reality of transhistorical female suffering as romantic subjectivity. The point is important not only humanistically but theoretically. The female reproductive consciousness whose historical reality we are attempting to establish is a universal consciousness, common to all women. We are not at all engaged in a psychology of pregnancy, or in the subjective experience of one man who parts with his seed and one woman whose femininity involuntary creates and gives birth to one or more children. Pregnancy is the positive pole, as it were, of the negative pole of menstruation. These are the visible and communally understood signs of female potency, of the unity of potential and actual. All women carry the consciousness of this unity, just as all women carry the notion of suffering and labour and decisions to be made. Women do not need to bear children to know themselves as women, for women's reproductive consciousness is culturally transmitted. It is a tribute to the indelibility of male-stream thought that we should have to make this point. Man knows himself as some kind of universal being with all kinds of shades of power and promises of immortality which particular men do not and cannot demonstrate. Man as universal may indeed be rational and noble and creative, but in the particular man these qualities are quite often as invisible as ovulation or conception. It is precisely this capacity to posit himself as universal, to assert a brotherhood of man, which has permitted men to make the history of man. The historical isolation of women from each other, the whole language of female internality and privacy, the exclusion of women from the creation of a political community: all of these have obscured the cultural cohesiveness of femininity and the universality of maternal consciousness. Menstruation and pregnancy have been at times 'decorously' shrouded, at other times bravely waved as the flag of the potent male. Breasts have been sometimes flaunted, sometimes flattened, understood as sensual tit-bits rather than as purposeful instruments of nurture. All the while, men have fashioned their world with a multiplicity of phallic symbols which even Freud could not catalogue exhaustively.

These involuntary, feminine moments of reproductive experience are symbolically important in the development of female universality, so that we do not simply ignore them in our elaboration of the dialectics of reproduction. They represent, as it were, 'pure' opposition between male and female, an abstract and formal opposition which cannot be resolved. They are the biological manifestations of the material oppositions of female and male which must be worked out in a socio-historical way by real, live men and women. Menstruation, ovulation and pregnancy represent the integrative potency of all women, which may terrify men, but the history of male supremacy is a great deal more than male psychological response to ignorance, terror and envy of the womb. The history of male supremacy is the history of the real domination of women, and to understand man's power to proclaim the triumph and universality of his potency over her organic and particular potency we must move on to the analysis of the more complex moments of reproductive process. We shall have to deal in a rather artificial sequence with the four moments which our taxonomy has isolated from each other, but which are in fact related in a dynamic and dialectical way. These are the moments of alienation, appropriation, nurture and labour. This alteration of sequence is deliberate. Alienation and appropriation are the male pole of a process to which female labour stands as the opposite: this is an opposition of separation and integration, but that abstract statement needs to be explained, and will be. Nurture, the sharing of responsibility for dependent infants between men and women, is the synthesis of the male/female opposition in social terms, which in turn creates a new opposition, the opposition of public and private life. This, too, is an abstract formulation to which we must give human and historical content. Perhaps we can come to grips with these complex moments of reproduction if we examine them separately, and then analyse their relationships.

Much has already been said about the alienation of the male seed in the act of ejaculation. Perhaps we should make it clear once more that we are not speaking here about some kind of psychological process, a sense of loss or something like that. Alienation is not a neurosis, but a technical term describing separation and the consciousness of negativity. We have criticized Freud for his reduction of reproductive consciousness to anxiety neurosis, but we do not, of course, deny that there are important psychological dimensions to reproductive experience. Our interest, though, which we have derived from Hegel in a way which neither he nor his followers would like very much, is in a more fundamental view of the nature of human consciousness and the form of process of that consciousness. Consciousness, we have argued, resists alienation, the separation of the thinking subject from 'the world and from experience of the world and the negation of the self. It is in this sense that we speak of the alienation of the seed. Men experience themselves as alienated from reproductive process, and the questions we have to ask are these: What exactly are men alienated from? What do men do about it?

Fortunately, we do not have simply to guess at the answers. They are written in the history of patriarchy and in the philosophies developed by male-stream thought. We shall be looking at some of this evidence presently, but here let us state possible answers in a way which catches the fundamental dialectical sense of separation and opposition.

First, we note that men's (or women's) discovery of physiological paternity is the discovery *at the same time* of men's inclusion in and exclusion from natural reproductive process. This opposition of inclusion and exclusion must be mediated by praxis.

Second, men's discovery of physiological paternity is the discovery of freedom. Men are free in both the senses of freedom which liberal thought has developed: there are positive and negative aspects of paternal freedom, freedom *from* and freedom *to*. Men are aware of parenthood but free from reproductive labour. They are also free to choose paternity, or, as they have liked to put it, to 'acknowledge' the child as theirs. Yet, to borrow a famous phrase from Rousseau, men are 'forced to be free'. This is a further contradiction, for, of course, to be forced to be free is to render that freedom problematic.

Third, men are separated by the alienation of the seed from continuity over time. There is no tangible, experiential link between generations, no mediation of the time gap as women experience in the act of reproductive labour. Men are isolated in their individual historicity, the dimensions of their own lifespan. The notion of man as a historical creature has been a very important component of male philosophical activity since Giambattista Vico first articulated the theory that history constitutes what men can 'hope to know',[31] for men have created history. The notion of man as a historical being is also, of course, a fundamental postulate of both Hegel's and Marx's social theory, to say nothing of Heidegger's powerful ontological assertion that Being *is* Time. Yet man's relationship to history, to continuity over time, is fundamentally problematic. At the primordial level of genetic continuity, of the continuity of the species, men are separated from natural continuity. Male reproductive consciousness is a consciousness of discontinuity. Underlying the doctrine that man makes history is the undiscussed reality of why he must. The alienation of his seed separates him from natural genetic continuity, which he therefore knows only as idea. To give this idea substance, man needs praxis, a way of unifying what he knows as real with an actual worldly reality. Men must therefore make, and have made, artificial modes of continuity.

The significance of the alienation of the male seed, then, lies in resultant forms of male reproductive consciousness. This is a consciousness of contradiction, a series of oppositions which must be *mediated*. Men are separated from nature, from the race and from the continuity of the race over time. This brings us to the second question: What do men do about it? More properly, perhaps, the question should be framed in the past tense and in a collective way: What has man done about it?

Over against the alienation of the seed we find posed, in the first instance, the moment of appropriation of the child, the almost universal mode of paternal mediation. Paternity is a universal phenomenon, though, unlike maternity, it takes versatile forms, as the anthropologists have shown us.[32] The appropriation of the child defies the uncertainty of paternity, yet it cannot do so in biological terms. It must do so in social and ideological terms. Unlike maternity, which is fundamentally social in so far as it involves at the very least the dyad of mother and child, paternity becomes social historically. The appropriation of the child cannot be made without the co-operation of other men. This is, in the first instance, because of the true 'universality' of paternity: some man, any man, has fathered this child. The assertion of one man's right to a particular child has to include some means of excluding all possible fathers from this relationship. There are several possible ways of doing this, which include:

1 Relations of trust between men and women;
2 Relations of trust between men;
3 The limitation of physical access to women;
4 The definition of paternity in a non-biological way:
   e.g. as related to the social role of husband.

Historically, all of these can be found in developed relations of reproduction, but two factors militate against the first. One is the strength of the sexual impulse in both men and women: trust and lust make uneasy bedfellows, and there is little evidence to support a view that humans are 'naturally' monogamous. In the second place, the relation of men and women within reproductive relations is a relation of the free and the unfree, the non-labourer and the labourer. Relations between men have an objectively causal base: they are relations of those who are forced to be free, a *brotherhood* of free appropriators. At the same time, they are rivals, and the guaranteeing of paternity forces co-operative agreements between men in relation to access to 'their' women.

Paternity, then, is not a natural relationship to a child, but a right to a child. 'Right', of course, is a political concept, which makes no sense in anything other than a socio-legal-political context. The assertion of right demands a social support system predicated on forced co-operation between men forced to be free. It is the historical movement to provide this support system which transforms the individual uncertainties of paternity into the triumphant universality of patriarchy. This is also the point at which the notion of potency expands far beyond a merely sexual connotation. The creation of a patriarchate is, in every sense of the phrase, a triumph over nature. The notion of man as nature's master is often regarded a product of the modern age and the development of science. This is too limited a view. Men did not suddenly discover in the sixteenth century that they might make a historical project out of the mastery of nature. They have understood their separation from nature and their need to mediate this separation ever since that moment in dark prehistory when the idea of paternity took hold in the human mind. Patriarchy is the power to transcend natural realities with historical, man-made realities. This is the potency principle in its primordial form. It simply is not an accidental fact that politics has been generally understood as an exercise in power. We cannot say categorically that paternity was the first historical development of the concept of right. We cannot say categorically that man's discovery of the problematic freedom embedded in his reproductive experience was his first notion of the concept of freedom. We cannot say categorically that the discovery of the ability to rearrange nature's more problematic strictures was man's first taste of potency and power. What we can say is that, if these things are true, then the history of patriarchy makes a great deal more sense than it otherwise can. Men have resolved their separation from nature in a new integration which at the same time conserves their 'natural' freedom. This has been a very tricky business, for at its heart there remains the reality of alienation and exclusion which is the soft core of the potency principle.

The question of a right to appropriate children does not exist in an inert theoretical vacuum, nor is it without its own tensions. It is the translation of this right to real social relations and the internal stresses inherent in reproductive process which both relate and divide male and female reproductive consciousness. This complexity leads us directly to consideration of the moments of nurture and of parturitive labour.

As a political concept, and as a major concern of political theory, right has usually been posited as one side of a coin of which the other side is the doctrine of responsibility. This relationship is by no means so consistent in terms of actual experience, for the assertion of right without responsibility is the hallmark of naked power, a phenomenon not entirely unknown in human history. The old question of the relation of right and responsibility has always exercised liberal theorists, who have historically sweated over the fine distinctions between liberty and licence, to say nothing of the tangled problems of the dichotomy of responsibility and free will. Despite these difficulties, 'right' by itself remains an abstract concept which has to be given a manifest presence in the world, an appearance which is recognizable. This can be done in symbolic terms, and has been done in this way, from the trappings of monarchy and the X on the ballot to the certificates which proclaim the right of obstetricians to exclusive access to women's reproductive anatomy, or the rights of husbands to the exclusive sexual use of women's bodies and the right to the title of father of a particular woman's children. The symbols, though, are not in themselves enough, nor can the important development of real property right say all that can be said about rights. Rights must be related to actual social relations between people, and it is in these social relations that the question of responsibility arises. The appropriation of an infant is the appropriation of a helpless creature. This does not necessarily mean that women must turn to men for help. Quite apart from nature's own provision of nutrition for the child, there is nothing to stop women turning to other women where they need assistance, and historically they have always done so in varying degrees. Paternal responsibility grows out of the fact that appropriation of the child requires a community of actively co-operating men, and the creation of social institutions to buttress the abstract notion of right.

Man the procreator, by virtue of his need to mediate his alienation from procreation, is essentially man the creator. What he has created are the institutional forms of the social relations of reproduction, forms which mediate the contradictions in male reproductive consciousness. Obviously, the most persistent and successful form is marriage, with all its variations. Yet marriage in itself is not an adequate expression of the right to appropriation. We must recall that the need to co-operate with other men in the creation of the conditions of appropriation is at the same time a relationship with rival potencies. The appropriation of the child symbolizes the rights of the father, but does little to reduce the uncertainty of paternity in experiential terms. The exclusive right to a particular woman is therefore buttressed by the physical separation of that woman from other men. In creating the right to the appropriation of children, men created that social space which political theorists have called the private realm. Whether mud hut or extended household, the private realm is a necessary condition of the affirmation of particular paternity, while the public realm is the space where men fore-gather to make the laws and ideologies which shape and justify patriarchy.

This separation of women from the larger social and natural world separates them from other men, most women, the means of expanding production and the developed political realm. It is an enforced separation, a condition and a result of the potency principle in action. It is as lord of the private realm that man gives substance to the right of paternal appropriation as a proprietary right. The need to appropriate children is specifically human, and men's participation in nurture emerges from the exercise of proprietary right. This is not simply because men partake in nurture; so do many male animals. The difference is that in one sense, with his knowledge of his separation from reproductive process, man sees his participation in nurture as voluntary. All wolves, for example, assist in nurture; some men assist in nurture. Further, and unlike papa wolf, men can assist in nurture indirectly. They can enslave or buy the labour power of others to assist in the task of rearing children. What men and wolves do share is *recognition*.[33] They both have status as providers, but to the wolf in his pack accrues neither the addition to status of political right nor moral righteousness, for he is doing what he must necessarily do. Men, on the other hand, have choices. To be sure, these choices come to be circumscribed in customary and legal ways, and the claim of a *right* to the child has in most societies entailed obligations towards the child, most particularly in societies and social classes where the separation of public and private is most effective. This developed pattern of right and obligation confirms paternity as both a political and a moral phenomenon. The 'good father' is admired on ethical grounds, and rewarded with domestic power and, in many societies, with political citizenship. The 'good mother' is merely natural, though family law provides safeguards to ensure that she stays so. Yet male participation in nurture also has symbolic social significance: it confirms a right to the child and a recognition of paternity which in fact rest on shaky biological foundations.

None of these considerations should be construed as implying some kind of rejection of any notion of affection, warmth and love between people and children. The family has frequently been defined as the realm of affective life, and it would be perverse to deny this. To be sure, affective life includes powerful emotions which are hardly loving, and both dramatists and psychoanalysts, for example, have found tragedy as well as romance and comedy in the endless generic accommodations of men and women in intimate relation with one another. Millions of men have loved their children, just as the unfeeling mother is not exactly an unknown phenomenon. These are the relations of *particular* families, and they vary in different societies. What this analysis is doing, in a still abstract way, is attempting to show the *general* relationship between the biological substructure and the social superstructure of reproductive relations, and to begin to indicate the real historical development of mediations of the contradictions in reproductive process. This includes the need men have to gain recognition of themselves as parents. The combined historical development of the right of men to appropriate children and the separation of social life into private and public realms are the significant means of mediation which men have adopted to this end. The forms that these mediations have taken are matters for empirical enquiry.

'Appropriation' has become a pejorative word, especially on the left of the political spectrum. Here, in the sense in which we have thus far used it, it simply means the assertion of a proprietorial right to a child which nature has omitted to provide for male parents. Given the historical attempts to combine this right with some level of responsibility for nurture of the infant, it does not seem in any logical way to entail the suppression of women. This suppression, it has been suggested, is tied to the need to ameliorate the ambiguity of paternity by the creation of a private realm, and the distrust of other men which complicates the necessary co-operation of patriarchs. Even then, there is still no irresistible process of domination involved in this development. There is no obvious or inherent reason, for example, why the work performed in the private realm should not have equal or even superior status to work performed in the public realm. We have noted that male reproductive consciousness has developed the notion of potency, but the ideological aspects of the potency principle itself have to stand over against the real potency of women whose labour actually reproduces the race. Further, we have argued that appropriation is the appropriation of a helpless infant, but that infant does not stay helpless; the edifice of patriarchy could not be built on the temporary helplessness of the very young. We thus must examine this act of appropriation a little more closely, and in doing so we must move from the generically shared moment of nurture to the female moment of reproductive labour.

The male appropriation of the child is more than the transformation of the infant to a rather troublesome piece of individual property. Embedded in the child is the alienated reproductive labour of the mother. Men claim more than the child; they claim ownership of the woman's reproductive labour power in a sense recognizably similar to, but by no means analagous with, the sense in which capitalists appropriate the surplus labour power of wage labourers.[34] Men are naturally alienated from their children; women are wilfully alienated by men from their own reproductive labour power.

Yet what does it mean to say that reproductive labour power is alienated and appropriated? It means, among other things, that the dialectical structure of reproductive consciousness is reaffirmed in the social relations of reproduction, and thus in female reproductive consciousness. At the biological level, reproductive labour is a synthesizing and mediating act. It confirms women's unity with nature experientially, and guarantees that the child is hers. Labour is inseparable from reproductive process in its biological involuntariness, but it is also integrative. It is a mediation between mother and nature and mother and child; but it is also a *temporal* mediation between the cyclical time of nature and unilinear genetic time. Woman's reproductive consciousness is a consciousness that the child is hers, but also a consciousness that she herself was born of a woman's labour, that labour confirms genetic coherence and species continuity. Male reproductive consciousness is splintered and discontinuous, and cannot be mediated within reproductive process. Female reproductive consciousness is continuous and integrative, for it is mediated within reproductive process. The fact that this integration has been labelled as 'passivity' by male-stream thought is part of the ideology of male supremacy. It is now hopelessly outdated, for the introduction of freedom of choice in a potentially universal way by the development of contraceptive technology means that women must create their mediations with procreative necessities.

Reproductive labour, like all human labour, creates value. What sort of value can this be said to be? Historically, instances can be found of the attribution to children of use value and exchange value, but this value inheres in the potential of the child. It is in its own potentiality as a labourer, an object of sexual gratification or as a reproducer of extra children that the child can have and has had a market value. This value is a socio-historically developed value which is not the product of reproductive labour, nor is it necessarily the value which men appropriate. Paternity is not theft. Further, the child has a human value simply by virtue of being human, of growing and maturing in all the wonder of nature's most stunning performance. For this, the child is not appropriated: it is loved. This is the value of the child's distinct personality, and is not the product of reproductive labour. It represents the unity and eventual separation of both parents and their child which

Hegel talked about, and is considerably enhanced by relations of mutual trust.

The value which is produced by reproductive labour might be called 'synthetic' value.[35] It represents the unity of sentient beings with natural process and the integrity of the continuity of the race. These are what men lose in the alienation of the seed, and, in a very real sense, nature is unjust to men. She includes and excludes at the same moment. It is an injustice, however, which male praxis might reasonably be said to have overcorrected.

The fact that synthetic value is the product of reproductive labour power means that the appropriation without labour of the child is, at the same time, the appropriation of the mother's labour power, embodied as synthetic value in the child. It is in a very real sense the appropriation of both a product of labour and of its 'means of production', the woman and her reproductive labour power. Women are not privatized solely to guard them from other potencies. They are privatized because their own reproductive labour power must be appropriated along with the child in whom it is embedded.

The complexity of male participation in reproductive process is such that it has presented challenges to men which it has not presented to women. Historically developed paternity represents a real triumph over the ambiguities of nature. It is achieved by masculine praxis, a unity of knowledge and activity integrated in an act of will, and objectifying the idea of paternity in the social reality of patriarchy. Men understand themselves as sharing a power over nature, a potency to give to their dualistic reproductive experience a unity which defies nature's injustice while it treasures her gift of freedom. In vulgar terms, fatherhood is a paradigm case of the possibility of getting something for nothing. The social forms which emerge from this complex series of mediations are therefore governed by what we have called the potency principle. They are relations of labourer and non-labourer, of appropriated and appropriator, of dualism and integration, of artificial potency and actual potency, of continuous time consciousness and discontinuous time consciousness, of female and of male. Yet the potency principal remains profoundly problematic, in constant need of revving up and redefining, of symbolizing and justifying. A huge and oppressive structure of law and custom and ideology is erected by the brotherhood of Man to affirm and protect their potency, and it is a structure which must be actively maintained, because at the heart of male potency lies the intransigent reality of estrangement and uncertainty.

The question of temporality, which has cropped up steadily in this analysis, deserves some further comment. The appropriation of the child and its synthetic value plugs men in, as it were, both to the cycle of nature which is completed in the birth of the child, and to the unilinear continuity of species time, which is a properly 'material' base of human history. All of women's reproductive moments except the ones she shares with men – copulation and nurture – are cyclical moments. Copulation and nurture are linear but episodic. Gestation does not automatically follow copulation, and the operations of sex-drive are unpredictable. There are thus three time modes involved in reproductive process: cyclical time, unilinear time and irregular episodicity. There are additional important considerations which emerge from this situation, which we can now elaborate in tidier form.

Female sexual receptivity differs from that of all other animals: women are immune to the cyclical compulsions of oestrus, and their sexual receptiveness, like that of men, is episodic. No other animals have this motivation to keep a sexual partner constantly at hand, but it should be noticed that this is not an exclusively male motivation, but applies equally to men and women. As one area of natural generic equality, this may well be a significant factor in the transformed social relations of reproduction which must emerge in the Age of Contraception. Liberated from the twin threats of unwanted pregnancy and the lumpen sensualist, women now share with men not only sexual needs, but the potentiality of shared sexuality and chosen parenthood.

Additionally, the differentiation of male and female time consciousness is a fact which male-stream thought has not sufficiently noticed, and which feminist scholarship must explore. The differentiation of natural time and historical time has been performed often enough, but the generic differentiation has not. Female time, we have noted, is continuous, while male time is discontinuous.[36] The discontinuity in male time consciousness partakes of a now familiar ambivalence: it frees men to some extent from the contingency of natural cyclical time, but deprives them of experienced generational continuity. Historically, men have clearly felt compelled to create principles of continuity, principles which operate in the public realm under male control and are limited only by men's creative imagination.

The problem of continuity over time has developed in western societies as a political problem, a quest for an 'order' of procession which transcends individual life spans in some self-regenerating way. Principles of continuity appeal either to cyclical time, and appear in all organic theories of the state, to an idealized form of continuity, such as the notion of eternity, which are a component of theocratic formulations, or to a practical instance of stable continuity, such as an economic order or a hereditary monarchy. The notion of history as a principle of continuity is a modern one to be discussed in Chapter 5, but time, separated from its biological roots, appears as a philosophical problem, which it undoubtedly is. However, thought about time is distorted where it neglects the generic differentiations in human time consciousness.

Finally, the time lapse between copulation and parturition exacerbates the uncertainty of paternity, and may well be a factor in man's conception of time as an enemy, to say nothing of the hardiness of the fear of the stranger which is a staple of the history of male domination. The idea of time as an enemy no doubt has connections with the fact of mortality, but it has roots in natality too. The shadow of lapsed time is the separation of men from the destiny of their seed. Paternity is, in a real sense, an alienated experience in abstract time: for men, physiology is fate.

This preliminary, and still very crude, analysis of the dialectics of reproduction is intended to be suggestive and heuristic, and by no means definitive and complete. The ultimate aim is to develop a feminist theory of historical process which can transcend the unsatisfactory reductionism which has bedevilled male-stream thought. The most interesting and promising socio-historical theory, it has been suggested, is that developed by Marx, and some further criticism of the limitations and strengths of Marx's model are offered in a later chapter. What we have been doing so far is attempting to develop a conceptual apparatus with which to ask our questions from a feminist perspective. Just as men have put nature to the question, women must now put male historical praxis to the question. This is not because women have suddenly decided not to put up with all this nonsense any more. The institutions of patriarchy are vulnerable because the Age of Contraception has changed the *process* of reproduction, and the social relations of reproduction must therefore undergo transformation.

Prior to the Age of Contraception, the most recent world historical change in the substructure of material necessities which determine the course of history took place in the productive rather than the reproductive mode. This was, of course, the development of capitalism. That event produced a new science, the 'dismal' science of political economy, developed by the revolutionary class of that struggle, the bourgeoisie. The changes wrought by the possibilities inherent in the mind-blowing capacity for rational human control of reproduction will no doubt also produce a new science. There are signs that this is happening: the development of feminist theory and feminist practice is still at a rudimentary level, but not so rudimentary that it is not recognizable as an irreversible historical force. However, we may have to be patient for a while before an Eve Smith joins Adam in the annals of intellectual history. The new mode of reproduction radically transforms the social relations of reproduction, and in this historical movement women constitute the progressive social force. This fact will take quite a bit of getting used to.

Here, we do not claim to have discovered the new and still nameless science which can provide the theoretical component of feminist praxis. Our perspective is a limited one, growing out of the discipline of political theory, and growing furthermore in a still partial and idiosyncratic way which will no doubt infuriate many political theorists. Yet the shadow of a theory is beginning to emerge. There is no need to develop a new vocabulary. The notions of power, of continuity and stability over time, of the opposition of individual and collective interest, of the separation of the public and private realm, of the organic state, of freedom and responsibility, of dialectical process, of the brotherhood of man: none of these notions are foreign to traditional political thought. The suggestion that these concepts are related to reproductive process is not new either, as I hope to show in subsequent discussions. What is new is the standpoint of analysis; the standpoint of women.

There is one further conceptual notion which will be examined in some detail, a concept which has not yet been utilized, but which in a sense summarizes the series of contradictions and the essential dualism of male reproductive experience which I have attempted to analyse. It relates to perhaps the oldest and most persistent problematic that has jiggled the ruminations of political philosophers, which is the human nature question. It is no longer quite so fashionable to argue for a fixed human nature, and such arguments as do persist have taken a woeful fall from heavenly Edens to those steamy jungles where sociobiologists discover their own smiles on the faces of tigers and fruit flies. No attempt will be made here to argue a theory of fixed human nature. What is interesting is that such arguments have never proved adequate: from early days, male-stream thought has toyed with the notion that man, in fact, has two natures. The nature of these two natures has been the subject of endless debate. It went on in the Athenian polis, and the notion of 'second nature' is embedded in ordinary language: it is 'second nature' to stop at a red light, to love children, to pursue survival, and so forth. In philosophical terms, the Greek view that man is divided between his first (biological) nature and his second (cultural) nature has remained a tenable proposition. What has never been clear is whether or not women have a second nature. Probably not: women, by virtue of their reproductive function, are 'closer' to nature, and by virtue of their passivity have never bothered to develop a second nature.

This is an important theme. The difference between man's first and second natures is that he makes his own second nature historically. Included in that historical view of himself is his sense of superiority over women, even though the sociobiologists are now defensively arguing that he is actually also superior by virtue of his first (animal) nature. Our analysis of the dialectics of reproduction suggests a more concrete foundation for man's felt need for two natures: they emerge from his real separation from the natural world and from species continuity. This is a hypothesis which is probably worth testing, for it is related to the persistent dualism of male modes of understanding, to which I have already referred. The testing of such a radical hypothesis will require a great deal of philosophical effort, and no claim is made to have 'proved' it here. Yet in a world in which the need for reintegration with nature is becoming more and more apparent, it may well be an urgent task, and one for which integrated female consciousness is pre-eminently suited.

2 Sorry, we forgot your birthday

There is fairly widespread agreement that the first trumpet call of the contemporary women's movement was sounded in a reverberating and marvellous way by Simone de Beauvoir. *Le Deuxieme Sexe* appeared in Paris in 1949, and three years later had been translated into several languages: the English version, *The Second Sex*, was published in 1952.[1] The work became, properly, an instant classic, and since its publication de Beauvoir has been perceived as the prophetess *extraordinaire* of feminism. Yet the homage paid to this fine mind has been, one suspects, a homage which de Beauvoir herself must regard in an ironic way, for it is curiously evasive of both her real project and her actual achievement. What she was quite clearly up to was the mounting of a sustained attempt to lay a theoretical foundation for feminism, and for the understanding of the ground and history of the oppression of women. This attempt simply has not stimulated a theoretical dialogue: instead, her work has been almost immune from the creative critique for which it cries out, and the subsequent avalanche of feminist writings has tended to evade the theoretical implications of de Beauvoir's work. Shulamith Firestone, whose own work we shall examine in a moment, has rather diffidently hinted that *The Second Sex* may not quite be the definitive work, on the grounds that it is perhaps 'almost too sophisticated, too knowledgeable'.[2] Here, Firestone is uneasily acknowledging one of the real difficulties inherent in the notion of praxis: if theory is to be useful it has to be intelligible to a wide group of actresses who do not all have a philosophical education. I don't want to play down this problem, but I don't want, either, to accede to the implication in Firestone's remark, which is that gender relations and their history are relatively uncomplicated affairs. We can see a comparable and instructive situation in the socialist movement: the tendency to reduce the prodigious philosophical propositions of Karl Marx to a few simple-minded slogans has resulted in the dreary inflexibilities of orthodoxy, which offers a troubling concoction of intellectual inertia and strident 'revealed' truths.

One problem here is the ancient and erroneous assumption that profound knowledge is accessible only to elite superior minds, an implication which Marxists, as uncompromising egalitarians, must deny. The actual situation is that profound knowledge has been, throughout history, a class and gender-bound prerogative, a prerogative defended by, among other things, the ability to control the institutions, and subject matters of education, and the access to a particular vocabulary. The solution to this problem, however, is not simply to open up access to education, though this certainly helps, nor to simplify the vocabulary, though this, too, helps. It is doubtful that the Leninist notion of a 'vanguard' to lead the working class to the fountains of wisdom and the certainty of revolution is practically effective, either. Even if this did work, political ideological control by class is still qualitatively different from male supremacy.

In both cases, for feminism and for socialism, there are historical and epistemological questions of extraordinary complexity to be dealt with, and as far as the theoretical comprehension of male supremacy is concerned, the task certainly is in its very early stages. There is no easy route into the defended redoubts of male-stream thought: there is only the way of intellectual effort and critical practice. Simone de Beauvoir has never shrunk from such implications.

So let us take de Beauvoir seriously, and on her own ground. Firestone argues that the complexity of the theoretical propositions in *The Second Sex* comes from the fact that these are bogged down in existentialist preoccupations. If this is true, the correct critical approach would be to specify major existentialist tenets and then subject them to systematic critique. Firestone does not do this; she simply observes that de Beauvoir leans too heavily on Sartre.[3] To be sure, it is a major irony of de Beauvoir's work that she is herself critical of women who accept unquestioningly the philosophies and ideologies of male associates, while she does rather uncritically embrace Sartre's brand of existentialist philosophy. She does, however, use that philosophy creatively. Neither the German progenitors of this philosophy nor the French connection ever waver in their pursuit of authentic Man. Heidegger's *Dasein* never transcends *Das Man*; under Franz Fanon's white mask is a black man's face; and the presiding but depressingly elusive Muse of existentialist poesy is Frederich Nietzsche's Superman. It seems that Man Alone is a figure of profound, tragic and noble philosophical significance, while woman alone is a welfare problem. De Beauvoir is explicitly in rebellion against the generic assumptions of existentialism, but she wants women to share the quest for the authentic human life rather than question the concept of authenticity itself, with its extreme individualist and subjective biases.

A further ambiguity in *The Second Sex*, which Firestone notes, is that de Beauvoir writes a history of women based on the fundamental postulate that women have no history. This is not so contradictory as Firestone thinks, for what de Beauvoir is actually arguing is that the activity of 'making history', which is also the making of values, is an essential component of authenticity, and that women have let men make their history and their values for them. Their history is shot through with their acceptance of masculine values. In the existentialist view of things, this constitutes 'bad faith'. Bad faith is the inactivity involved in the refusal to 'make oneself' freely and responsibly, preferring the passive acceptance of the definition of one's reality proposed by others. None the less, bad faith is something rather more complex than a mere cop-out. It has an ontological foundation resting in the intransigent dualism perceived as inherent in the human condition. De Beauvoir does not question the actuality of this pervasive notion of dualism, which I have suggested may be a specifically masculine experience. She accepts dualism as a common human experience, and attempts to give meaning to generic divisions in the light of this universal need for mediation of the dualism inherent in the human condition. She believes that the historical and cultural manifestations of human attempts to mediate the dualism of experience are ontologically rooted, are implicit in what it means 'to be', but that the mediating consciousnesses which have tried to do something about their fractured realities have been masculine consciousnesses. Women and their female consciousnesses are primordially Other, and have been *objects* of male mediation, one pole of the intransigent dualism of male/female, rather than subjects actively mediating their own subjectively experienced dualism. If de Beauvoir is to be criticized, it is her model of a common, dualist but genderically differentiated consciousness which must be considered seriously, and her insistence that woman is primordially Other, an object and never a subject in her historical development: one lonely leg of a dualism which she somehow shares with men who have courageously and freely faced up to the risky job of mediating their two-legged existential fate.

As dualism is perceived as 'natural', the mediation which men must perform to overcome this condition takes the form of resistence to nature, and de Beauvoir argues that the significant movement in masculine history is *anti-physis*, that male values have been created in the course of a historical struggle to overcome nature. Life by itself, without humanly created values, can have no meaning, and the re-creation of life is but the mindless urge of the species to persist, without even the consciousness of persisting *in time*. What stands between women and the knowing recognition of the significance of temporality is, predictably, reproductive process, which makes women dependent on men and obscures their knowledge of themselves as historical beings. They remain immured in natural process, by definition irrational.

De Beauvoir's version of the dualism of the human condition posits a space between mere biological life and 'existence', understood as a unity of responsible creative experience and subjective understanding of this experience. The key concept in understanding this distinction between life and existence is 'transcendence'. Man transcends his animal nature by his ability for projection, apparently in its double sense. He devises 'projects' and 'projects' a future, thus developing the sense of time which the notion of a future implies. He is able to do this because he is inventive and unrestrained by the 'painful ordeal of childbirth' which to women in prehistoric societies, must have 'seemed a useless or even troublesome accident'.[4] Birth, de Beauvoir claims, was never perceived as so important in primitive forms of human society as manual labour. This was because the self-evident need to provide food and shelter ensured that man was forced into creative activity. Giving birth, according to de Beauvoir, is not an activity in the human sense, and carries with it no pride of creation. Further, male activities which transformed inert brute life to historical human existence were often dangerous: in performing such activities men risked their lives, and risking one's life is much more prestigious than merely giving life: the former is transcendence, the latter mere immanence. One is a human choice, the other a natural burden. Prestige is, of course, a created social value, and, indeed, this is what transcendence is; the ability to create value and to be recognized by others as so doing.

De Beauvoir acknowledges the origin of this analysis in Hegel's celebrated philosophical myth of the encounter of master and slave.[5] In fact, she claims that in some respects Hegel's arguments apply much better to the relations of man and woman than to those of master and slave. Hegel's parable has concerns which are multifaceted and cosmological in their scope: it attempts to encompass factors which are epistemological, anthropological, social, moral and biological. The life-risking confrontation of master and slave is, for Hegel, the beginning of history; a journey towards the universal union of the rational with the real.[6] Incorporated in this formidable vision is Hegel's criticism of the empiricism of the Enlightenment, which had failed, in his view, to give a satisfactory account of problems about knowledge which had been raised in antiquity. To do this, Hegel posits self-consciousness as an active mediator between subject and object, rejecting the notion of a merely passive receptivity of experience. Whatever the merits of the master and slave parable, Hegel's achievement is profound and important, and sadly unknown to the stimulus/response generations, which are content still to gaze at the squiggles on the *tabula rasa* of human cognition with no interest in how they got there beyond immediate stimuli. This model of consciousness leaves no space between life and existence to mediate, and incidentally plays havoc with the notion of free will, which its progenitors were much concerned to propagate. Hegel had, of course, taken on the task of unifying subject and object in a dialectically structured continuum of rational and historical mediations. Having established the form and the reality of self-consciousness in the early chapters of *The Phenomenology*, he had to make the shift from individual self-consciousness to a social life in which free will and reason could be objectified, and the master and slave parable signifies the movement from undifferentiated to differentiated self-consciousnesses, illuminated metaphorically in his account of recognition by one self-conscious being of another, and the ensuing struggle for affirmation of being by self and other. Yet Hegel's scenario remains a recognition and a struggle for recognition between two adult males. Master and slave are inaugurating human history and the transcendence of nature in conditions under which the institution of patriarchy is already established for all time, and from time out of mind.

De Beauvoir's claim that the master and slave passages are applicable to men and women is, therefore, problematic.[7] Theoretically, the problem is one of what sort of historical model emerges. Hegel's parable is very significant in the class struggle model of history, as Marx was able to see, but it said little about the history of generic struggle. In substituting the latter, de Beauvoir, who posits socialism as the condition of generic equality, loses sight of class distinctions. Both accounts are one-sided, which suggests a need for a model which can embrace both of these realities of human history. De Beauvoir points out that Hegel says that the advantage to the master comes from his 'affirmation of Spirit as against Life through the fact that he risks his own life; but in fact the conquered slave has known the same risk'.[8] It is only women, she argues, who take no risks and gain no recognition. She does not consider the risk inherent in childbirth, for women do not choose (or did not choose) to take these risks. She also implies that no known society grants recognition to women as the reproducers of the people who must be born before history or value can have any meaning at all. Hegel perceived that, by the enslavement which was the price of withdrawal from the freely chosen risk of death, the loser of the battle for mastery was presented with the humanizing and rational opportunity to re-create his world through productive labour, a world from which women were excluded by their preoccupation with essential tasks related only to the survival of individuals in the circumscribed world of the social relations of reproduction, namely the family. Yet de Beauvoir cannot, like Hegel, abandon women to immanence and animality, so she proceeds to make a rather unconvincing distinction between a dependent consciousness and a relation of subjugation.[9] Women, she claims, as potentially authentic existents, *recognize* the values which men are busily creating. They do not make their own values, but this is not because they exist 'naturally' in the realm of immanence, but because men, in defence of their privileges, have created the private realm and imprisoned women in it.

De Beauvoir does not tell us why or how men did this in the first place, except to claim that women were prevented by their reproductive imperatives from participating in this making of values which is at the same time the making of history. She does not really rescue women from the sort of ontological passivity which Freud and others have decreed as female destiny. Transcendence, for Hegel's slave, is the affirmation by an existent of a project and the ability to realize that project, a process mediated by labour. It is low-level but authentic architect work rather than mere bee work. De Beauvoir's female existent simply cries 'Me, too!' She has been shown by men the possibility of freedom and wants it, but she has not, like Hegel's slave, discovered that possibility for herself.

De Beauvoir's model of consciousness and female immanence is too rigid. There is no way of escape, except by an undignified catch-up scramble along the paths which men have beaten. She does not analyse with sufficient rigour how much of 'immanence' is natural and how much historical. She assumes an immanence which rests, on the one hand, on an intransigent and unalterable biological function and, on the other hand, on certain transcendental assumptions about the nature of social life, such as the hypothesis that women are too weakened by childbirth to participate in production or to demonstrate inventiveness. She is, in fact, less aware of the difficulties of an analysis of human history which gives a negative value to the process of reproduction than Hegel himself was.

The *raison d'être* of the master and slave dialectic is fundamentally social, and the object of the struggle is 'recognition'. Again, this is ambiguous, with the calculated ambiguity with which Hegel uncovers contradiction. It is 'recognition' in the perceptual sense, the sense of 'facts of consciousness', but it is also recognition in the reputational sense of political and social reality. Reputation needs social relations and the light of day, but for Hegel women were a negative 'dark principle', a romantic notion which appears to owe quite a bit to Eve.[10] He was convinced that the confrontation of master and slave cannot ensue until the biological opposition of man and woman has been dealt with. The reason that this relation is eternal is that it is constituted by an opposition which is natural and not properly dialectical. Women are negated without a struggle because they have no potential for self-consciousness: they are a dark and self-negating principle of nature, and, as Hegel argued later, nature is impotent (*Ohnmächt*). Women cannot be either masters or slaves because, in the first instance, they do not have a contradiction between themselves and nature to negate and, in the second instance, they cannot 'risk life' because, as helpless and compulsory bearers of children, they are the amoral principle of life itself. The control over beasts and women which God gave to Adam, Hegel has already given to pre-self-conscious man. It is the pre-condition of the move from an unawakened to an awakened consciousness. In effect, the office of father is man's first political office; political in the sense that it permits him to move from inchoate self-preservation to the knowledge of others which, given Hegel's contention that 'no relation to an object is possible except mastery over it',[11] becomes the realization of the other, not only as an object for knowledge, but also as a challenge to govern. In his knowledge of power over others, united with concern for their helplessness, the primordial patriarch becomes the progenitor of political man, unifying his power with his moral sense, the still inchoate sire of Platonic man in all his splendour. The superiority of men over women remains rooted in the natural order, which does not require political and ethical acts of will and derring-do; it is immediately apprehended. The superiority of men over men, on the other hand, requires recognition, self-consciously willed and running the gauntlet of death in life-risking struggle. De Beauvoir is wrong in attempting to annex the symbolic saga of master and slave for relations between women and men, for the attempt is inconsistent with her theme, so often expressed, that women have no history; Hegel's master and slave both make history, and discover the values of struggles for power over other men and power over nature. She and Hegel are in agreement as far as women's immanence is concerned, with the important exception that Hegel is quite content to allow this 'natural' situation to persist, with the addition of a limited infusion of domestic ethics from the moral reservoir of *Geist*. De Beauvoir, of course, is not.

The question is not, however, the adequacy of de Beauvoir's interpretation of Hegel, or, for that matter, of my own reading. What is involved is the much wider question of de Beauvoir's theory of sexual supremacy, and the strategies of liberation which such a theory indicates for women. The final chapters of *The Second Sex* are consistent but disappointing. De Beauvoir is anxious that women project a new social order, but nervous of the charge of mere utopianism. Her female projectionist, however, seems hopelessly disadvantaged, torn as she is between a project to ensnare man in her immanence and a project to struggle out of his gaoler's grasp, his 'project' of perpetuating her convenient and useful immanence. De Beauvoir's woman is perpetual natural object seeking to wrest an authentic human subjectivity from men who have neither the will nor desire to give it to her. The subjectivity which she seeks, the individuality which can project and transcend, is one she knows only at second hand. Freedom for women is finally an act which imitates men, rather than a confrontation and struggle with masculine otherness.

De Beauvoir acknowledges that economic freedom is a precondition of emancipation, and she also understands that economic freedom is not enough. Women, she notes correctly, find that joining the work force subjects them to the exploitation of all workers in capitalist society, yet does not relieve them of domestic responsibility. Women, she says in her concluding chapter, are only just beginning to develop a political and social sense. She does not, however, pursue the question of political action, and pays scant attention to the authentic potential of women wage-workers. Instead, she reverts to a long discussion of the difficulties in store for the very few emancipated middle-class, educated women.[12] The major problem addressed is the question of sexuality and its expression; her female existent is an erotic existent too schooled to inferiority to assert her sexual needs. De Beauvoir is right in believing this situation damages men and women alike. She is right in thinking that changing this situation will require prodigious activity – transcendence, if you will – by men and women alike. What she does not consider seriously is the co-operation of women with women. Authenticity remains an individual affair, as does freedom: to each her own. The notion of a real female collective consciousness, transformed by objective change in its reproductive base, is excluded by the ahistorical and abstract dogma of immanence.

Sartre has claimed that existentialism is a transitional stage in the movement to socialism, filling a historical gap due to 'the decay in bourgeois ideology [and] the temporary arrest of Marxism'.[13] Marxism is only one choice open to each existent. This is a view which predictably horrifies orthodox Marxists, but it is an attempt, however imperfect, to deal with some very real difficulties in the Marxist inheritance. These difficulties are historical and practical, and relate to tensions in Communist theory and practice, of which the non-appearance of proletarian revolution is simply the most obvious. Events which can at least theoretically be forced into a model of capitalist perfidy, such as the horrors of totalitarianism of the Right, are subjected to a dishonest 'analysis' which ignores totalitarianism of the Left. Other phenomena which elude dogmatic analysis — and Freudian psychoanalysis and contemporary feminist struggles are cases in point — can be dismissed as bourgeois prejudices. For Sartre and his comrades of the Resistance, the experience of fascism and its works, and the descent into irrationalism and the Stalinist terror, constituted the commanding historical problems which cried out for explanation. Such an explanation also had to take account of the collapse of the fraternalism of the Resistance after the war. Marxism provided a theoretical framework, but some revision was needed in the light of actual experience.

The related question was the vexed one of consciousness. Marx's prophetic account of a revolutionary transition from false to the true proletarian consciousness has not been fulfilled. Existentialism seeks clarification of this problem by returning to an attempt to understand individual consciousness as the ground of class consciousness, but it fails to move back again to the collectivity. Subjectivity falls into the melancholy void which is its essence and its opposition. Existentialism stretches liberal individualism as far as it will go, and where it goes is nowhere. Bad faith is not just the particular manifestation in the individual of the false consciousness of one's class. It emanates from immanence, and immanence is the transcended ground of the ontology of the individual male existent. Marx's brilliant and useful epistemological concept of alienation becomes problematic. Marx analysed the moments of alienation inherent in the process of wage labour, a self-estrangement from the self as producer. Existential alienation is alienation from the self as thinker. Bad faith therefore relates to what one thinks (or does not think) of oneself, and one's action becomes a matter of subjective individual projection not related necessarily to production or any other social necessity. It is the sad and empty triumph of the autonomous but totally isolated will.

De Beauvoir falls into this trap of subjective determinism, just as she succumbs to the more serious failure to relate female authenticity to reproduction. Giving birth, it will be recalled, is, in her analysis, not an activity, and brings no pride in creation. De Beauvoir comes very close to saying that for a woman to understand her reproductive function as creative is an act of bad faith.

Gestation, for de Beauvoir, is woman eternally in thrall to contingency. Her analysis suggests that the denial of this contention, the assertion by woman of creative pride and satisfaction in the birth of her child, or an understanding of nurture and child-rearing as authentic project, are simply evasions. They are defensive contentions, at best merely sentimental, perhaps rationalization of necessity, at worst an act of bad faith. In the Age of Contraception, whose significance for de Beauvoir lies primarily in freedom of sexual expression, this position is problematic. Effective contraception entails the choice of parenthood, the voluntary acceptance of a real as opposed to a philosophical risking of life. Yet it must also be asked if passivity is an accurate description of any form of reproductive consciousness at any time, in any society. The implication of de Beauvoir's model of human development is not only that parturition is non-creative labour, but that the product, the human child, *has no value*, that the value of children must wait to be awarded by the makers of value, men. She sees human reproduction as indistinguishable from that of other animal species, making reproductive labour a labour immune to the interpretations of a rational consciousness and incapable of forming an authentically human consciousness.

It is man, de Beauvoir insists, who turns his productive labour to the creative praxis whose product is value in the normative sense. She does not note that those who create values can also negate values. The low value of reproductive labour is not necessarily immanent in that form of human labour, but may well be assigned to it by those who are excluded from it. Men assign low social value to 'mere' biological reproduction, yet value children. Uncritical acceptance by women of the male deprecation of reproductive process, however garbed by the moth-eaten cloth of venerated Motherhood, becomes itself an instance of bad faith. The low social and philosophical value given to reproduction and to birth is not ontological, not immanent, but socio-historical, and the sturdiest plank in the platform of male supremacy.

Similarly, men value sexuality in the erotic sense. This value is more than the mere gratification which women share; sexuality represents the male moment of inclusion in genetic continuity, a recognition of male participation in continuity which is also his moment of exclusion.

Sexuality objectifies the potency principle in action. De Beauvoir shares the masculine evalution of sexuality and sexual freedom as having value superior to reproduction, thus accepting the measuring of an individual existent's experience in the light of another's values, even where it contradicts the experience of the individual existent in question, the experienced reality of procreating women. This is, by definition, bad faith. This core of bad faith is the negative component of de Beauvoir's important legacy to feminist thought.

Sheila Rowbotham has a better understanding of the historical significance of the social relations of reproduction. As a Marxist, she is concerned with the failure of Marxism to comprehend the inadequacies of a rigidly economist historical model of class struggle, a problem I have already noted.[14] She notes that capitalism has eroded the patriarchal foundations of social life, yet has managed to maintain unequal exploitation of men and women, with a different value attributed to household tasks and child-rearing on the one hand and industrial labour on the other. Women who seek liberation have therefore a double task; the revolutionary action necessary to destroy capitalism, and the equally revolutionary task of developing a socialism which abolishes sexual inequalities, 'control not merely over the means of production but over the conditions of reproduction'.[15] Rowbotham believes that the intense vulnerability of women under capitalism has created the current raising of feminist consciousness, and will continue to do so. She calls for a unification of the exploited – by class, sex or nationality – which at the same time recognizes the particular problems of women. This is to be a political task, wholly dependent on the creation of a mass movement of working-class women. Rowbotham seems confident that the continued and exacerbated contradictions of capitalism will bring about the transformation of consciousness which will produce the desire for a socialist society among women, and stimulate the active intervention necessary to bring this about. She recognizes, of course, the enormity of this task. One of her posited preconditions of such a development is 'to work out the precise relationship between the patriarchal dominance of men over women, and the property relations which come from this, to class exploitation and racism'.[16] However, while she recognizes the antiquity of patriarchy, she discourages a 'chimerical pursuit of origins',[17] and in her own descriptive history of women as a revolutionary force she is mainly concerned with modern feminine revolutionary activity. The strengths of Rowbotham's work are the recovery of female revolutionary history, which rejects the notion that women are and always have been politically unconscious; her awareness of the problems of the transformation of consciousness; her insistence on the social significance of reproduction; and her understanding of the particular form of genderic oppression which emerges from capitalist property relations. The weakness of her work is theoretical. She is critical of the shortcomings of Marxism, but never develops a theory of history or consciousness by which the task of working out 'the precise relationship between the patriarchal dominance of men over women, and the property relations which come from this', might be comprehended. Perhaps the initial step is neglected: the comprehension of the relationship of men and women in its original historical development. Rowbotham appears to despair of such an enterprise, owing to the obscurity of the origins of such relationships. This is Firestone's position too. The whole argument about early matrilinear societies, it is claimed, is irrelevant to contemporary problems.

Rowbotham argues that Marxism in general, while providing an adequate historical analysis of modes of production and a valid critique of capitalism, has failed to pursue Engels's view of the socially formative aspects of production and reproduction, or to clarify the relationship between these processes and their social manifestations. She calls for theoretical reconsideration of both the process and relationships of production and reproduction, but, as noted, does not herself offer a dialectical analysis of such relationships. Historically her work is invaluable, just as, anthropologically, Evelyn Reed's work, to be discussed later, is provocative and importantly informative. What is lacking in both writers is a theoretical model which might both comprehend a feminist commitment to Marxism and, at the same time, provide the material basis for the contention that productive and reproductive functions cannot be simply collapsed into the ditch of a problematically dialectical 'substructure'.

Shulamith Firestone tackles the problem presented by dialectical materialism by simply rewriting passages from Engels to demonstrate that his definition of historical materialism omits, but could include, a more acceptable cognizance of the historical force of the relations of reproduction.[18] This procedure has the effect of conflating the two processes. Eleanor Burke Leacock, in a thoughtful introduction to a recent reissue of Engels's classic, calls once more for theoretical understanding, without which, she says, the women's movement may dissolve in arid confrontations and irrational rage.[19]

The difficulties of Marxist 'revisionist' feminism are threefold. First, there is general agreement that capitalist society is intransigently patriarchal, and that the cessation of the exploitation of women would create insurmountable problems for capitalism, which is dependent on this form of cheap and/or unpaid labour, both in industry and the family.

Second, there is general agreement that Marx's view of the unification of theory and practice as the essential prerequisite of effective social change is correct.

Third, there is a general sense that Marxist theory itself is not an adequate basis for feminist praxis. The problem is to specify what revisions are necessary, to analyse the historical base for such a revision and to clarify how far such a revision can proceed without the destruction of Marx's own theoretical achievements.

Firestone attempts to evade these problems by suggesting a selective approach. Marx's general theory of history is to be approached in a very guarded way in view of its economic determinism and male prejudice, while the dialectical 'method' is to be retained. *The Dialectic of Sex* enjoyed a large readership and a considerable influence in the early days of the contemporary North American feminist movement. Firestone extends to its logical conclusion de Beauvoir's view that the essential basis of women's inferiority lies in the immanent nature of childbearing. As it is the case, Firestone argues, that social inferiority rests upon a biology which is intransigent, then clearly women's liberation depends on the transcendence of biology. Modern science offers not only the choice for women as to whether or not to bear children, but the possibility of release from childbearing altogether, by means of extra-uterine pregnancy and developed methods of technological reproduction of the human species. Indeed, we have now seen the male-controlled media sing the birth anthems of the first test-tube baby, voices cracking between jubilation and hysteria.

Firestone does not recommend a universal march into Huxley's brave new world, but she does insist, correctly, that women will soon have the choice between bearing children or acquiring cybernetically produced infants. She attempts to develop a theoretical basis for this revolutionary event, compounded of a revised historical 'dialectic' and a consideration of psychoanalysis shorn of Freud's male-supremacist distortions. She is too astute, and perhaps too bored by Oedipal excesses, to argue simply that biology is or is not destiny; she wants to marshal her argument for feminist revolution on a more sophisticated theoretical foundation which incorporates the 'good' Marx and the 'acceptable' Freud. One of the curiosities of her unevenly luminous and episodic book is that, having attempted this, she then abandons her embryonic theory. Finally, her argument for the abolition of biological reproduction rests on the claim that 'pregnancy is barbaric' and that 'childbirth hurts'.[20] Any dispute about this can be attributed to a male chauvinist conspiracy rather than women's lived experience. This is a rather utilitarian notion; childbirth is devoid of pleasure and is wholly pain. Jeremy Bentham would appear to be a more suitable theoretical mentor than Karl Marx.

It is not disputable that women are now able to choose whether or not to have children, though this choice is circumscribed by nationality, class and religion. Women's ability to make such a choice is clearly an event of enormous historical significance. None the less, the reader of *The Dialectic of Sex* might well feel some misgivings about Firestone's rather naive reliance on technology, and it should be noted that her selectivity in the adoption of Marxist concepts appears to have rejected the analytical concept of alienation. She does not address the question of how mechanized reproduction can transcend the human alienation inherent in mechanized production in general. More important than these considerations, from both a theoretical and practical standpoint, is Firestone's use of the 'method' of dialectics. She considers that all social contradiction emerges from sexual division, that the man/ woman, yin/yang relationship is the root of the dialectical motion of human history. In other words, she does not analyse the relationship of the processes of production and reproduction, but substitutes generic determinism for economic determinism, then divorces generic antagonisms from any material substructure in favour of an abstract functional dichotomy. The opposition male/female is seen as the true basis of dualism which permeates western thought.

While a simple opposition of male and female is significant in human relations, it hardly accounts for the longevity of male supremacy. Firestone confuses mere dichotomy for dialectical contradiction. Mere unlikeness does not command mediation, and opposites can be complementarily coexistent. Hot does not take action to mediate its relation to cold. Firestone notes the objective basis of sexual differentiation; reproductive processes are common biological processes, but are at the same time generically differentiated. She is less successful in demonstrating in theoretical terms why this differentiation is also a dialectical opposition, or how it is mediated in socio-historical terms. She rejects metahistory of the Hegelian and Freudian variety; and she is especially scornful of Eros and Thanatos: it is therefore a little surprising that her own theory of history comprises a struggle of a couple of abstractions which she calls the 'Aesthetic Principle' and the 'Technological Principle'.[21] She does not, however, appear to consider these terms to be abstractions, on the grounds that they are rooted in the 'material' realities of the sexual differentiation inherent in biological reproduction. Men permit women to participate in activities governed by the aesthetic principle, but keep the technological principle to themselves, thus gaining enormous advantage in both sex struggle and class struggle. The reality of class struggle is one to which Firestone does concede some validity, though it remains a growth from the fundamental sexual dichotomy.

The brief theoretical section of Firestone's work might be called the trivialization of metahistory by metatheory. Firestone is not, and does not claim to be, a historian. A cursory and derivative account of American bourgeois feminism serves her as an adequate vehicle for the demonstration of the working of the dialectic of sex through human history. In her discussion of the joint exploitation of women and children, she roams a little farther back in time. 'Let's review the development of the nuclear family – and its construct childhood – from the Middle Ages to the present',[22] she proposes. This 'review' occupies nine pages, which are both racy and readable. They are, however, hardly sufficient grounds for her contention, proposed in an approving way, that the new social forms which the feminist revolution is to initiate will have a medieval slant. Karl Marx has been accused, with some justification, of a tendency to idealize feudal social relations, but he never confused dialectics with eternal return.

Firestone's most interesting passages are related to her belief, shared by other feminist writers, that the traditional enmity between Marxists and Freudians is inimical to the formulation of a solid theoretical approach to genderic relations. Freud tells us more about the personal destructiveness of bourgeois family relations than Marx and Engels do: Marx and Engels provide a theoretical model of history as struggle rooted in the material conditions of life, but neglect the individual psyche. Firestone attempts a historical analysis of sex relations in 'psycho-sexual' terms. Her analytical tool is the above-mentioned pair of abstractions, Aesthetic Principle and Technological Principle, which govern history. These are principles which Freud failed to recognize, she claims, mistaking them for Eros and Thanatos. Engels simply impoverishes them in the one-sided conception of class struggle.

Firestone aspires to do for the social relations of reproduction what Marx did for the relations of production. This is in fact an important task for feminist scholarship, and the central concern of this book. Firestone is to be commended for taking this difficult enterprise seriously, and even though her theorizing is inconsistent, it is an important step in the collective historical task of developing feminist theory. Marx's analysis took the lifetime of an intellectual giant and several fat volumes, and it is not reasonable to expect that Firestone, age twenty-five, can produce, in ten and a half pages plus a diagram, a sophisticated dialectical analysis. In fact, Firestone's view of the 'contradiction' inherent in sexual relationships is distilled in one brief sentence: 'The biological family is an inherently unequal power distribution',[23] a classic instance of the use of that which is to be explained to explain itself.

The conceptualization of sexual relations in terms of power politics is an article of faith with many feminists. Power is not, of course, irrelevant to either political or sexual relations, but power as such is an abstraction which can only be rendered analytically useful if it is given a material base and a historical content. Firestone does not succeed in doing this in a satisfactory way. The connection between the biological base and its conceptualization as a power relationship remains obscure. To her, it is self-evident that 'the biological family is an inherently unequal power distribution'. This is not offered merely as an empirical observation of either contemporary or historical family relationships in actual societies. As such, it would be valid description: it is offered, however, as a theoretical generalization which is to account for the history of male supremacy and relate that history to a material base. The problem, of course, is that the relation of male sexuality to power is not self-evident. What I have called the Potency Principle is a complex phenomenon, which has important political implications, but it has a base in male reproductive experience which must be analysed and not simply asserted.

Firestone's insistence on sexual relations as a primordially unequal power struggle leads her to an attempt to negate generic distinction, at least in theory. Sex distinction is to be 'eliminated'. What class struggle will negate, according to Marxist theory, is class itself, a historical and cultural creation. What sex struggle must eliminate, according to Firestone, is a biological distinction upon which history has festooned neuroses. This will then produce the new cultural system which Firestone calls 'cybernetic society'. Women must therefore aspire to 'the seizure of control of *reproduction*: not only full restoration of ownership of their own bodies, but also their (temporary) seizure of control of human fertility'.[24] The bracketed '(temporary)' is presumably inspired by Marx's notion of a transitional dictatorship of the proletariat. Firestone admits that her prescriptions for the resultant society are utopian. She is right, but, as always, utopianism has its basis in theoretical inadequacy. In the last analysis, Firestone wants women to become men, with a vague implication that the absence of sexual differentiation will result in the abolition of power as such and thus harmonize human relationships. Shulamith's baby is ultimately a theoretical waif, programmed for the theatre of a disturbingly mechanistic future.

Kate Millett is also concerned with sexual relations as power relations.[25] Unlike Firestone, she does not attempt to ground sexual power in biological reality. On the contrary, she quite strenuously rejects the notion of a biological base for male supremacy, maintaining that such a view is a bulwark of conservatism and reaction. By 'biological base' she understands mainly the doctrine that physical strength, rather than reproduction, is the historical explanation of men's place in the sun. Male supremacy, in Millett's analysis, is an almost wholly cultural phenomenon, and efforts to give it a 'natural' status are usually bad news for women.

Millett's *Sexual Politics* is a competent and passionately sincere denunciation of the psycho/cultural ramifications of feminine inferiority and male superiority. With as much shock value as she can muster from pretentious pornographers like Lawrence, Mailer and Henry Miller, she elaborates the ideological components of male supremacy, its dogmas, its modes of social control, and particularly the dehumanizing and destructive effects of male socialization. Her book has had considerable social impact, and is credited with playing a substantial part in the escalation of feminist concern for women's place in contemporary North American society. It is important to make these points before launching a critique which will centre around the ahistorical and atheoretical aspects of Millett's work, while fully recognizing that historical and theoretical issues are not her central concerns.

The title of Millett's book is a little misleading, in so far as her analysis is sociological and literary rather than political. It was noted above that Millett rejects a biological basis for male supremacy. None the less, she claims that copulation, which certainly has biological aspects, is 'the fundamental level of sexual politics'.[26] For Millett, politics and power are virtually interchangeable terms. Sexual relations can be best understood 'as a case of that phenomenon Max Weber defined as *herrschaft*, a relationship of dominance and subordination'.[27] Hers is a claim to a realistic definition of politics: 'The term "politics" shall refer to power-structured social relationships, arrangements whereby one group of persons is controlled by another.'[28]

Millett's approach is pragmatic — an approach which she reasonably claims to share with Mill and Engels — and her choice of materials eclectic. She selects some historical events to support her demonstration of the immense structure of male social control but the bulk of her evidence is literary. Her section on 'Historical background', mandatory in American sociological studies of this type, starts only in 1830. Like Firestone and Rowbotham, she is impatient of theories of origin, on the grounds that they are always and only can be speculative. This does not prevent her from summoning Bachofen, Morgan and Engels to support her cause. However, Millett does attempt to differentiate her own pragmatic stance in social science from the claims of 'objective' or 'value-free' approaches, and she has a reasoned critique of the functionalist persuasion.[29] Here, she does not follow Weber, but publicizes her passionate commitment to the feminist cause in a manner and method which owe much to the late C. Wright Mills.

Millett's second chapter is called 'Theory of sexual politics', later modified in the text to a more modest 'notes toward a theory of patriarchy', which is to be 'descriptive' theory.[30] She then proceeds to analyse sexual relations in terms of conventional sociological variables: ideological, biological, sociological, class, economic and educational, force, anthropological, myth and religion, and psychological. Her conclusions from this descriptive exercise are that all human societies are patriarchal; that the social and sexual relations in any society, both in terms of the individual and the group, are relations of dominance; that culture and its most reliable bearer, the socialization of children, perpetuate a patriarchal ideology; and that the restraints upon the liberation of women are mainly psychological and due to this process of cultural indoctrination.

This is impeccably and powerfully done, but there are several aspects of Millett's work which are less satisfactory. The first of these is that it shares a general inadequacy of 'empirical theorizing'. Such theorizing aspires to a pragmatic view of reality and a methodological purity by the collection and examination of positive and observable variables within a specified conceptual framework. The difficulty is that very complex social phenomena which are 'observable' only in terms of human behaviour, such as religious faith and political ideology, are recruited as variables with only the most cursory recourse to their historical development, or to the question of the formation of consciousness. 'Attitude' and 'behaviour' cannot be understood merely as more scientifically objective equivalents to 'theory' and 'practice'. They are concepts which attempt to freeze dynamic realities in an isolated, inert and unreflective objectivity which leaves out both historical meaning and subjective content, retaining an icicle of brute presence immune to critique simply by virtue of being there. Millett is aware of this limitation, but she does not succeed in transcending it by the device of defiantly adding normative judgments to the data of a methodology which categorically deplores such judgments. Her unspecified theory of knowledge wavers between mechanical stimulus, intuition and the pedagogical and heuristic prowess of determinist culture. There is considerable confusion as to whether sexual domination is a physical, historical or psychic phenomenon, or, if it is all of these, how such factors are subsumed in the general concept of the political. Thus, while the 'most fundamental level' of sexual politics is copulation, it must also 'be clearly understood that the arena of sexual revolution is within human consciousness even more pre-eminently than it is within human institutions'.[31] None the less, the institutions of patriarchy have as their principal result 'the interiorization of patriarchal ideology'.[32] Presumably institutions are prior but not pre-eminent, causal yet subordinate to their powers of psychic suasion, but Millett's descriptive methodology cannot make sense of these dialectical relations.

Second, these categorical confusions, together with a notion of history as 'background' rather than process, create difficulties for Millett which are common to bourgeois-liberal social science in general. It may seem unfair to tag Millett as a liberal when she is clearly aware of the increased exploitation of women within the framework of capitalism, but there is no systematic critique of capitalism. She admires Mill, seeing him as a 'precursor of revolution', whose conclusions that the liberation of women will make the whole human race happier are 'rational' and 'full of a new and promising vigour'.[33] While she generally approves of Engels's radical analysis of patriarchal marriage and the family, she is critical not only of his economic determinism but of his socialism. She rather slightingly notes that 'Engels, in the time-honoured manner of socialists, appears to romanticize the poor'.[34] This latter is not untrue, for Engels does indeed display this tendency on occasions, though socialists as different as Shaw and Marx do not. Millett's phrase, however, indicates that she disassociates herself from socialism. In the last part of her book, she accuses Marxism of failing to notice that oppression corrupts the oppressed. She is clearly unfamiliar with either *The Condition of the Working Class in England* or with Marx's chapter on 'The working day' in Book I of *Capital*.[35]

Millett would clearly like to avoid ideological labelling altogether, on the grounds that all political ideologies and theories are tainted with patriarchalism. As she does not herself present an alternative and coherent social theory, her ability to be prescriptive is limited. She therefore falls back on the old liberal stand-bys of reform and education. Her notion of 'revolution' is radical reform which will grow out of consciousnesses reformed by 'true re-education'.[36] She speaks of Plato's 'liberal' suggestions on education without noting that Plato's educational aims are 'liberal' only in the sense that they are intransigently elitist.[37] None the less, the dilemma which produces these ambiguities is a very real one, relating to both the theory and practice of social change.

In strategic terms, the issue is that of the advocacy of radical change in a peaceable form which will not terrify nervous voters, while in fact the changes sought are too profound to be brought about by anything other than a violent revolution. Millett's dilemma is similar to the continuous dilemma of democratic socialism, which expects to abolish capitalism in rational co-operation with capitalists. Her position is complicated by her assertion that violence is a specifically male behaviour. Violence, she claims, is the cultural expression of the phallic consciousness which male socialization instils and lauds. The happiness which she and J. S. Mill believe will emerge in a sexually equal society will be a fruit of women's capacity for peaceable solutions to human problems. Millett, like most feminists, rejects the enduring categorization of women as passive and men as active, arguing that men suppress women by engineering consent while they keep their police and military powers ever ready. Having argued that violence is not the alternative to passivity but is essentially a male cultural value, Millett is obliged to find an alternative mode of social transformation for women. Like a reluctant Fabian, she has no position to fall back on except education.

This problem of women and violence is a very real one, not only for Kate Millett, but for all feminists. Friend Hegel contended that women are 'the principle of life' and that makers of life cannot consistently be takers of life. This is no doubt a consoling thought, but very problematic indeed. Women have, historically, practised personal and political violence. Millett's problem is in rooting patriarchy to an abstraction called culture without relating it to its material and dialectical ground in reproductive process. Whether, however, the radical change in the social relations of reproduction brought about by the technology of contraception can be accomplished peacefully is, as yet, by no means clear. What is clear is that there will be a struggle, but Millett's narrow definition of politics as power actually precludes any notion of struggle other than violent power struggle. A politics of movement and resistance among women to the conceptualizations of power as the definition of politics and politics as the definition of power cannot be built on male-stream thought's insistence on power as the desirable dynamic of social order. Education, as we know it, is a tool of power held firmly in the hands of the ruling classes, but there is a potential exception in the socialization of young children. It is at this level of consciousness formation that women individually do have 'power' which waits for the collective mobilization which can mediate the division of public and private and create new values. There are revolutionary and collective possibilities inherent in reproductive politics which are quite different from those inherent in the personal wars of sexual politics.

There is a heavy dose of sexual determinism in Millett's analysis, particularly where she resorts to the literary evidence which is the largest part of the book. The male penis becomes both the pennant and the coercive weapon of male supremacy, and the sex-act itself a mode of exploitation. Millet admits the difficulty of moving from the individual sex-act to metacultural patriarchy, but she is unable to provide any other basis than sexuality itself for this phenomenon. The principle intermediary is her problematic psyche, floating free and undifferentiated from rational consciousness and doomed to be nailed by patriarchal indoctrination. Her abhorrence of the appeal of patriarchal ideology to 'nature' leads to a lurking implication that sexuality is in some sense unnatural. Early in her book she quotes with apparent approval the studies of Money and Stoller on sexual identity, including Stoller's dictum that sex is biological while gender is 'psychological'; and Millett adds, 'therefore cultural'.[38] She does not, however, maintain this distinction of sex and gender, and it is sexual revolution which she consistently calls for. Millett is not alone among feminists in being ambivalent about the whole question of 'nature'. Nature differentiates women from men, yet at the same time is the basis of their lowly social status. Men, on the other hand, have consolidated their supremacy by the overcoming of nature. For Millett, this latter warfare appears to have been carried out under the 'natural' and therefore oddly inappropriate standard of the Penis Rampant.

In 1885, August Bebel published a work which identified women's liberation with the emancipation of the proletariat, seeing no differentiation in the historical destiny of these two groups.[39] Rosa Luxemburg held this view, too, and was impatient of feminism in general, believing that true and rational liberation through the action of the proletariat must bring universal liberation.[40] Truly human, universal liberation can only come through the dialectical momentum of class struggle. So far, it has not shown up. Indeed, the position of women and their depressing history in the Soviet Union and under other communist and crypto-Marxist regimes is the oft-quoted source of feminist disillusionment with communist theory and practice.

Such disillusionment has not led to a universal cry for theoretical revisions from women socialists. The feminist movement is tremendously diverse: not all feminists are Marxists, not all women are feminists, and not all feminist Marxists are revisionists. Evelyn Reed, a committed Marxist, argues from an anthropological standpoint that what is missing in the comprehension of sexual relationships is a properly materialist interpretation of existing data. Reed's materialism combines a Trotskyite economic positivism with the yearning for a dignified history which has inspired other minority groups in recent years. She would not agree at all with de Beauvoir's position that women have no history, and, indeed, would be quick to point out that de Beauvoir's posited ontological otherness implies that men have always been the subjects of history, which Reed denies. Women's history is abundant, albeit somewhat distant, and has been either neglected or wilfully suppressed.

In her book, *Woman's Evolution*,[41] which is the fruit of twenty years of study of a disappointingly limited selection of anthropological data, Reed attacks the prejudices of male-dominated bourgeois ethnography. She is particularly critical of Levi-Strauss's attempt to liquidate totemism, and presents a fresh view of that controversial social phenomenon.[42] Male preoccupation with incest taboos she sees as a onesided and perverse prejudice emanating from an exaggeration of the importance of sexual relationships and the neglect of economic necessity. She argues that neglected evidence shows that the totem originally signified more compellingly those who must not be eaten, rather than those with whom carnal relations were forbidden. She interprets totemism as a device to control cannibalism, the initiators, she claims, probably having been women defending their young against male marauders who were not yet capable of distinguishing human from other animals. Reed credits women with the ability to make this distinction. She does not analyse the material basis for such a true consciousness, but is content with the idea that women would not eat what they have borne. This is simply sentimental. What is needed is a demonstration that reproductive labour is capable of forming in human consciousness the conception of a proprietorial relation between mother and child. To be sure, female animals protect their young, but they do not create socially sophisticated structures equipped with a mode of norm-enforcement strong enough to be able to modify 'natural' male behaviour.

Kinship is generally claimed to be the basis of totemism, but kinship is not in any sense a sexual phenomenon, Reed claims, because the relationship between sexuality and parturition was not understood in early times. The formative influence on kinship is cannibalism, which Reed interprets in an uncomfortably ghoulish way as a 'mode of production'. The reason why totemic taboos are directed against foods as well as sex is simply that primitive minds make no distinction between these two primordial hungers. Reed notes several languages in which one word serves for both functions. Sexual prohibitions are perceived as being added rather routinely to the far more important prohibition of cannibalism, simply because of the joint status of sex and eating as human necessities. As this simple parallelism is clearly an inadequate explanation for the realities of incest taboo, Reed, who dislikes psychological explanations, is none the less forced into such an explanation, though she attempts to leaven it with economic and biological determinants. She claims that the 'dominant male' indeed exists in the animal world, but he is the product of 'the individualistic and competitive character of male sexuality'.[43] Evidently, not only men but male animals bring a marketplace morality to the act of coition. They also fight, Reed says, for the females' territory.

Reed is properly critical of Ardrey, Tiger and the school of patriarchal ethology, but here she comes close to the notion of a territorial imperative and 'innate', or at least biologically determined, aggression. Where she separates again from the would-be lions of the anthropological jungle is in her claim that, far from leading to male bonding, such antagonisms create 'jungle law', and constitute a destructive and antisocial force which in fact precludes co-operative action by men.[44] As cannibalism was one aspect of this behaviour, the behaviour had to be modified, and women performed this modification. They had two reasons for doing so: to protect their young from hungry male teeth and themselves from equally hungry sexual appetites. One may wonder how creatures sufficiently undifferentiated as to be able to distinguish other species from their own are still capable of strong individualism, but Reed's onesided conceptual framework rides rather roughly over such questions. In her anxiety to show that totemism is a twosided phenomenon, embracing both subsistence and sexuality, she overcorrects what she sees as patriarchal anthropology's preoccupation with sexuality. Cannibalism is no doubt one mode of production, and may well have been a strong evolutionary force, but this does not mean that reproduction is of no importance at all. Once again, we see the need for a socio-historical model which can give recognition to both spheres of necessity. There is an opposition between the general need to eat and the need of particular individuals to eat, which Reed understands perfectly well. This opposition of general and particular has led, historically, to actions which may be either co-operative or competitive. This is the nature of dialectical contradiction: it creates new oppositions. What Reed does not analyse is the qualitatively different opposition in sexual and reproductive relations: all people are sexy, but only women are reproducers. Reed's analysis posits a mediation of the productive opposition in social labour, which leaves the social relations of reproduction dangling helplessly in its wake. Instead of analysing the contradictions within the material basis of reproductive relations, Reed posits a contradiction between male and female nature, a device which she finds objectionable when Freud utilizes it.

Reed's work has the merit of attempting to root women's oppression in women's history, which is a different procedure from the more general preoccupation with the analysis of domestic labour which most contemporary Marxist analysts have favoured, and which will be discussed when materialism is considered in Chapter 5. Reed's notion of incest taboos is original and quite frankly speculative, which is why I consider it among feminist rather than Marxist works, a distinction Reed herself would not, probably, find pleasing. None the less, Reed's failure to consider reproductive *process* has some odd results. She argues, for example, that the relation between copulation and birth was not discovered until quite late in history, but argues elsewhere that women in early societies limited their childbirth by segregating themselves in women's houses.[45] This leads her to a rather bizarre variation on evolutionary theory, in which female sexuality simply disappears for a few centuries, to be restored vigorously in modern times.

Reed finally has men abandoning cannibalism simply by following the good example of women, a tendency which has not been noticeable in the history of male supremacy in general. There is no reason to suppose that men did not abandon cannibalism for the same reason that women did: namely they learned that the children were their own, in the discovery of physiological paternity. At the same time, of course, they discovered that their estrangement from the process of reproduction imbued the 'own-ness' with uncertainty. It seems to me less likely that men copied brotherhood from sisterhood than that they developed it in response to their own worldly experience.

This selective discussion of feminist writings displays both the strengths and weaknesses of the search for a feminist philosophy: strength in the commitment to a still rather abstract cause; weakness in theoretical perspective; ambivalence in relation to the proper critique of male-stream thought. In the last six or seven years, many women, including myself, have struggled to redefine the possible grounds of feminist theory. This new body of work owes a great deal to the women we have discussed, and many more. At the same time it is quite different. The empirical situation has changed, especially in relation to modes of sexual expression, and the notion of sexual freedom alone as a liberating force has dissolved in the bawdy laughter of Erica Jong's satire. The theoretical problems remain, and the relation of feminist theory to intellectual history is by no means resolved. None the less, there is an increasing move towards a different standpoint. Women like Adrienne Rich, Mary Daly, Dorothy Smith and Nancy Chadorow are working from a new standpoint, the standpoint of women and women's personal and political experience.[46] Necessarily, the pioneers we have been discussing have worked from an academic and sometimes abstract perspectives: the new body of theory *grows from the women's movement*.[47] It is vitally concerned to unify theory and practice, not necessarily prescriptively, but in a living unity of thought and action. Grand strategies of liberation are not yet emerging, but utopianism is retreating. One result of this is a refocusing of the central female experience, the experience of motherhood. In practical terms, it has become quite evident that a widely based women's movement (I have trained myself not to say broadly based), cannot emerge from the devaluation of the intimate, humane, exasperating, agonizing and proud relations of women and children. The feminism of the pseudo-man is passé. The need to grasp theoretically the historical significance of the social relations of reproduction, a need which is a robust but not yet articulate embryo in the work I have just discussed, is emerging as the central concern of feminist theory and practice.

Birth is a subject and object of an integrative feminist philosophy. The nurture and care of children is as essential to the continuation of human life as is the need to produce. A new value for these activities must be the goal of feminist praxis, a goal which means the breaking down of the age-old distinction between the personal and the political, between private and public life. Marxism's call for the socialization of child care is far too superficial. Decent day care is an important feminist objective, but it is but a stage in the revaluation of true human necessity. Feminism will be ill served if we simply create another class division: women who bear and care for children serving with small status and reward women who do not do these things.

What has been absent from feminist theory is a sense of the specific social form which emerges from and embodies the dialectics of reproductive process. The family by itself cannot do this; family forms are buttressed by law, custom and ideology, and all of these are the fruits of political activity. Yet it is not enough to say that Man's world of politics, the public realm, moulds the forms of the social relations of reproduction. The forms of the public realm itself have material roots in reproductive process. Genderic oppression is the outcome of centuries of effort to mediate the contradictions within and between the relations of production and reproduction.

It is therefore to the relation of public and private, and to the political significance of reproductive consciousness, which we must now turn our attention.

3 The public and private realms

If it is the case, as I have argued, that the oppositions within a dialectically structured process of human reproduction take the social form of a separation of the private and individual realm from a public and political realm, then it must be demonstrated that this separation has empirical validity, that it actually appears in the social world. It can be argued that this separation is only a theoretical one, that the actual organization of social relations have never made this kind of clear distinction. If the separation of public and private is to the social relations of reproduction the same kind of conflictual and dynamic relation as that in which class struggle objectifies the social relations of production, then it should be possible to analyse and describe the forms which this particular struggle has taken.

Operating at the theoretical level, it is relatively easy to see the separation of private and public as an abstract dialectical opposition of particular and universal, of individual and social, of the domestic and the biological, standing opposed to political and historical development. This is a commonplace sort of understanding, but male-stream thought has added the wrinkle that, as the biological is fixed and unchanging, development and change must take place in the public realm of politics where man makes history. This does not mean, of course, that the private realm never changes: on the contrary, such themes as the decline and erosion of the family and the destruction of family-based economies appear as perennials in both revolutionary and conservative thought. What is disputed with considerable vigour are the reasons for such changes, with a huge bias in favour of change in family resting

93

helplessly on developments external to the social relations of reproduction. The history of political conservatism, for example, is tuned to a continuing coda of despair for the fate of the family. Much of this despair is rooted in the contradiction which insists that the family is the locus of the 'natural', but at the same time has laid upon it responsibilities related to moral values and the maintenance of moral stability. This dual function of the family is the root of the arguments in the Greek polis which insisted that nature and the Good were identical. In practice, the family clearly needed a great deal of policing, and the moral values had to be articulated by men in the public realm. This conflation of the unchanging natural and the ideologically moral functions of family made the family a constant source of anxiety to thinkers and moralists in general. The family appears as the prey of forces of moral instability, including of course women's 'natural' built-in propensity to moral turpitude. This 'unreliability' was in fact a facet of the failure of male schemes to mitigate the uncertainty of paternity, for venal exacerbation of this uncertainty has always been quite clearly understood as chief among feminine wiles, as generations of mutilated male slaves attest. Added to the perceived opposition of nature and morality is the longstanding clash of family-based morality and political reality. This particular conflict, as it appeared to the classical male imagination, was dramatized with tragic grandeur by Sophocles in the confrontation of Antigone and Creon.

For many centuries, the moral right of assorted authority figures was perceived as being grounded in the natural soil of family morals and paternal authority.[1] This view was not seriously questioned until the bourgeois revolution in seventeenth-century England, when John Locke articulated the need to move the rationalization of political sovereignty and political obligation from the generalized rights of man as patriarch, which Filmer had argued, to the particular rights of man as property owner.

This process, which seemed quite self-evident to Locke, was perceived as a much more complex affair by Jean-Jacques Rousseau, for whom the integration of the particular and general wills was an elusive but essential condition of rational public life. There is a phylogenetic pattern in Rousseau's work which lends it a canonical consistency which has not always been appreciated. The *Second Discourse* provides a sort of civil creation myth, *The Social Contract* a utopia, and the *bildungsroman* of *Emile* a means of proceeding from one to the other.[2] Emile is something more than the recipient of a natural education: he is a progenitor, whose reproductive activities are to provide a stock of citizens, as opposed to the ordinary but extraordinarily decadent people whom Rousseau sees peopling his world. The path of mere people is a downward one, but the citizen sons of Sophie and Emile will reverse this process and travel upward towards the natural society, in which the decent values of domestic life will modify and perhaps replace the grossness of civil society.[3]

Book V of the *Emile*, in which Rousseau draws his picture of Sophie, has proved such an embarrassment to Rousseau's admirers that in several editions of the book it is simply omitted. It has also excited understandable feminist wrath,[4] but it cannot be suppressed, for it is crucial to Rousseau's vision of the good society. Rousseau understands that the nastiness of first nature and its animal lusts cannot be negated by a wishful or theoretical denial of first nature, for biological reproduction is a necessary component of human history. He also understands that the premise of natural universal freedom cannot omit women and retain its universality. Much misunderstanding of the social operation of the general and particular wills can be avoided once it is grasped that Rousseau, *prior* to the foundation of his rational contractual society, has already made arrangements for the defusing of the irrational propensities of particular wills. The potency principle is shut up in the private realm, freely, willingly and perpetually guarded by Sophie. Sophie understands that her freedom finds its best expression in the guardianship of her husband, who is equal in freedom but superior in the rationality required to express the general will. Functionally, Sophie's act also assures the children that Emile is in fact their father,[5] permits the application of moral norms to the otherwise destructive promptings of sexual passion, and enables Sophie to educate her daughters in this correct disposition of their natural freedom. Marriage purifies the passions of particularity, thus making the private realm truly ethical and the source for a more humane citizen body, which can then express the general will in the public realm.

The great strength of Rousseau's analysis, a strength which does not excuse but partially transcends his vulgar misogyny, lies in the fact that he aspires to a politics which is not cut off from the virtues which are commonly regarded as domestic, and which were traditionally ascribed to the private realm. Rousseau wants to bring to public life sympathy, love, affection and the supportive solidarity of family relationships. George Armstrong Kelly has remarked that the state in Rousseau's conception is to become a surrogate for nature.[6] In our terminology, the state is to become a principle of asexual, self-generating continuity, which is both rational and humane. Rousseau's mysterious and controversial Legislator is the political metamorphosis of the unity of Sophie and Emile, as androgynous a character as Pallas Athene herself. The Legislator represents political continuity, while Sophie guarantees genetic continuity. The Legislator relates to the general will which Emile must express, while Sophie relates to the particular will which Emile must repress. This accounts for the Legislator's peculiar passivity and abnegation of his own will. He has rationally conceded his freedom to the General Will of the polity; Sophie has gifted her freedom to a Particular Will, that of her husband.

Rousseau's work is of course paradoxical, but the traditional problems of political theory which are vital to feminist understanding are very clear in Rousseau's paradoxes. He understands the biological base and moral dilemma of the separation of public and private life. He proposes a programme for the development of a second nature, and in doing so incidentally demonstrates a profound awareness of the power of the process which we now call socialization, the educational clout of the private realm. Rousseau also recognizes the need for men to create a principle of continuity, an artificial continuity, an abstract but eternally binding contract, which transcends male separation from genetic continuity. He faces up to the implications of this artificiality, accepting political continuity as the reification of biological continuity which in fact it is. Yet he wants to retain for this idealist structure that authority and authorship of nature for which classical political theory yearned: herein lies the perplexity which is the ground of paradox. Reifications of continuity must somehow be able to command intellectual respect and a claim on political obligation, the capacity to make men obey their dicta.[7] Second nature or custom must also be able to make demands upon free men, to create the duty and the will and the instruments to maintain an actual, workable political order. The artificial continuity which replaces natural continuity must be a factual, socially confirmed reality.

Rousseau does not relate this problem to the dialectics of reproduction, but simply to the question of nature in general. The order of orderly nature, the massive mathematical dignity of the planets in their courses, the harmony of the spheres: these constitute but one side of nature. It is set over against finite and contingent nature, red in tooth and claw, the river in which no man steps twice, the radical uncertainty of paternity. Rousseau understands this dichotomy, though he does not express it in these terms. He yearns for the realization of the superior order of nature, a moral order, rational, desirable and above all authoritative, but authoritative in the sense that it requires an obedience to a non-experienced, ideal reality of orderly continuity. Its only hope of success lies ultimately in fraternity, and the ability of the Brotherhood to unify and humanize their potent wills in the public realm and for the public good. Rousseau wants to maintain and conserve the creative dynamic and the freedom embedded in the potency principle, while he tames its individualist excesses. What he in fact proposes is the fertilization of its enigmatic roots in the private realm. The only way to mask the oppressiveness of this kind of male supremacy is to make women *choose* to give up their freedom in defence of rational life, in much the same way as Antigone was compelled to choose death in defence of ethical life.

The importance of the relation of public and private life to political philosophers is by no means the product of an abstract thirst for metaphysical puzzles. To be sure, revolutionary liberalism in its early enthusiasms thought it had solved these problems by the happy discovery that individual and private interest coincided neatly with collective and public interest, and the articulation of this harmony of interests was the important ideological task of Adam Smith and his followers. It is a comforting doctrine for entrepreneurs, who to this day insist that their individual pursuit of profits is, happily, the best thing that can happen to society: what is good for General Motors being good for America, and then presumably what is good for America being good for the world at large. The failure of this radical utilitarianism to reflect the realities of lived lives was already apparent in the early years of the nineteenth century, and paved the way for the new political ideologies of socialism. The critique of conservative preoccupation with the preservation of the family will be dealt with later in the context of a discussion of Marxism. The important points to be made here are these: the relation of public and private life and the historical changes of these spheres have been the subject matter of political thought for a very long time; the fact that this dualist construction of reality is of profound significance to women has been the topic of masculine apologetics or heroics, rather than serious analysis; the division of these realms does represent some kind of experienced reality; the processes by which forms of public and private life change historically have never been related to a materialist view of the actual structure of reproductive process.

In the context of a Marxist materialism, it has been customary to relate changes in the family to changes in the economic substructure, a doctrine which, too rigidly applied, falls into the trap of economic determinism.[8] Over against this, structuralist formulations of models of analysis have tended to view the family as functional, a function based on the uncomplicated and obvious needs of society to do such necessary things as make provision for the nurture and education of children, be responsible for moral teaching and normative maintenance, regulate sexual passion and make provision for the physical needs of the biological individual. The need to conserve the principles and practice of male supremacy are not usually included in lists of family and political functions. It is, however, abundantly clear from masses of research activity in the social sciences that some kind of division of labour and institutional activity around the necessary realities of reproduction and production is common to all known societies, though the strength and form of the institutions and the value of the labour in question varies a great deal. None the less, the social practices which embody and express the social organization of human survival do not 'prove' that the dictates of necessity entail male supremacy, or the development of political power or the control of the economic forces of any given society by a particular group. Historically, of course, they have done so, and societies which have not followed this pattern tend to be thought of as anachronistic and quaint refugees from the triumphs of modernization, grist to the mills of ethnologists but, in the large historical picture, not very significant.

A major complicating factor in social analysis is, of course, that of socio-economic class. It is much easier to see and analyse the relations of classes as an antagonistic one than it is to see that the separation of public and private is the material locus of generic struggle. The separation of the domestic from the political, of the biologically necessary from the freely and rationally created, of personal need from public good; all of these may present important theoretical problems to the moulders and shapers of culture and opinion. They may equally well appear to the men and women on assembly lines as just as unreal and insignificant as they were for the medieval serf and his family. The impact of the public realm on the lives of the working classes was, for centuries, a reality only when they were called upon to fight and die in the power struggles of their paternalist masters. In the age of democracy, the experienced sense of ordinary people of shaping and forming public affairs is very problematic indeed, and a preoccupation with the household as the realm of commodity consumption is easy enough to understand. Clearly, an analysis of these very complex historical realities cannot be grounded in abstract models of socio-historical process which separate out the various 'factors' involved in historical change, and arrange them in neat hierarchies of significance or regressive causal chains. Understanding must come from the perspective of the actual experiences and social practices which people continue to develop to deal with the conditions of their lives. It is no more true that all women live in the private realm and all men live in the public realm than it is that we are all, quite unproblematically, either bourgeois or proletarian. Yet because of women's 'special relationship' to the private realm, we must have some kind of theoretical standpoint from which we can understand the social practices of the private realm, its internal structures, its relation with the public realm. Such a theoretical standpoint must clarify both the core of stability constituted by biological reproduction in the changing structure of the private realm, and the relation of this to the dialectically structured realities of class struggle. It is also important that we understand that this core of stability is not a peaceful, passive oasis in a stern and cruel world, but an arena of economic, political and ideological struggle where the male potency principle and the integrative feminine principle take real and antagonistic social forms, and where actual generic struggles are fought out.

In the preceding chapter, we considered the work of feminist writers who sought to understand this struggle from a limited conception of the dialectical dynamic of reproductive process. In an attempt to understand the dualism of the relation of the public and private realms, it might be useful to look at the work of Hannah Arendt, a woman who accepts the normality and even the necessity of male supremacy, and who, far from bemoaning sentimentally the decline of the family, believes that the functions and structures proper to the private realm have expanded historically in a way which has well-nigh destroyed the public realm.[9] As the public realm, in Arendt's view, constitutes the only social space in which we can command and create a human destiny which conserves human freedom, its invasion by the private realm constitutes a grave threat to that freedom.

Arendt understands the private realm as resting on necessity, but human activity, she argues, is not exclusively or even primarily a response to necessity. The grounds of activity are ontological rather than biological. This, she claims, was understood in antiquity, but modern history is the history of the wilful loss of that crucial understanding. It is consequently the history of the dehumanization of man and the corrosion of the public sphere by the acid of necessity itself. Man has permitted himself to be abstracted from his created world by his preoccupation with the limited 'science' which he has brought to his unsuccessful attempt to conquer nature. This abstraction has left the political space which the ancients so lovingly created to the ravages of untamed necessity, which self-abstracted man can only contemplate impotently and facelessly from an abstracted Archimedean point outside the real world. Thus, the only action left to him in the real world is labour, that aspect of activity which he shares with other animal species, and which precludes the kinds of human work and action which permit men to rise from species anonymity to individual excellence. Arendt's method of proof of these contentions is phenomenological analysis of the *vita activa*, in which phrase she generalizes the totality of the activities of labour, work and action. The *vita activa* moves men from the private realm of enforced necessity to the public realm of created freedom.

It is proposed to argue here that Arendt's view of the human condition is in fact a view of man in the literal as well as the generalized sense, and that the lack of analysis of the human condition of women is ultimately a failure to analyse adequately the *vita activa* itself.[10] Arendt is engaged in an endeavour which is commonplace within traditional theory; she is speculating on man's second nature. Unlike many of her predecessors, she does not posit second nature as first; she arbitrarily separates the two natures of man on the grounds of the humane superiority of second nature as opposed to the mere animality of first. She then provides worldly lodging-houses for these separated natures in the public and private realms. The separation of nature and society is not an arbitrary one: Arendt argues that it is an ontological dualism embedded in the human condition. Human freedom, on the other hand, is not an ontological given. It is possible only if man can isolate his political activities in a public realm uncontaminated by life process. This is precisely the separation which, I have argued, has its real ground in the dialectics of reproduction. Arendt stands in a long line of social and political thinkers who, in failing to analyse the significance of reproductive consciousness, are able to find all kinds of ontological, metaphysical and ultimately ideological justifications of male supremacy. Arendt's version of man's dualism is based on a distinction between the activities of both subsistence and reproductive labour, which are shared with other animals, and productive work and political action, which are specifically human.

Arendt's understanding of the political realm is that it is the public 'space' in which those men who are able to escape from the thrall of necessity are able to show forth their uniqueness. This uniqueness exists primordially in the human condition, along with the mere species-being shared with other animals. This is Arendt's formulation of particularity and universality. The objective manifestations of uniqueness are speech and action, the modes by which the individual reveals himself to others and gains the recognition which is the condition of fame, fame being the worldly recognition of political excellence. To this desirable end, man must break violently with the necessity which enfolds him in the stifling womb of species-being, and exert control over necessity so that he may be free.[11] Thus, the political actor *par excellence* is the father of the family; this was the case in the Athenian polis, but it is emphatically not the case that what takes place is a simple transfer of paternal power to political power. Arendt dodges the trap which engulfed Filmer. She argues that there is a qualitative difference between patriarchal and political power, a distinction arising from an inseparable existential gulf between necessity and freedom, the first animal, the second human. Paterfamilias on his way to the freedom of the political realm has to cross this gulf, or, as Arendt says, 'rise' from one realm to the other.[12] The public realm is evidently not only apart from but superior to the private realm.

Not least among the difficulties in Arendt's analysis is that she has deliberately excluded human thought from the analysis of human activity. This is perfectly acceptable within the canons developed for phenomenology by Husserl and his followers, where the intention of the analyst is unified with the object to be examined. The difficulty, however, is that Arendt does not really examine physical activity as such, the real live doings of real live men. She examines only what Greek philosophers thought activity was, what she calls 'the Greek understanding' of the *vita activa* and the separation of public and private.[13] As this 'understanding' remains unanalysed *qua* understanding, Arendt's ontology is an epistomological *non sequitur*. Questions of the unity of theory and action are thus bracketed, but the evidence for an account of the material conditions of family life in the polis is mainly derived from theories which are shot through with ideological presuppositions unrelated to their cultural workings out.

Arendt criticizes Plato and Aristotle for inverting the hierarchy of action and contemplation, but at the same time appeals to them as authorities on 'the Greek understanding'. She notes, for example, that Aristotle differentiated between the private power of the father, based on violence, and political power. This is correct, but it is not correct to assume that Aristotle thus separated absolutely private power and public authority. Presumably antiquity had its Filmers, and Aristotle is anxious to refute them. Not having access, like Locke, to an alternative conception of regenerative propriety, Aristotle's refutation is couched in teleological and ethical terms. Yet he does not abandon the analogue of the family. Tyranny, he says, corresponds to paternal power, but statesmanship is analogous to husbandly rule:

> [The husband's] rule of his wife is like that of a statesman over
> fellow-citizens; his rule over his children is like that of a monarch
> over subjects.[14]

This is not just because women possess only an 'inconclusive' form of 'the faculty of deliberation'.[15] Aristotle elsewhere attempts to justify the claim of natural male superiority in biological terms, maintaining in *De Generatione Animalium* that the sperm contains the essence, spirit and final form of the human being to be produced, whereas women contribute only 'material'.[16] Aristotle's view of public and private is that both are rooted in *nature in general*, whereas for Arendt the separation of the two is grounded in an existential dualism of *human nature in particular*. She believes that reason as such cannot, as Aristotle thought, confirm the differentiation of the animal and the human. Reason is not satisfactory because it has a regrettable tendency to lapse into mere contemplation, a capacity to take off, as it were, from the world of men, losing touch with its essential ontological roots. Metaphysical flight of reason is precisely what Arendt believes happened to Greek philosophy.

In normative terms, however, Arendt's recommendations remain very similar to those of the great political thinkers of antiquity, but on different grounds: the effect of her analysis is to move the rationale for political elitism from an ethical metaphysics to an action metaphysics. Perceived metaphysically, the category of action in Arendt's analysis remains predictably abstract and unsatisfactory; it is never quite clear, for example, what these fathers of families who are to spend their 'whole life' in the public sphere are actually doing there.[17] Aristotle creates a hierarchy of values, to be sure, but it is an articulated hierarchy which, however imperfectly, attempts to encompass the pluralistic realities of the polis as Aristotle experienced them. Necessity has its place, inferior to virtue as it may be, and virtue itself is at least accessible to thought. Arendt inserts between public and private precisely that vacuum which Aristotle abhorred, but the gulf over which paterfamilias establishes his shuttle service extends its vacuity into the political: the political space is strangely empty of politics. Yet it is this putative 'gulf', this posited vacuum, in which she rests her extraordinary claim that violence, which in fact permeated Greek public life within the class struggles of the polis itself and in the execution of imperialist ambitions abroad, *really* belongs only in the private realm. Violence is needed to overcome the imperiousness of biological necessity. From this axiom emerges her odd and ahistorical contention that violence has nothing to do with politics, but belongs exclusively to the private realm. She simply does not see that the violence needed to maintain the separation of public and private in both the reproductive and productive spheres must have a political component. Paterfamilias, to preserve his freedom, requires family law, fraternal co-operation and ideological legitimization. He also, then as now, retained the option of brutality to enforce his domestic power. Far from being a paradigm of political power or the social precondition of public renown, patriarchy and the doctrine of potency are the products of political power, the creations of a brotherhood of fathers acting collectively to implement their definitions of manhood in social and ideological forms.

Believing that force and violence were 'felt' in antiquity to be 'pre-political', Arendt cannot and does not logically claim that the defence of the freedom which is the basis of public life can ever be a rationale for violence in defence of that freedom. The polis could not exist until necessity had been separated off in the private realm and 'Under no circumstances could politics be only a means to protect society'[18]

The clarity of the separation of public and private which is so clear to Arendt does not seem to have been quite so obvious to the Greeks, and the men of Marathon and Salamis certainly perceived 'circumstances' in which the protection of the polis became the only political objective. According to Thucydides, Pericles dealt with these questions in a very straightforward way in his celebrated funeral oration, which Arendt herself quotes as evidence of her contention that the Greek notion of political action was pre-eminently that of guaranteeing the immortality of otherwise ephemeral words and action.[19] Thucydides is more sensitive to the tensions within the private realm.[20] He senses that Pericles' particular view of manliness, of which 'the first revelation' is an honourable military death, might sit ill with the woman who gave that life and the women who sustained it, even if it can be sold as an idea to the men who are actually to do the dying. To be sure, his words to wives and mothers are cursory and come as a somewhat casual postscript to his elaboration of man's second nature as free, noble and adventurous, and of political continuity as more human than biological continuity. He reminds the women that they too can be glorious, and that 'the greatest glory of a woman is to be least talked about by men'. Here, Thucydides inadvertently gives us a glimpse of what men showing themselves forth in the public realm actually talked about; it clearly included gossip about women, a far cry from Arendt's austere view of the nobility of public speech.

Pericles also recognizes the highly practical bond which unites public and private; he forthrightly instructs surviving men to go home and make babies to replace the lost. Indeed, Pericles, unlike Arendt, does not seem at all confident that men will regard their property as valuable only in so far as it guarantees access to the public realm. That life and property are of less value than honour is not self-evident, and Pericles notes that it is difficult to convince men that they are. He argues, in

exact opposition to Arendt, that what in fact makes public life possible
are the relations of reproduction:

> All the same, those of you who are of the right age must bear up and
> take comfort in the thought of having more children. In your own
> homes these new children will help you from brooding over those
> who are no more, and they will be a help to the city, too, both in
> filling the empty places and in assuring her security. For it is
> *impossible* for a man to put forward fair and honest views about our
> affairs if he has not, like everyone else, children whose lives may be
> at stake [my italics].[21]

For Pericles, or for Thucydides, it is clear that the relation of the public
and private realm is a vigorous and practical articulation, and not only
because of the obvious consideration that immortal glory is a damp
squib if the race which is to recognize and cherish it dies out. Pericles
appears to understand that the appeal to nobility, to man's second
nature, remains an ideological appeal, and one, moreover, which cannot
rely on unquestioning acceptance. Arendt maintains that the polis is 'a
kind of organized remembrance'.[22] That it has this dimension is
something which Pericles wishes to stress, but as a practical and shrewd
politician he knows quite well that tunes of glory must be orchestrated
to the necessities of human life, from which they cannot in practice be
separated by an evasive coda of elevated thoughts. For Pericles, the
polis is a practical principle of continuity, but it has not yet lost touch
with its reproductive roots. His last word is an exercise in that welfare-
stateism which Arendt believes to be a modern post-political regression
to pre-political forms:

> For the time being our offerings to the dead have been made, and for
> the future their children will be supported at the public expense by
> the city, until they come of age. This is the crown and prize which
> she offers, both to the dead and to their children, for the ordeals
> which they have faced. Where the rewards of valour are the greatest,
> there you will find also the best and bravest spirits among the
> people.[23]

Pericles quite obviously realizes that the 'rewards of valour' must take a
substantial and quite mundane social form before their acceptance in
terms of reputational immortality is likely. He knows that the separation

of public and private is limited and artificial, can be maintained and enforced only by large public doses of justificatory propaganda, and direct appeals to the potency principle as a base of military valour.

It is quite clear that family and economics played a large part in the public life of the polis. Thucydides noted the value of reproduction. Economic concerns were also of public import, but Arendt's view of the glamour of political action excludes such commonplaces as collecting and spending taxes, of which the necessity to finance public works, such as fortifications and harbour facilities for the visible, physical protection of the polis, were but one instance. For the funding of cults and games, the huge temple treasure was 'administered', which, then as now, quite often meant plundered, by secular authorities. Indeed, Ehrenberg suggests that the political economy of the polis rested not only on taxes but to quite a large extent on heredity, in that the accumulation of wealth for public use came to the Athenians as 'the heirs of the Mycenaean kings'; the temple treasurers became primitive 'bankers'. For Ehrenberg, examining historiographically what is known of the real historical conditions of the polis, a conclusion almost directly opposite to that of Arendt is reached. He argues that the action of the state tended to replace private action, and that Greek objection to tyranny was less a matter of principle than objection to direct taxation.[24]

In truth, Arendt's own insistence on the separation of public and private, of necessity and freedom, has far more to do with the present than it has with the past. It is a necessary component of her critique of socialism in general and Marx in particular, a critique which is hardly free of polemical overtones. Arendt recognizes that the 'burden of biological life' is one which technology cannot eliminate, but she appears to believe that Marx thought that it could. This putative lapse in common sense occurs because Marx, in her view, failed to analyse the *vita activa* with sufficient rigour, but lumped all human activity under the heading of 'labour'. This is the source of the major contradiction Arendt sees as woven into the fabric of Marx's thought; labour defines the human, whose greatest effort and only possible freedom lies in the negation of labour. That such a dialectical tension is present in Marx's work need not be denied. However, Marx, unlike Arendt, includes the operations of reason within the category of specifically human activity, and his last word on the subject, at the end of Volume III of *Capital*, is that men can never escape the realm of necessity entirely, but *can* 'regulate their interchange with nature rationally'.[25]

Arendt's use of historical evidence tends to be cavalier, but she makes no claim to be a historian. Her main concern is to argue that the destruction of the public realm is an offence against the human condition, while the interpretation of social life from the standpoint of history rather than that of ontology is an intellectual and social disaster. This inversion she traces to the activities of Plato and Aristotle, who, she argues, substituted contemplation for action. She cannot, of course, say why they did this: 'It seems unnecessary to my present purpose', she claims, 'to discuss the reasons for this tradition'.[26] Given the ontological burdens which her phenomenological analysis of the *vita activa* has to bear, it would have been more satisfying had it been complete. Her proposition that major philosophical propositions emerge from particular historical occasions 'almost incidentally' is rather casual,[27] particularly because the ultimate effect of the movement from action to contemplation will be to destroy man's comprehension of his own *eidos* and his own world.

Arendt does, however, find herself forced to refer to historical developments, though she does so in passing and without analysis:

> It was not just an opinion of Aristotle but a simple historical fact that the foundation of the *polis* was preceded by the destruction of all organized units resting on kinship, such as the *phratria* and the *phyle*.[28]

Here, 'simple' is too weak, 'destruction' is too strong. This 'simple event' appears to have taken several centuries to reach its culmination in the polis.[29] It required at least two episodes of major legal reform to establish a territorial and patriarchal rather than a tribal and matriarchal basis for polis life. Solon's reforms of 594–3 were concerned with remedying the ravages which debt had wrought upon the peasantry, with the modernization of the military and with the regulation of slavery. His greatest concern, however, was family law. Solon appears to have been a political moderate, who was willing to let the aristocracy preserve the genealogies which were their pride and their elite justification. He was, as we know from Aristotle, much concerned to protect the family, and ensure male inheritance.[30] The effect of his inheritance laws was to free individual property from clan control. The proposition which Aeschylus dramatizes so effectively – that kinship organization knows no law but that of bloody revenge – may well have been true, but by the time of Solon the kinship in question was already patriarchal, and the historical protagonists were aristocrats intent on enlarging hereditary holdings by the appropriation of peasant land and the enslavement of its former owners.

To be sure, we do not know much about the great crisis which precipitated the Solonian reforms, but it seems clear from the laws themselves that problems had arisen in the relations of production and the relations of reproduction. The accomplishments of Solon in law were concurrent with religious developments in which the old chthonic and fertility cults had been consciously replaced by the Olympic heavenly patriarchs, and life-process celebrations in which women participated were 'rationalized' in the all-male mathematical mysteries of Orpheus and the intoxicated liturgies of Dionysius. In any case, Solon's attempts to mediate the claims of family and polity included harsh retribution upon sexually errant women, measures which had the clear effect of mitigating the uncertainty of paternity.

Cleisthenes' reforms from 608 onwards were a masterly exercise in politics, and, while they did not create democracy, they went a long way to making it possible. One can acknowledge the achievements of this great statesman without losing sight of the fact that the net result of his new political organization was the exclusion of the old tribal and cultic communities from political activity, and the absolute exclusion of women from politics, both as persons and as mothers. Citizenship became a matter of registration in one's *deme*, and a man stayed with the same *deme* irrespective of where he moved to throughout his life. A man and his descendants were to belong to the same *deme* for all time to come, a principle of continuity which tended, in a mobile population, to weaken neighbourhood ties and strengthen individuality, while a second nature was invested in male citizens in a confection of law, custom and rite. None the less, Cleisthenes laid the foundations of a pluralist society, for citizenship appears to have cut across class as well as tribal divisions, and Cleisthenes called his new order *isonomia*, which Ehrenberg describes as 'equal distribution and thus equality among citizens, equality before the law as well as equal political rights, equal shares in the state'.[31] *Isonomia* did not cut across generic barriers but fortified them. The definition of a citizen passed historically from the child of an Athenian mother, through two Athenian parents, to the need for a citizen father only.

The *deme* was intended specifically as an arrangement which would transcend individual lifespans and guarantee stability over time. It embodied a principle of continuity. Arendt is surely right in insisting that the question of continuity over time was a matter of considerable importance to the Greeks, but she does not see the connection between this quest and male separation from biological continuity. She claims that the fabrication of permanence was seen in terms of works and deeds and words. Certainly, the laws of Solon and Cleisthenes are admirable illustrations of works and deeds and words. They did not, however, destroy kinship; they simply substituted and legitimated patriarchy for wider forms of kinship. As it was sons of particular fathers who were admitted to citizenship, the uncertainty of paternity required that the new laws provide a mechanism whereby the mothers of these sons must be sexually reserved for the use of one man.

The question of continuity over time is very important to Arendt's analysis, as it is to this critique. She analyses the question of continuity in terms of the inversion of the *vita activa* and the *vita contemplativa*. The best, 'albeit somewhat superficial', way to understand the rift between active statesmen and contemplative philosophers, she tells us, is by analogy with the concepts of immortality and eternity.[32] Immortality, briefly, Arendt sees as the prize of the active man whose products, including his reputation, outlast his mortal span, whereas eternity is an object for mute contemplation, and cannot be rendered in speech. Contemplation was a discovery of philosophy, which was confirmed as valuable, Arendt says, when the fall of Rome demonstrated the futility of striving for immortality. This disappointment created the permanent hegemony of passive contemplation as the optimum mode of doing philosophy. For the philosopher, it seems, politics became a bore and a distraction as he struggled to escape not only from dismal caves of carnal ordinariness and domestic violence but from the now broken promise of enduring political fame. This kind of analysis is itself a parade of phantoms, for thinking and doing can have no meaning in the world if the thinkers and doers never get born into the world.

Arendt's attempt to ground the separation of public and private life in an arbitrary stratification of human activities is undertaken from an exclusively male perspective, a fact which is itself a tribute to the strength of the tradition of male-stream thought. The artificiality, the literal thoughtlessness, of her analytical categories blurs the real tensions within the realm of human necessity. Arendt's strictures on the project of taming and defeating nature are strictures only upon a historical and social commitment to that task, not at all on a notion of the possibility of the integrative view of the relation of society and nature which feminism is currently developing. Arendt would control nature, but by private violence. She does not appear to understand that this private violence is possible only where it is legitimated by public action, and that in this sense it is always political violence.

The ideology of male supremacy offers to female prisoners in the private realm two consolations. The first is biological: the sacred role of 'legitimate' maternity. The second is ethical: a solemn and honourable conservatism. Women are given the task of conserving these very values which men create to legitimate female privation, the religious and customary sanctions which sanctify the family in a single standard of female behaviour, but which are not applicable to the double standard of male behaviour. Women usually perform little ritualistic roles in the celebration and conservation of life-process events such as birthdays, marriages, funerals. They also have a traditional aversion to such mechanisms of *vertu* as violence, war and revolution. As Thucydides noticed, women do not like to have their children killed, an assertion of the value of private over public which shows women's unfitness for politics. Given such tasks or resistances women are deemed to be 'naturally' conservative. The effectiveness of this ascribed conservatism is real enough. Today, the most frightened critics of feminism are sometimes women. None the less, female conservatism has shown historical signs of fragility, and has, under conditions of public excitement and radical social change, exhibited a tendency to crumble. These are the same historical occasions which produce new departures in political theory, as philosophers attempt to comprehend a world in which established values are transformed, and poets like John Donne mourn the loss of all coherence. At these 'heights of times', as Ortega y Gasset has called them, or nodal points in the class struggle, as Marxists call them, women are drawn into overt public conflicts, shaking off their conventional conservative image and startling the public realm with protest, prophecy and profanity.

Sheila Rowbotham, who notes this tendency, has also noted that women's concern for biological life has established the bread riot as a common though not exclusive form of female political activity.[33] The economic factor is clearly vital, and both women and men have traditionally shown considerable resistance to the spectacle of their children dying of starvation. Starvation is not the only fuse for female political passion, however, nor does starvation necessarily lead to revolt. Marx and Engels, among others, documented the mortality of malnutrition in nineteenth-century England, but hunger did not lead to revolution. Women eventually emerged into the public realm, but in the form of mainly bourgeois cadres calling not for bread but for the vote. Starvation can as often produce profound lethargy as public excitement. The former response to hunger has been seen in recent years in Central Africa, whereas in Ethiopia and other areas revolutionary activity ensued. There are clearly many factors involved, including imperialistic exploitation and the *necessita/fortuna* of geography, and the theory of the level of maturity of class struggle as the major triggering mechanism, while enormously fruitful, is by no means unproblematic.

One predictable and persistent refrain in dramas of social and economic stress is the outcry against what is generally called 'the breakdown of public morality'. This is a euphemism employed when women conduct their sexual lives like men, and one factor of the conservatization of female consciousness is that women often join this chorus. We see this in our own time, in the activities of 'sacred ladies' like Anita Bryant in opposition to progressive feminism. Moral turpitude has, apparently, a direct relation to uppity women, a relation which often seems much clearer in the minds of men than in actual social conditions. The Women Question was clearly more important in the Athens of Plato's time than the actual helplessness of women can explain. It was a source of much concern to conservatives like Plato and Aristophanes, and of inspiration to the tragic dramatists. Women appear to have been important but not active in the polis, which suggests that their inactivity was relatively recent, or less well established than historians believe. In declining Rome, there appears to have been female activism at all class levels: the wives of the proles joined in the bread riots, the wives of the plebs joined the religious cults which were reviving and debasing ancient earth goddesses in rather nasty ritualistic celebrations of fertility, while the wives of the patricians were refusing to bear children.[34] In this latter context, it is instructive to compare the work of Ovid and Juvenal, writing just one hundred years apart. The urbane and confident Ovid lives in a society still so sure of itself that women can be considered human beings. To be sure, Ovid is a gay and fickle blade, but he is not terrified by either intelligence or sexuality in a woman: 'Let the woman feel the act of love in her marrow. Let the performance bring equal delight to the two.'[35] This is a sentiment which would have puzzled Engels, who did not believe that women experience sexual pleasure.

Augustine thought that evil feminine influences attended the birth of Rome, and indeed that all secular cities proceeded from the wombs of whores.[36] For Juvenal, one hundred years after Ovid, the behaviour of women was not a symptom of Rome's decline but an important causal factor in that decline. His animadversions are scurrilous but deeply felt. His saga of woe for the rape of public weal includes the breakdown of the double standard of sexual behaviour, with women outrageously abrogating its permissive level; the pernicious influence of women in high places; and the effeminization of the military by adultery, homosexuality and the meddling of wives in the administration of the provinces. Women were said to have been engaged in posting election propaganda on the walls of Pompeii during Juvenal's lifetime, which is thought to have been somewhere about AD 60 to 140, and were presumably part of the riots and civic disturbances of the times. Juvenal is not just reporting, though; he is claiming that women in politics are evil, and at the same time attacking imperialist assertions of right to power through the hereditary principle.

He pictures the Empress Agrippina in a brothel, 'displaying her golden tits and the parts where Britannicus came from', a rather more explicit but hardly less vulgar version of a new society appearing from the womb of a whore than that proposed by Augustine. Perhaps Juvenal's most bitter satire was reserved for the abortionists, who were the busiest men in Rome, with the possible exception of genealogists offering parchment patricianship for a suitable sum. The patrician families had been decimated by the whim of mad emperors, by battle casualties and internecine strife, but that this decline was exacerbated by a declining birthrate is a fact supported by many sources.[37]

Juvenal's satire is extravagant, but his response to increased female activism is not atypical. Little is known of him, but he is believed to have come of old, conservative, plebeian stock, exalting the virtues of love of land tied to domestic bliss ensured by modest, good women and hard work. He hated the newly emergent bourgeois class with a vitriolic virtuosity comparable only to his enraged contempt of women in the public sphere, harlots by definition. He was, in a sense, a puritan, though this is misleading if we do not remember the different class structures and religious organization of first-century Rome and seventeenth-century England. Juvenal's puritanism is that of the countryman who lives submerged in urban rejection of rural values.

In the English Civil War, however, women espousing puritan values were again bursting into the public realm, and starvation does not seem to have been a factor. The London mob, formidable as always, took to the streets, but they were calling for the blood of bishops rather than the bread of life. The period shows a marked increase in female public activity, which extended over all classes. It was almost exclusively sectarian:

> when all the obvious objections have been made, it still remains true that in the sects women played a disproportionate role; and they received from them correspondingly greater opportunities.[38]

The opportunities of which Keith Thomas speaks here do not appear to have been solely economic. These women called for spiritual liberation, the right to preach and the right to interpret Scripture, but they also called for sexual liberation, the right to choose their mates and discard them if that choice turned out badly. Attacks on the institution of marriage not only alarmed the authorities; they alarmed fellow sectarians. Likewise, in 1789, Olympe de Ganges's view that the French Revolution should entail the end of masculine privilege was snuffed out on the scaffold.

The significance of these events, largely neglected by historians until quite recent times, should not be exaggerated. However, there are three points which might be noted. The first is that analysis of women's political activities in terms of class struggle cannot account for the fact that such activity crossed class divisions, and was clearly seen by the women themselves as related to sex and reproduction. The second is that women are not 'naturally' conservative. Let out of the private realm women attack that realm with vigour. 'Almost every apartment', claimed Juvenal 'is Clytemnestra's address'.[39] Female sectarian activity in the seventeenth century was widely recognized as a threat to conjugality. 'Next to the debauching of women into forbidden embraces', in one Puritan observer's hierarchy of sin, came 'this alienation of those two, whom God had made one, and no person has power to put asunder in body and mind'.[40] Women sectarians finally learned that the obedience due to the father from wives and children could not finally by abolished by an appeal to a God who in fact ordained it, and Puritan preoccupation with the Fall made theology a poor debating ground for female liberationists. Nevertheless, as a generic historical development, the enthusiasm of these Puritan women made an indelible mark on the social relations of reproduction.[41]

Third, and most importantly, the infrequency and brevity of these occasions is the most significant thing about them. Only under intense social upheaval does the strength of the abstract wall between public and private tremble, and its fetishistic nature stand exposed as male invention. As soon as the tremors diminish, men move in to rebuild the wall, to re-establish and redefine their generic supremacy. Though the social forms grow progressively weaker, yet the centre holds so long as the changes which have taken place have left untouched the process of reproduction. These struggles have not lessened the male need to institutionalize the potency principle or to mediate the uncertainties of paternity. They have not created objective tensions within the female experience of reproduction which challenge women to elaborate a second nature for themselves, or provide the freedom to do so. Such truncated female revolts were premature children. The objective conditions which are necessary for the cancelling of the dualism which is embedded in the theory and practice of male dominant history are (1) the technological capacity to control the process of reproduction, and (2) evidence that man's definition of the human condition as the endless struggle with nature will lead not to the subjection of the natural environment but to its destruction. It may also require, in economic terms, a more powerful social representation of universal man than we have heretofore seen, and such an objectification of universality is emerging in the form of the multi-national 'corporation', man's latest and most lethal self-perpetuating invention. In the process of the irrational destruction of the environment for the profit of multi-nationals, real men stand helplessly by, their politics unable to resist their own alienated creations. All that stands opposed to this is what Angela Miles calls 'the feminist principle',[42] the principle which upholds the value of individual lives against collective death, of integration with the natural world against the 'masterful' destruction of that world, of the abolition of the phoney wall between public and private, first nature and second nature, continuity and discontinuity. This political principle is not the exclusive property of women: just as some women have 'succeeded' in the world of men, some men recognize feminist politics as the movement of the future, seeing the translation of the feminist principle into political praxis as the most urgent of contemporary tasks.

4 Creativity and procreativity

The idea of second nature is an old one, and seems at first sight quite uncomplicated. It is embedded in our conceptual and expressive apparatus in a proverbial way: it comes as second nature to me, we might say; it's second nature to stop at a red light, or set aside the rent money or vote Tory. When we say such things, we refer to some action which is habitual, done without thought, rooted in custom and habit, some facet of language or behaviour which has been engraved in human personality by the experiences and needs and duties of the lives we lead. In a common-sense way, we all, men and women, have 'second nature' of this kind. It may seem, therefore, that nothing much is added to this everyday experience if it is noted that the debate as to the nature of second nature has been continuing since the days of the Athenian polis. So what? seems to be the only possible response to that. It may also seem to be a quibble to ask why, if indeed the behaviour which we describe as second nature is determined by culture, we assign it to some kind of natural origin. We may answer impatiently that this is simply a traditional linguistic flourish: we do talk of 'the nature of things' in a sense which has nothing to do with organic nature. Obviously, we still talk too about 'human nature', yet nowadays, in our enlightened times, we all know, surely, that there really is no such thing as human nature. There are, of course, certain instinctive and anatomical imperatives in our existence, but the idea of some kind of fixed human nature, involving such notions as spirit and soul and all that antique metaphysics: that was all rejected when the great wave of Enlightenment swept over the European intelligentsia in the eighteenth century. In fact, it has been asserted, this 'human nature' fallacy is one of the reasons why traditional political philosophy is no longer relevant to modern lives. Behind every theory of politics, a venerable old cliché has it, lies a theory of human nature. The way in which the traditional political theorist proceeded was to say what Man was by nature and then prescribe a society to suit him. If, in fact, the evidence showed that men were not at all like the postulated pattern, the theorist simply retreated to the position that this was what men ought to be like, or what they would be like if the proper sets of political institutions were created in which their true nature, their essential nature, could emerge.

The fact that male-stream thought has abandoned speculation on the nature of man (first, second or combined) does not mean that the history of these concepts can or should be ignored by women. This whole question of the status of nature is one which has been important to the development of the ideology of male supremacy, and plays a crucial part in the assorted 'concepts of man' which have raised that ideology to impressive heights. It has also been an important part of 'concepts of woman', where some kind of special relationship with nature is that glory which puzzlingly appears to guarantee our inferiority.

I do not propose to attempt to reinstate nature-of-man theorizing. On the contrary, I have asserted that concepts of man have at all times a material base in lived male lives. We are attempting to unravel the specifically reproductive determinants in male experience, wherein man's biological nature (first nature) exerts identifiable constraints upon his modes of developing his socio-historical (second) nature. We should note, however, that contemporary women have not been averse, in some cases, to tangling with sweeping generalizations about the nature of man. To be sure, the metaphysical presuppositions embedded in the proposition that man is a chauvinist pig are not always self-evident. It is a proposition certainly much less elegant than generalizations relating to rational man, spiritual man, universal man or man alone, but it does belong to this same dubious speculative genre: it attempts in a crude way to integrate a first-nature metaphor (pig) with a second-nature behaviour complex (chauvinist) in a generalization about the nature of man. What is absent, as it so often is in speculation about fixed human nature, is a bridge between the imputed and the actual and between the particular and the general.

Here, our interest lies in quite specific and delimited aspects of second-nature theorizing. First, we are interested in the fact that while men have two natures, however great their difficulties in getting them together, women have only one. If we take only two of the multi-faceted meanings of the word nature – organic/biological on the one hand, transcendental/essential on the other – we note that these have not generally been thought to present philosophical problems in the female case. Women have been perceived as integrated with first nature so completely that they do not need a second nature. As the expression of second nature takes place in the political realm, this is one reason why politics is man's world. Women's special relationship with nature has not evidently prevented them from displaying some 'essential' characteristics; impetuous, unreliable, sentimental, 'kind of dumb', the whole familiar catalogue. These characteristics, however, are firmly related to women's reproductive capacity, which does not differentiate them from animals in any case, and are therefore first-nature universal characteristics. It is misleading even to call such characteristics essential, given the philosophical significance attached to essence: femininity is, rather, accidental, and subsequently a matter of necessity. The second point about man's second nature which therefore interests us is the fact that this powerlessness is not apparent in the male case. Man makes himself. This stimulating notion has not always been so important as it became with the development of Liberal and Existential concepts of man. Man does not make himself self-consciously until quite late in history. The philosophers of antiquity, noting the usually depressing performance of the politically powerful, were rather nervous of this notion, hence the attempt to root second nature in some metaphysical realm prior to both ontogenesis and phylogenesis. The philosophers were equally nervous of the argument that human nature was basically 'natural' in an organic, animal sense. Analogies with the animal world did not have to wait upon modern ethology. In the first book of *The Republic*, Socrates has to deal with Thrasymachus, who proclaims the 'might is right' law of the jungle with a great deal more political realism that Lionel Tiger has ever managed. None the less, whether each man makes himself or lets a philosopher or a masculine deity or a lawgiver do it for him is not too important. For our purposes, it does not really matter whether male-stream thought argues that second nature is already potential in first, or whether second nature actually precedes first, or is made by men or by society. What we want to do is to see more clearly why men, or at least those men who attempted to give theoretical substance to the idea of man, formulated the proposition that men have two natures, for it is within his second nature that Man has found his assurance of generic superiority. In doing this, we can perhaps add a depth of more specifically feminist perspective to de Beauvoir's analysis of men as makers of themselves and of history, as successful transcenders of their biological limitations, and as superior to women.

Let us therefore return to the nitty-gritty of Arendt's version of this ancient argument about the dualism of human nature, which shares biological being with the beasts and at the same time finds ways to publish abroad before an audience of the ontologically elite the splendours of human being. For Arendt, as for many traditional thinkers, this was precisely what was the matter with first nature; it did not distinguish human from animal nature. Imputed to man is a quality, a property or an essence which makes him specifically something more than a featherless biped, a something which transcends mere existence. Nature in the organic sense simply exists. She was for the Greeks the source of life, yet somehow not quite so clearly the source of being. Man's relationship with this potent force was his fate and his glory, and it was an endless challenge to know himself as a natural but also a transcendental being.

Nature was therefore, in Greek thought, the legitimizer of ethical lives and political organizations. At the same time, she could be an unruly and wanton old lady. To be good was to act in concord with nature, which is very different from modern views of man and nature as antagonists, and as the overcoming and taming of nature as the most human of tasks. It was possible for the men of antiquity to hold their ambivalent view of nature because of the estimation of nature's greatest gift to men, perceived to be the gift of reason. This in a sense cancelled out the ambivalence implicit in nature's actual performance. The dualism associated with spring and life and order as opposed to woeful winter, disorderly accident and irrational death seemed to the philosophers to appear, in individual and social life, as an opposition of rational and creative behaviour to the thoughtless and destructively selfish satisfaction of animal desires. Human nature could, however, overcome the dualism of nature in general by exercising reason to overcome the wild animal in our bosoms. Man is naturally rational, and one of the consequences of this is that he is able to create the conditions under which he can be a good man in the teeth of Mother Nature's more depraved legacies. Thus, both Plato and Aristotle held that man was 'naturally' social, for the state of moral goodness which his reason told him was the desirable way of life for him could only be attained in community with others who were of the same rational nature as himself. Man, as Aristotle famously remarked, is a polis animal, essentially sociable in that only political community can provide a rational ambiance in which animal desires can be subjected to the rule of law in a decent, orderly, ethical and 'natural' way.

Thus, the philosophers recommended that men build on the foundation of their obvious animal naturalness a superstructure of lived conditions in which the subtleties of their essential human nature could be born. Where it is argued that first nature includes the capacity to reason within the second-nature condition of natural sociability, there is complete harmony between first and second nature, and for Plato and Aristotle this division is only a deceptive appearance of the essentially whole nature of man. There is, of course, the practical difficulty that this admirable harmony is rarely visible to the naked eye, but it was the conscious cultivation of the real synthesis which the philosophers and even some of the politicians appeared to see as the purpose and glory of political life. Political and ethical life are entwined in the task of realizing the conformity of man and his nature,. even where real men have to be thumped a bit to remember this. There was something more to this, however, than mere theory. In Greek society, as in many other societies, the unification of first and second nature required a bit of all-too-human help. It required, for example, a second birth, qualitatively different from biological birth, and evidently only required by males. Women, with one nature, only needed one, natural birth. George Thomson, whose work we shall be looking at in more detail in the next chapter, claims that prior to the Classical Age puberty rites were common to children of both genders. These rites were simply celebrations of the transition from childhood to adulthood. In classical Greece, the older ceremonies were for a time retained, but females were progressively and systematically excluded. Males not only became adults, they became citizens, in a strange tangle of sacred rite and secular bureaucracy. They were symbolically and sometimes mimetically reborn. The conditions of this second birth, given powerful symbolic expression in the myths of Second Coming which are an integral part of many male dominant religions, are very different from the conditions of first birth. They are conditions created and controlled by men, both human and divine, and no female reproductive labour is required for this significant genesis.

Obviously, the conceptualization of the differentiation of the animal and the human or of first and second nature has changed historically. The beautiful simplicity of the notion of the polis as man's natural sphere is that it deals with the uncertainty of paternity and the absence of experienced continuity in one fell theoretical swoop. Animality is controlled by rational social institutions implemented by the political community, while that community itself, persisting as it does over and beyond the lifespan of individuals, both realizes and symbolizes a continuity over time which defies nature's real indifference to men's post-coital fate. Other historical forms of man/animal differentiation can be analysed: it has been argued at various times, for example, that the distinction rests on putatively 'natural' abilities such as the capacity for grace through faith, or for producing tools, or for acquiring property. The Greek notion of human nature as encompassing an innate capacity for polis life is the one that Arendt wishes to restore. The limiting 'first-nature' questions of bodily need and species continuity are banished to an ahistorical and quite unnatural realm in which dualist ontology defeats undifferentiated biology in the interests of an abstract concept of man the Creator. In this scenario, biological necessity guarantees more than species continuity: it guarantees economic and genderic inequality maintained by violence *in perpetuo*. Arendt does not tell us how those who master their first nature by violence will be able to leave that unpolitic characteristic at home. Freedom and equality are deemed possible only for a select band of successfully violent men. Somehow, an existential craving for fame and immortality will enable these tyrants to cast off the dark robes of the oppressor, as they cross the mystic gulf between private and public life to don the shining armour of excellence, which is the proper raiment of their second natures.

The actual relationships of the public and private realms in the Athenian polis appear to have been different from the subsequent historical breakdowns in genderic apartheid referred to in the previous chapter, where women have been actively involved in political struggles.

There is no record of public female activism in the polis; indeed, there are only the slimmest records of any women's activities outside of the domestic treadmill at all. In terms of the fame which Arendt claims is the prize of uniqueness, only the redoubtable and tormented Sappho has left a mark in the 'strangely physiological' verses in which she hauntingly records her vision of the physical destruction of her body.[1] The other woman 'most talked about', to use Pericles' derogatory term, was Socrates' much maligned wife, Xanthippe. The Lesbian and the Shrew stand in pale and perversely comic relief against the backdrop of the powerful dramatic fictions of ancient womanhood. Clytemnestra and Antigone, Electra and Medea, Phaedra and the Eumenides played out their tragic aesthetic destinies before a male audience whose own women were insignificantly toiling back home in the safety of the private realm.

The situation and aspirations of the men of the polis were not the same as those of their descendants who utilized general social havoc to recruit women as day-labourers in a variety of revolutionary causes, confident of their ability to re-establish the integrity of generic apartheid when the fireworks had burnt out. In this early stage of generic struggle, the Greeks were engaged in the quite different tasks of creating the socio-legal forms and the justificatory ideology of a quite recent male supremacy. There are many indications of a conscious mediation of the real problems posed by the dialectical structure of reproductive process. Drama faithfully reflects men's agonistic activities in religion, in law, in politics and, above all, in family life, as they struggled to come to terms with their relatively newly acquired generic hegemony.

The reality of the historical supersession of matrilinear kinship forms has been obscured by vague abstract formulations, such as Maine's 'discovery' of the move 'from status to contract', and by the unseemly squabble which has developed within the discipline of anthropology.[2] Further, the whole question has been seared with ideological passion since Marx and Engels seized upon the work of Bachofen and Morgen as additional evidence for a materialist view of historical evolution. It is not proposed here to enter into these gladiatorial lists. We posit the existence of ancient societies in which matrilinear kinship was the practical ground of social order and tribal continuity. We hypothesize that the historical event which triggered the eventual overthrow of these social forms was the discovery of physiological paternity. We argue that the creation of polity was a development whose roots lay in the dialectical relations within and between the necessary processes of production and reproduction, and that the part played by reproduction has been neglected to such an extent that we lack a theoretical perspective from which to understand it.

It seems reasonable to assume that the overthrow of ancient social and kinship arrangements was a traumatic affair. This is, in fact, something more than mere assumption. The early mythical forms of the ideology of male supremacy are replete with rape, murder, incest, castration, fratricide, matricide, parricide and the cannibalization and sacrifice of infants. Zeus did not take over Mount Olympus without a battle, a battle fought with truly repulsive ferocity betwixt blood relations and between truculent and vengeful spouses. The polis was not, however, the arena of these struggles; it was their culmination. The great political thinkers of antiquity were as aware of this as the dramatists, and Plato would have liked it better had the poets stopped going on about it and left its interpretation to philosophers. Like the patriarchal composers of the book of Genesis, the intellectuals of antiquity found ambiguity and confusion in the movement from an order and continuity grounded in human procreativity to a surrogate order and continuity grounded in male creative potency. It was precisely because the latter is not 'natural' that ideological inversions were required to make it seem so.

Plato was a member of the aristocracy, and a defender of aristocratic values, which include commitment to a hereditary principle. He was therefore in the difficult position of having to defend class-conscious devotion to patrilinear elitism which quite clearly was rendered problematic by the uncertainty of paternity. His solution was radical. He attempted to extend the uncertainty of paternity to both parents: motherhood was to be made as uncertain as fatherhood. In Book V of *The Republic*, females are offered a form of equality in that some can earn a place in Plato's elite class, the Guardians, but the condition of that equality is that 'children should be held in common, and no parent should know his child or child his parent'.[3] Plato makes it quite clear that precautions must be taken to see that even suckling mothers cannot recognize their own children.

Arendt's charge that Plato wanted not to abolish the family but to set up the state as a super-family is an idiosyncratic reading. It always has to be remembered that Plato's recommendations in *The Republic* are for the Guardians only: what Plato is doing is setting up a ruling class which is *supra* family and relies on class regeneration rather than individual birth for a controlled continuity. He says little about the social organization of the ordinary people who do not complete his pedagogic marathon, although by the time he came to write *The Laws* he is a bit more practical, and a peasant-proprietor and firmly patriarchal family is restored as the basic unit of a repressive political organization.[4] Plato in his old age was evidently less sanguine about the capacity of reason to rule over rapacity.

The recommendations in *The Republic* have led some feminists, including de Beauvoir, to conclude that Plato was on the right side in terms of generic equality.[5] This is a short-sighted view. In fact, this argument that women can be Guardians is born of the intransigence of biological nature, and is the only occasion on which Plato had anything even grudgingly comforting to say to us. Women are part of a utopian plan which is dictated by the dialectics of reproductive process and a real historical tension between democratic polity and aristocratic family, which created special problems for the hereditary aristocratic class. Democracy can ignore women, for heredity theoretically plays no part in the right to rule, though it sneaks in the back door in the form of property laws. Aristocracy simply cannot pretend that the uncertainty of paternity is insignificant.

The Greeks had developed real social institutions to reduce the uncertainty of paternity. The separation of public and private may well have been enforced by private violence, and it may in fact have been mainly a feature of upper-class life, but it was buttressed by publicly legitimized institutions centred around monogamous marriage, a marital police, the *gynaeceum*, the castration of male domestic slaves and heavy penalties for adultery and other misconduct. These measures were effective enough to create wives so deadly dull that prostitution and homosexuality flourished, and were eloquently defended among the intelligentsia. For Plato, such socio-political institutions were not enough. The purificaiton of such first-nature vulgarities as sexual lust and family squabbling clearly needed some form of rational control over the social relations of reproduction. So, less obviously, does the problem of male alienation from species and from time.

Plato's concessions to the strength of the sexual impulse and the social need to reproduce his stable of elitists are grudging and impractical in the historical absence of contraceptive technology, for only with such technology can the rational control of reproduction be understood in a non-utopian way. Plato, to complicate things, appears to have an almost pathological dread of sexuality. In the *Timaeus* he talks of the 'terrible and irresistible affections to which flesh is heir'.[6] He claims that the Ideal Form of the human organism recognizes this danger, and attempts to guard against it by creating a corpus in which the human neck guards the head against contamination from the inferior regions. In this way, the mind can rationally control passion without the danger of sexual distraction. For reinforcement, the soul takes up a watching brief at the midriff.

The *Timaeus* is indeed a strange piece of work, demonstrating clearly that the idealization of the carnal, and the substitution of the abstract time of eternity for the cyclical and historical time of experience, are intricate theoretical tasks. Plato does, however, perceive metaphysics as an antidote, quite specifically, to man's reproductive problem. Cyclical time is both maintained and transcended, while creation itself becomes the generated fecundity of ecstatically and mysteriously cavorting forms of a 'nature' whose nature partakes of formlessness. The reality of maternity as opposed to the ideality of paternity is simply inverted, and motherhood becomes passively abstract while male creative imagination becomes a potent and regenerative force:

> Wherefore, the mother and receptacle of all created and visible and
> in any way sensible things, is not to be termed earth or air or fire or
> water, or any of their compounds, or any of the elements from which
> these are derived, but is an invisible and formless being which
> receives all things and in some nysterious way partakes of the
> intelligible, and is most incomprehensible.[7]

It does not come altogether as a surprise that the best that this passively immaculate receptionist can finally give birth to is a series of triangles.[8] However, even the most dramatic metaphysics has to account for real flesh and blood women, and Plato is equal to the task:

> ... of the men who came into the world, those who were cowards or
> led unrighteous lives may with reason be supposed to have changed
> into the nature of women in the second generation.[9]

Plato's mystification of natural biological process leaves him with the task of creating an alternative mode of human regeneration, a new principle of continuity. He waffles between the needs of the aristocrat and the dreams of the metaphysician. In the latter role, he abandons even the circumspect sexuality of his Guardians, and transfers the dynamics of procreation to creative intellectual intercourse between men. Arendt's argument for male hegemony in politics has more in common with Platonic modes of understanding than she thinks. Both she and Plato deprive reproduction of consciousness and of humanity. The mysterious gulf which male-stream thought has found separating animal from human, appearance from reality, spirit from matter, necessity from freedom and so forth does make sense, but it makes sense if and only if it can be materially grounded in real human experience. Otherwise, it remains 'most incomprehensible'. Such material grounds do exist, and they exist in the estrangement of male life from the act of giving life and the comprehension of that reality. This unity of experience-consciousness is ignored where reproduction is considered to be either wholly physical or wholly metaphysical.

The polis and its philosophers did not create male supremacy, but encountered it, and encountered it as problematic, as requiring the justification demanded by an imputed 'naturalness' having no visible and certain natural roots. The effect of the creation of a private realm in practice was to exclude women from politics, but polity as a substitute for family is hampered by the fact that it cannot do without sexuality and procreation, and therefore cannot do without women. Male praxis can denigrate physical birth and restrict access to women, but male supremacy separated from genetic continuity must equip itself with ideological principles of continuity, and also a non-biological account of beginning. Arendt claims that Plato loses the sense of 'beginning' by abolishing the 'linguistically determined' sense of *archein*, which means both ruling and beginning.[10] As is clear from the passage from the *Timaeus*, Plato did not 'lose' the sense of beginning, he idealized it on the grounds that it was incomprehensible. The Greeks, including Plato, were far more conscious of the problems of 'beginning' than are modern heirs and heiresses to centuries of male-stream thought. The thinkers of antiquity had not 'forgotten' that beginning is birth, and that the comprehension of birth process is a necessary and complex philosophical challenge. Plato initiated a process developed historically in such elaborations as that of, for example, God the Father with his only begotten, but sexually untainted, Son. The Christian God copulates and gestates by saintly proxy. Hegel, by his time, can talk solemn nonsense about the Son separating from the Father and returning again to the Holy Spirit, and thoroughly indoctrinated male readers will not blink or even notice that this is a pathetic travesty of reproductive process.[11] Hegel's effort has respectable intellectual origins, for his work is in a tradition inaugurated by Plato in the *Symposium*, which makes a literately lovely attempt to etherealize that robust old fertility god, Eros, into a worldly immortal saved from ordinariness by a yen for philosophy. It is worth examining this particular effort of Plato's in more detail, for it is here that he makes a fateful contribution to the history of the ideology of male supremacy, in the assertion of the natural superiority of intellectual creativity over carnal procreativity.

The participants in Plato's banquet, replete but sober, decide to forego the usual entertainment provided by dancing girls in favour of some intellectual discussion.[12] The topic chosen is love. The greatness of Eros, says Phaidros, the first speaker, is by virtue of his birth, for he had no parents. This distinctly unnatural dissociation from life process evidently makes Eros stronger than death, for it is only for love, Phaidros argues, that people, even women, are prepared to die. Eros, evidently, is a life-force but is not to be confused with birth process. Pausanias, who speaks next, carefully distinguishes the love of Common Aphrodite from that of Heavenly Aphrodite. The latter is motherless; she firstly had no share of the female, but only the male, and she loves philosophy and virtue in general. Common Aphrodite, of course, loves sexuality in particular, and uses men for mere physical gratification without understanding how important their minds and souls are.

Note that Plato has moved us from a conception of Eros as a life-force totally divorced from biological reproduction to a conception of single male parenthood, in which reproduction has nothing to do with women because female sexuality presumably sullies the purity of masculine moral potency and philosophical prowess. The next speaker, Eryximachos the physician, agrees with the distinction between the two Aphrodites, but hastens to turn it to a vulgar and startlingly modern plug for the all-male medical profession. The good doctor extols the physician's moderating art, which is able to harmonize physical and spiritual love in such a way that Heavenly Aphrodite triumphs over

Common Aphrodite in the production of good health. Men were clearly the beneficiaries of the healing arts, then as now. One wonders how Common Aphrodite would have fared with a hefty dose of valium.

Aristophanes, whose contribution to the discussion has been delayed by an attack of post-prandial hiccups, eventually manages to give a witty account of an old creation myth. There were originally three sexes, male, female and hemaphrodite, all with four legs and two heads, who were very strong and ambitious and attacked even the gods. Zeus solved this problem by the simple expedient of slicing them all down the middle, but the parts were very distressed, and constantly sought their other halves. In an uncharacteristic burst of compassion, Zeus moved their privy parts outside and to the front so that they might unite briefly and then get on with more important human business. Those who are cut from hemaphrodites are adulterers and men who like women, or are women who are mad for men. Those who are slivers of original women are Lesbians and strumpetesses. Best and brightest are those who came from the original men; they are homosexual and would never stoop to reproduction, did not law and custom compel it. Being undistracted by family and the dangers of heterosexuality, these make the best politicians.

Agathon, an aesthetic youth, claims earnestly and eloquently that love is a wise poet, and everyone he touches becomes a poet. After Socrates has spoken (and we shall discuss what he says in a moment), Alcibiades arrives on the scene, a bit drunk, and speaks not in praise of Eros but in praise of Socrates. The suggestions that Socrates really *is* Love, and that wisdom is the true life-force, are emphasized in a skilful literary way. Alcibiades' account of his encounter with Socrates, which gives birth to virtue by sexual abstention, is structurally similar to Socrates' earlier account of the encounter in which Poverty and Plenty give birth to Love by sexual indulgence. Before Alcibiades' arrival at the Symposium, Socrates had told the story of how Eros' mother, Poverty, hungry and cold and miserable, had crept into the bed of his father, Plenty, who was luxuriantly sleeping off a juice which the nectar gods drank before wine was invented. Poverty seduced Plenty, and their child, Eros, was therefore a golden boy, the mean between his mother's poor nature and the rich nature of his father. This paternal nature was one which loved the true, the good and the beautiful, a nature which belonged to a great hunter who hunted wisdom as well as animals, and which was fertile of ideas and dedicated to philosophy. It is from the nature of this splendid and potent creature that Eros gets his life, but because his mother's nature is deficient in the capacity to give life, the life he inherits from his father is always dribbling away. Thus, the nature of the father is to give life abundantly, the nature of the resourceless mother is to deny life. So poor is she that the *actual sex-act is all she has to contribute to life*. This is a quite stunning inversion of the real process of reproduction, in which the sex-act is all that *men* actually contribute to biological life. Poverty, the mother with only a first nature to contribute, is presented as separate from the truly human unity of first and second nature in which Plenty, the father, is happily integrated. Here is a dramatic symbolization of the potency principle at work in defiance of its own biological reality.

Plato cleverly arranges things so that the late-arriving Alcibiades has not heard this tale, so that his story is, as it were, independent evidence of an experiential version of the truth implicit in the myth. The encounter with Socrates of which Alcibiades tells also takes place in bed after a good meal, but both are nourished and so there is no taint of prostitution. Further, Alcibiades the bold is so overcome by a giddy shyness, that it is only on a second attempt that he can make his sexual proposition to Socrates. Socrates exchanges his threadbare cloak for Alcibiades' rich and warm one, for his Poverty is neither proud nor wasteful: further, he spurns the sexual advances of the younger man, for, though sensual, he is above all moderate. Foolish Alcibiades – and gone is the arrogant ranter whom Thucydides portrayed – tells how he had humbly thought that some of Socrates' wisdom might rub off in sexual encounter, but wise Socrates knew that Alcibiades *really* sought wisdom rather than sexual titillation, but he was poor in understanding. Socrates shows the young man that a meeting of minds is what is necessary for the birth of what is essentially, rather than merely biologically, human. Unlike Poverty, he had the potential to become rich.

Alcibiades' adventure with Socrates does not negate sexuality as such. It simply relegates it to a different, lower sphere of existence and defers it in temporal terms. This is not the time or the place. What *is* negated is woman. Temperance conceived in true wisdom is the blessed product of all-male creative intercourse which transcends the sexuality and messiness of procreativity. The stretched-out intellect has replaced the palpitating womb as the cradle of the life-force.

This translation of Eros from body to mind and spirit is by no means void of political significance. Socrates presents his view on love as having been culled from a wise woman: Diotima of Mantinea. Her name, according to W. D. H. Rouse, means something like The Prophetess Fearthelord of Prophetville.[13] This redoubtable character holds the only sizeable female part in the Platonic canon, although it is not a speaking part, for Socrates reports what Diotima said. Plato here uses the literary device later adopted by Rousseau and finally debased by Kate Millett's dreary collection of literary rape artists:[14] he puts the arguments for male superiority into the mouth of a woman.

Diotima first teaches Socrates, according to his account, that Eros is not really a god in the proper sense, but is a mediator between mortals and immortals. Diotima's Eros is a philosopher who seeks wisdom because he does not have it, as gods do, but is not wholly without it, as some mortals are. Eros is miscalled if he is thought of as a god of love only in the carnal sense. Further, lovers always desire that which they love to be theirs 'forever', which is to say that the ownership of the 'good' loved must persist over time. How can this be done? 'All men are pregnant, Socrates, both in body and soul, and when they are of the right age, our natures desire to beget.'[15] Begetting, Diotima claims, is related to the quest for beauty which is certain and permanent, and mortal nature has only one way to ensure immortality, which is to replace the old with the young. But this is the way of beasts. However, says Diotima, knowledge is not immortal either, for it too becomes and passes away. The love of immortality, as opposed to the uncertainties of crude mortality, comes from the love of knowledge, for one cannot love what one does not know. The love of immortality is closely allied to the love of fame, which happens to be more important to men than their children. Men are further blessed in that it also happens to be the case that the immortality of fame is ethically superior to that which comes from having children, and the most potent manifestations of this superiority are political:

> So those who are pregnant in body turn to women and are
> enamoured in this way, and thus, by begetting children, secure for
> themselves, so they think, immortality and memory and happiness,
> 'providing all things for the time to come', but those who are
> pregnant in the soul, for there are some who conceive in the soul

more than in the body, what is proper for souls to conceive and bear. And what is proper? – wisdom and virtue in general – to this class belong all creative poets, and those artists and craftsmen who are said to be inventive. But much the greatest wisdom ... and the most beautiful, is that which is concerned with the ordering of cities and homes, which we call temperance and justice.[16]

Arendt might seize upon the phrase 'cities and homes' as evidence of Plato's tendency to conflate the two, but it must also be noted that Diotima is making Arendt's own distinction between labour, work and action, except that she does not speak of reproduction in terms of labour, but of 'begetting', and she does not speak of ordinary productive labour at all. This is no doubt because, like Arendt, she believes these functions of women and slaves to be indistinguishable from 'the way of the beasts'. None the less, we must note just exactly what it is that is being touted as man's greatest creative venture: 'the ordering of cities and homes'. This does not mean, of course, that Plato is insensitive to the historical importance of economic issues, although his sense of the significance of the social relations of production is less astute than that of Aristotle. We must remember that in this society the household was the major *locus* of productive activity, and, as Marx has remarked, the true nature and mediating power of human labour was obscured by the institution of slave labour. Still, when all of this has been taken into account, what we have from Plato is the notion of the city and home, that is, of the public and the private realm, as products of male creativity, realms in which men unify their first and second natures in social institutions created by the inventive power of their non-biological second nature. Plato is correct in a very important sense; men do use their creative powers this way, and in doing so claim a superiority over those creatures who are unable to transcend their first nature, such as women, slaves and animals. But what is missing is any attempt at analysing why men behave in this way. The answer we propose here is that they must; they must resist the alienation from nature and from time which is inherent in their reproductive praxis, investing intellectual creativity with a power superior to ambiguous procreativity, and creating institutional and ideological modes of continuity over time to heal the discontinuous sense of man the uncertain father.

It might be argued that the *Symposium* is poetic metaphor, an elaborate literary conceit born of the double meanings of 'conception', the physical and the mental. But Socrates is doing more than weaving an analogy. He is claiming that both procreativity and creativity are significant in terms of temporal continuity and the expression of human reality, but he is performing an ideological inversion on actual as opposed to abstract manifestations of that reality. He is saying that procreativity and the genetic continuity which is the product of reproductive labour are illusory, unreal and without significance, while abstract proliferations of male ideas have a more concrete reality. What is in fact material becomes ideal and what is in fact ideal becomes material. Such inversion is not, of course, simple intellectual banditry, though Socrates was quite capable of a bullying kind of casuistry.[17] Plato is struggling with the biologically based realities of male reproductive consciousness. The products of female reproductive labour – species integration and genetic continuity – are deprived of their unity of understanding and action precisely because this unity is not immediately accessible to men. It must be mediated. The experiential moments of female reproductive consciousness, confirmed in actual labour, are thus denigrated and dehumanized, given a low value while they are quite frankly imitated in a 'higher' sphere, the creation of concepts in a male intercourse of spirit and thought. It seems likely that Plato was aware that this substitution might not be deemed very exciting for his followers, for he injects a little booze to liven things up.[18] Plenty had been drinking, so had Socrates and Alcibiades. One remembers the emphasis Plato gives at the beginning of *The Laws* to a discreet education in alcohol for young men. This is no doubt socially impeccable instruction, and gentlemen are still expected to hold their liquor; it probably has some relation, too, to the procreative mystifications practised in Athenian cults, especially those devoted to such products of rebirth as Dionysius and Bacchus.

This philosophy of tiddliness, in which the excitement of conceptual creativity stirs the blood like sexuality with a little help from alcohol, has had a long life. The Bacchanalian whirl erupts unexpectedly and colourfully into the Preface of Hegel's *Phenomenology*, on the heels of the anti-birth argument that essence precedes existence. There is nothing at all staid about philosophical idealism. Whether all this has orgasmic overtones or sublimatory dimensions is best left to psychoanalysis, but psychic phenomena have material roots. What we are examining is intellectualized mimicry of reproductive process, and it is the problematics of that process which structure both the social relations of reproduction and the ideological forms of male reproductive consciousness. We are not dealing simply with the neurotic mumblings of a celibate aesthete. We are dealing with Plato, a lavishly endowed intellect struggling with the meaning of masculinity. We are not at all interested in proving that Plato was somehow wrong, nor in denying the historical fact of male creativity. What we are attempting to do is to understand why it should have been the case that the historical move from matrilinear kinship relations to urbanized political relations should not only have denigrated women, but should have entailed the denial of creative properties to the act of reproduction of life, and the devaluation of the birth of a new human being. We are analysing a powerful and early expression of the doctrine of male potency. This is important, for if it is correct that the development of the polis and the idea of political community has material roots in male reproductive process, then we can understand the historical persistence within political institutions of the potency principle, the definition of politics as power which Millett notes as universally accepted. This is not to argue some kind of biological determinism; political forms have roots in the other pole of necessity, the realm of production. Power accrues to the appropriators of surplus product in a very tangible way, but one might argue that an important element in the capacity of ruling classes to exercise power over men lies precisely in the fact that no man is powerless. However exploited, however stupid, however brutal, however deceived, all men are potent in the realm of reproduction. No man is ultimately powerless. There are obvious psychological ramifications of this situation which ruling classes can and do exploit, giving, for example, to wretched male labourers dingy homes which are none the less private castles. The determinants of this power quite clearly do not lie within the realm of the social relations of production, where most men have been powerless for a long time. They lie in the sphere of reproduction, and just as the labour process is the fundamental determinant of economic and technological development, reproductive process is the key to the mysteries of the potency principle and the forms which the ideology of male supremacy takes.

This ideology conjoins the notions of male supremacy as 'natural' and of men having created for themselves a second 'nature', an ideological complex honed in the minds of the intellectual giants of antiquity which remains important precisely because it is still around. It has proven durable and powerful, which is hardly surprising, for its material base in reproductive process underwent no radical transformation until the development of contraceptive technology in our own time.

Ideology, to be effective, persuasive and persistent must have a discernible conjunction with lived experience, with the real lives of real people, even though that experience may be turned upside down in a fetishistic way. In making this kind of inversion, in spiritualizing the material realities of reproduction and genetic continuity, Plato becomes a potent 'father' of the ideology of male supremacy. He is not, of course, the only one, and one large task of feminist scholarship is to uncover the development of this ideology in all its historical forms. Plato, however, has had an influence on western intellectual life which might be said to be profound, and is by no means always explicit. Modern anthropology, for example, has appreciated the fact that paternity was perceived in early times in terms of magic, but such analysis has retained Platonic overtones. Even today, no serious attempt has been made to link reproductive forms of consciousness to their material base in reproductive process. The genderic implications remain largely unanalysed: it is taken for granted that men in primitive societies looked after the 'magic' – and ideology is strong on magic – while women looked after biological needs. Claude Lévi-Strauss, for example, working from Rousseau's speculative anthropology, attributes a 'binary' structure to human thought emerging from man's initial dim consciousness that other animals were different from human animals. It is difficult to know why the human species should have to step outside of their biologically differentiated selves to discover otherness, and de Beauvoir and Reed, from very different perspectives, have made this point. However, as Lévi-Strauss's theories of mental and social structures are binary and static, rather than dialectical and dynamic, he has to speculate upon the nature of a fixed primary dualism which can stimulate that intellectual activity which alone, he claims in a very Platonic way, can account for the passage from nature to culture. The primary dualism is universal/particular, and Lévi-Strauss says that it is not very important how one labels this essential dualism, which represents the actuality of lives which are at the same time social and individual. He is committed to the rescue of the study of kinship structures from a religious over-determinism which he detects in anthropological science. He is able to note the differentiation of male and female experience of temporality and continuity, and to recognize, but not explain, the magical component in these. Discussing the work of A. P. Elkin on Australian totemism, Lévi-Strauss remarks:

> He [Elkin] opposes the totemism of matrilinear clans to that of patrilinear clans, and with good reason. In the former case, the totem is 'flesh', in the latter it is 'dream'; organic and material in one case, therefore, spiritual and incorporeal in the other.[19]

While the empirical existence of these differentiations is a 'good reason' to consider them, it does not provide any reason why they should have been made in the first place, and Lévi-Strauss's 'therefore' suggests a logical procession which is not in fact there. He does not consider this functional generic distinction to qualify for participation in that dualism so dear to the French intellectual tradition. Far from opposition, generic roles are 'seen rather to be in a relationship of complementarity ... different but correlative ways ... of displaying parallel attributes of nature and society'.[20] He thus empties binarism, his basic epistemological category, of generic significance, assuming that there is nothing in the form of reproductive process which can move humanity to thought or to action. He simply does not recognize paternity either as historical discovery or as creative idea.

Lévi-Strauss's structural model of human culture permits variation, though it remains a little short on flexibility. He is able, for example, to deal with a great deal more ethnographic material than Engels could, with the latter's rigid correlation of kinship structures and economic development. Engels, of course, was working with much more limited data. Lévi-Strauss's structural correlations, however, do not and cannot account for sexual conflict: in fact, they do not account for social conflict at all. Having rendered nature abstract and non-dynamic, and having reduced reproduction to a generic complementarity of flesh and magic, Lévi-Strauss is left with structural generalizations empty of human content and lacking entirely any objective material base. Ultimately, his substratum of social structure becomes an interplay of affect and intellect: 'the advent of culture thus coincides with the birth of the intellect'.[21] Here is another of these asexual births beloved of male-stream thought. Biological factors alone, Lévi-Strauss believes, cannot reduce the opposition between the continuous and the discontinuous. He does not see that *male* reproductive experiences cannot, but that women mediate this opposition in reproductive labour. In Lévi-Strauss's work, the Platonic idealization of male reproductive process remains uncriticized and intact.

I have argued here that the development of male supremacy rests on the objective process of reproduction, not because that process is static and immutable, but because it is historical and dialectical. The supersession of matrilinear kinship was the historically necessary consequence of the undateable discovery of physiological paternity. This was a process which took a very long time, and the Greek polis was a fragile, brief but influential synthesis of massive and intransigent contradictions within and between the relations of production and reproduction. It was the relative recency of the overcoming of traditional kinship relations which made the 'woman question' urgent to Greek philosophers and dramatists. The change, in fact, was not complete, either in Greece itself or in Asia Minor. Among the people the Athenians liked to call Barbarians, the *ethnos*, a type of society still tribal in an artificial way, flourished, and Aristotle actually accused Plato of wanting to regress to this type of pre-political organization.[22]

It is clear that this radical turmoil, despite the political genius of the great legal reformers, did not resolve the questions of the relations of men and women, of parents and children or of the status and interaction of public and private realms. It could hardly do so. Patriarchy distorts and idealizes the realities of reproduction, but it cannot negate them. The social need for forms of order and ideological justification of the *status quo* which follows the development of political community and conjugal family cannot make a simple switch from matrilineality to patrilineality, for this throws into stark relief the core of uncertainty in male reproductive consciousness. Alternative modes of continuity must be created and institutionalized, not only in property relations, but in polity and constitutional law. All of these developments are strengthened by the ideology which they create, and which flowers in art, religion and philosophy as well as in ordinary, everyday custom and prejudice. These are vast changes. Social surplus product, the fruit of the alienation of productive labour, becomes petrified in the notion of inalienable property: the alienated sperm becomes the basis of paternal certitude. Both of these demand the defence of rights of appropriation which custom and law eventually provide, though clearly not without a struggle.

Of course, the question of continuity, unlike the question of hereditary rights, is not of importance just to an aristocratic class, but to any ruling class. It is not, however, the same question. Heredity is the justification and form of continuity of property rights. In politics, conservative minds see the question of continuity in terms of the problem of order. The political community, objectified in institutions and exploiting law in favour of persistence, does transcend the deaths of individuals and the succession of generations. It also, and this is less often noted, transcends the births of individuals, rejecting genetic continuity in favour of political persistence, though conservatives have argued for centuries that the family is the basis of the state. The great conservatives of antiquity, Plato and Aristotle, certainly wanted to argue the naturalness of polis life, to defend the polity against the ravages of discontinuity and political conflict, but they would not rely on anything so problematic as the family to do this. History indeed shows us that both political theory and family life have been powerless to impose continuity and order on political reality. Many men, and some women, have been quite willing to overthrow political regimes which they have found very unnatural indeed, and to overthrow them violently. The fact is that what is really 'natural' for men is discontinuity, and Plato understood this and understood its reproductive roots.

So far in history, political change has not transcended the potency principle. Change has been a transfer of power, and women, of course, have been involved in a smallish way in such events. It is too soon to say what effect the historical transformation of the reproductive substructure of human history will have on ways of understanding problems of continuity and change in political life, but we can at least cast off the shackles of traditional ways of thinking about the problem. To do this, we must have a theoretical model which apprehends the dialectics of reproduction and production as the substructure of human history.

Plato, casting his own compelling haze of aesthetic splendour and ethical longing over creativity and procreativity alike, still recognized, however reluctantly, that political action was the only means whereby philosophers could guarantee a society in which creators control procreators. This entails the power to compose and impose a speculative form of 'second nature' and a new principle of continuity on man's world of politics. If everyone shared Diotima's contempt for reproduction, there would be no posterity to bedazzle. An ideal continuity is proposed, composed of memory which looks back, aspiration which looks forward, and contemplation which looks upward into eternity. In this way, men transcend their first, animal nature by the introspective creativity of their philosophical second nature, shored up by the mutual admiration of brothers in freedom. Plato thus retains for men the extraordinarily powerful *ethical* legitimization which the natural still holds for a society close in time and space to natural kinship structures, and still unsure of the efficacy of its own social innovations. At the same time, nature is idealized, and the dynamics of ideal intellectual creativity invert the dynamics of biological procreativity. In the process, the nature of man is split in two.

Arendt comments that the political vocabulary of ancient Greece, whose perversion by the Romans she laments elsewhere, tends to the organic because exciting things were happening in biology at the time, and it seemed quite natural to use this new vocabulary. This is an unlikely accident; equally exciting things were happening, for example, in mathematics and drama. The political vocabulary is organic because of the close relationship of politics to reproduction. What Plato sees is that biological process, fraught with genderic oppositions, cannot provide the social unity which he insists is the end of politics. I. M. Crombie has called Plato 'the midwife's apprentice', and indeed that is the role of Socrates vis-à-vis Diotima.[23] He/she is midwife to the products of an intellectual potency operating continuously through both history and eternity. Aristotle, with a stronger sense of real history, turns to constitution and law to provide orderly political continuity. Rather than contingent plenitude or ideal form, Aristotle's God generates nothing. What Aristotle does add to this pure, abstract potential, says Arthur O. Lovejoy, is the conception of continuity:

> Aristotle did not, indeed, formulate the law of continuity with any such generality as was afterwards given to it. But he furnished his successors, and especially his late medieval admirers, with a

definition of the continuum: 'Things are said to be continuous whenever there is one and the same limit of both which they possess in common'.

Nature refuses to conform to our craving for clear lines of demarcation; she loves twilight zones, where forms abide which, if they are classified at all, must be assigned to two classes at once.

There are not many differences in mental habit more significant than that between the habit of thinking in discrete, well-defined class concepts and that of thinking in terms of continuity, ... so that the whole notion of species comes to seem an artifice of thought not truly applicable to the fluency, the, so to say, universal overlappingness of the real world.[24]

There are few twilight zones so murky as the realm of procreation. T. S. Eliot's 'shadow' still darkens the space between paramour and parent. The ideology of male supremacy has deepened that shadow, so that the dead core of impotence in the potency principle might wear a deceptively decent shroud. For men, physiology is fate, and the greatest among them have known this very well. For women, anatomy is creativity, and the ordinary among us have known this very well. Only now, however, does history present us with the challenge to express in theoretical terms the 'nature' of this lasting paradox, the material ground of the double standard which stretches all the way from the rapist's alleyway of terror to the ascetic philosopher's cave. Only by grasping the whole can women actively transform it, and Plato is not the whole. His work can be, however, what it has always been: a place to begin. If we want to know about the birth of male-stream thought and the ideology of male supremacy, it's a good idea to interview the midwives and their brighter apprentices. They have much to tell us, more still to keep secret in the cultic mysteries of the brotherhood of man.

5   Production and reproduction

Marxism and the polis

The Athenian polis was a mature and relatively coherent synthesis of
centuries of development in which humanity had grappled with its
consciousness of the dialectics of the necessary processes of material
life, the processes of reproduction and production. Karl Marx has
remarked that the great charm of the ancient world, still working on the
minds and imaginations of its cultural heirs and successors, was its
wholeness, its ability to present precisely this coherence in its
philosophy and literature. Marx is correct with regard to the imaginative
weight of the Greek achievement. Antiquity is the bejewelled heritage of
western man, which bathes him in an inherited translucence to which
Marx, who was rarely sentimental about anything except marriage, was
not immune.[1] The fact that this society, based on slave labour, was
imperialist, racist, sexist and quite often orgiastic somehow loses its
impact in an aesthetically supernal totality which presents its seamless
cloth of gold to entranced posterity. From a feminist perspective, the
seams of that fabric show through; it becomes a patchwork in which the
ragged edges of the rather crude articulation of an early ideology of
male supremacy can be seen quite clearly. Not least of Greek
achievements was the definition of humanity as man.

The wholeness of the classical world was never, of course, complete.
Greek thought and, to a lesser extent, Greek drama, idealized the
conscience of a wealthy and leisured class, and the intellectual riches of
a ruling class challenged by democracy and a ruling sex in the process of

consolidating its power tended to obscure the material substructures of their culture in productive and reproductive process. The wholeness thus renders women and slaves 'invisible'. Yet this 'invisibility' was itself an ideological product, a lack of appearance which was, paradoxically, mere appearance, a paradox quite at home with a Platonic philosophy which insisted that appearance was not real. Idealist thought notwithstanding, slaves and women visibly continued to produce and reproduce, while the creativity of labour power remained uncelebrated and unsung in the shadows of the private household, and in the noisome bowels of the silver mines.

The separation of life from necessity is in the first instance an ideological separation, a yearning and a dream of the sweet sunshine always outside the cave of the contradictions of carnality. The move to transform necessity to ideology, and ideology to social practice, entails tremendous struggles, and can be maintained only by continuous and active vigilance. The social structures which emerge from attempts to separate life from necessity are the *division of classes* in the productive realm and the *division of public and private life*, of family and polity, in the reproductive realm. The grounds of these separations lie in the dialectical structure of the processes of productive labour and biological reproduction, the series of alienations, negations and mediations which structure the way experience is thought about. In the classical world the cultural creations – economy, family, polity – which embodied free men's separation from nature, carried with them the additional paradox of an appeal to the natural for legitimacy. The ultimate ethical appeal of Greek thought is to the natural, which is the paradigm of the Good.

The social relations between classes and between men and women are therefore necessarily relations of struggle, the struggle of the upper classes and all men to conserve their freedom from labour. The quality of freedom from labour is of course quite different in terms of reproduction, in which men are forced to be free, and in terms of productive labour, the necessity for which must be forced on others. The struggles in each case are both ideological – the apologetics and rationalizations of private and public power – and practical – collective actions to objectify existential needs. This is so, too, of the struggles to overcome alienation from nature, which becomes a struggle to contain and exploit both nature and her servants, the productive classes and women. In the case of the struggle with women, the ideological creations are the 'principles' of patriarchy and potency, which serve to legitimate the realities of the segregation of women in the private realm, the creation of a public, male realm of freedom and control and the objectification of assorted 'principles' of continuity, including the public realm itself, which takes on a 'constitutional' capacity to transcend the individual lifespan.

The form and strength and visibility of these struggles varies historically, and varies in response to changes in the actual modes of production and reproduction. Clearly, change in modes of production has been more frequent in historical terms. This is partly because productive labour is a generalized human praxis: the whole human race is involved. Everyone eats. Nature, further, is both provident and niggardly in her provision of means of food and shelter. Productive labour is universally a synthesis of mental inventiveness and physical effort. Reproductive labour, on the other hand, is genderically differentiated; maternal labour is material but involuntary, while paternity is voluntary and essentially ideal. Another important factor in the uneven transformation of mode of reproduction is the fact that technological development in a male dominant society gives no priority to contraception. Indeed, there is evidence that contraceptive methods have been suppressed, in much the same way as technological know-how has been withheld from labouring classes and exploited races. The clearest instance of male reactionary reproductive conservatism is the huge legal and religious edifice erected to outlaw abortion, but feminist historians also claim that the distribution of herbal contraceptives was one of the 'sins' for which 'witches' paid such a brutal price.[2] Today, of course, contraceptive technology is maintained at a murderously primitive level, while reactionary ideologues gear up communications technology in opposition to any change in the oppression of women or the 'sanctity' of the private realm.

The argument that classical idealism has identifiable roots in reproductive dialectics constitutes a materialist critique of idealism, but not a materialist analysis in a conventional sense. The 'materiality' of reproductive process, which is the flesh-and-blood reality of the process, has been relegated by male-stream thought to a brute objectivity, shot through with a contingency more absolute than that of nature's providence. It is precisely this brute contingency which places man in active opposition to nature, obsessed with an ambition to control and exploit. When we turn to the modern materialism developed by Marx we find that the brute objectivity of biological reproduction remains relatively intact, though with a distinct tendency to become conflated with the processes of reproduction and production. The term 'material' is appropriated for the qualitative 'metabolism' of production, while reproduction is left to linger undialectically and a little sadly in the 'necessary' realm of biological intransigence.

The major Marxist statement on reproductive relations is that made by Engels in *The Origin of the Family, Private Property and the State*, a work which has offered both inspiration and irritation to feminist thought. Late in his life, Marx had received with great enthusiasm Lewis Morgan's evolutionary anthropology. Marx's death left it to Engels to attempt to draw out the theoretical significance of the transformations in kinship forms which Morgan had found empirically. Engels asserts the historical reality of an early genderic revolution, but he does not do so dialectically, and he sees 'material' change only on economic grounds. The passage from tribalism to polity is perceived in terms of the rise of the state solely as the defender of developed private property. Thus, the 'world historical defeat of the female sex', which was a forerunner to civic development, is given no material reproductive substructure, but is perceived in terms of a faintly melancholic naturalism.

Engels claims that although this massive genderic transformation was probably the greatest revolution of all time, it has left no trace of struggle and was likely to have been peaceful:

> Thus on the one hand, in proportion as wealth increased it made the man's position in the family more important than the woman's, and on the other hand created an impulse to exploit this strengthened position in order to overthrow, in favour of his children, the traditional order of inheritance. This, however, was impossible so long as descent was reckoned according to mother right. Mother right, therefore, had to be overthrown, and overthrown it was. This was by no means as difficult as it looks today. For this revolution – one of the most decisive ever experienced by humanity – could take place without disturbing a single one of the living members of a gens. All could remain as they were. A simple decree sufficed that in the future the offspring of the male members should remain within the gens.[3]

Engels does not consider that the historical edifice, male supremacy, itself constitutes something much larger than a mere trace of struggle, or that male supremacy is actively, forcefully and quite often violently maintained. He quotes Marx's marginal note to Morgan's text: 'Man's innate casuistry! To change things by changing their names!' Marx adds in another note that the eventual transition to father right to tidy up the social confusions created by property 'In general ... seems to be the most *natural* transition'[4] (my italics). Marx and Engels seem to accept quite complacently such notions as 'impulse' of a psychological nature, or simple decree, or semantic juggling, as sufficient grounds for immense social transformation, grounds which are specifically rejected in their analysis of subsequent history, whose dialectical laws are objectified in the much more concrete reality of class struggle. One would have expected that a major revolution which eluded the instrumentality of class struggle and the formality of dialectical process would have raised far more serious problems for historical dialectics than this. Engels is not above invoking a mixed bag of causalities, including moral factors, to explain transformations in kinship relations:

> How easily it [transition to father right] is accomplished can be seen in a whole series of American Indian tribes where it ... is still taking place under the influence, partly of increasing wealth ... and partly of the moral pressure of civilization and missionaries.[5]

It is not hard to argue that the whole question of reproduction remains for Engels essentially a question of sexual morality and sentiment, a problem for missionaries rather than materialists. The change which he believes a socialist order will bring for women is that they will not have to 'give themselves to a man from any other considerations than real love'.[6] The possibility that they might take unto themselves a man for sheer pleasure is not aired.

Morgan's fearless symmetry of kinship forms with productive modes obviously delighted Marx and Engels, but it has been demonstrated by subsequent anthropological research to be less satisfyingly orderly than they thought.[7] A more recent and less crudely reflexive attempt to flesh out, from a Marxist perspective, the details of the 'world historical defeat of the female sex' has been made by George Thomson.[8] In *Aeschylus in Athens* Thomson offers a historical and literary analysis of the events which Engels, following Bachofen, believed that Aeschylus had memorably dramatized in *The Oresteian Trilogy*. Orestes' matricidal exercise, the defeat of the female Furies as guardians of decaying Mother Right, the establishment of the mildly democratic Areopagitica as a juridical institution, the rationalization and civilized abolition of the bloody and vengeful struggles that are the only possible political relationships which can emerge from a social organization based on blood kinship: all of these sterling events are seen as a celebration of the historical defeat of women. They then serve Thomson's economist predilections by giving the great seal of historical inevitability to the actuality of the repressed condition of polis women.

Thomson's work is erudite and persuasive. He brings impressive classical scholarship to bear on the historical evolution of popular cultic activity into formal drama. He attempts to relate this development to the class struggles and slave economy of antiquity; but, like Engels, he strives for too close a fit. His commitment to an economist model disfigures a fine and valuable historical analysis with absurdities. For example, in his discussion of the *moirai*, the earthy goddesses known also as the Erinnyes, the Furies, the Fates, and the Eumenides, Thomson is puzzled by Atropos, the goddess of 'abhorred shears who slits the thin spun life'.[9] In his anxiety to relate this symbolic activity to productive process, Thomson evokes a weaving analogy, speculating that what may be represented here is the cutting of woven cloth from a loom, even though he has to posit a confessedly idiosyncratic etymology to make credible the sense of a gash in a web which 'cannot be unspun'.[10] There is an interesting coalition between idealism and materialism here, for it was this same Atropos and the other goddesses of necessity who presided over the corners of the spindle in Plato's myth of Er.[11] Plato has the web which cannot be unspun relate to the necessity of the soul and its transcendental circular tour. Thomson has necessity relate to production process. Where Plato etherealizes, Thomson materializes, but while Plato confuses first and second birth, Thomson substitutes loom for womb. Atropos is no weaver but a midwife. The thin spun cord to be slit is an umbilical cord. The connection between birth and weaving appears to have been associated with an early custom of embroidering kinship marks into the child's birth robes, a very practical instance of the relations of production and reproduction in operation.[12] Older societies knew the child must be

born before it need be robed. Thomson concentrates on the weaving
and neglects the midwifery.

The Fates lost their guardianship of birth process with the
transformation to patriarchal religion, when they suffered the
humiliation of having the upstart Zeus publicly claiming to have
fathered them. It is clear that they were originally associated with birth
and reproduction, but they were later subsumed in the sexy version of
Aphrodite, an interesting instance of symbolization of the male
experience of separation of sexuality and reproduction replacing
integrative femininity. The Fates, symbols of women's integrative
power of birthing, became angels of man's powerless dread of dying.
They were finally kicked downstairs to a sinecure in the Lower
Chamber, under the earth. Thomson's attempt to relate this mythic
female representation of life process to productive process is simply
bizarre. The interesting question of why patriarchy forces birth to give
way to death as the primordial human experience will be discussed
further in a moment.

Thomson also examines at some length such topics as adoption,
initiation and the various rituals of rebirth practised in antiquity without
ever noticing that these take the form of mock pregnancies. They are
celebrations of the nativity of men's second natures, asexual
reproductions which exclude women but have no self-generating
substitute for the experienced continuity of reproductive labour. They
are symbolic ritualizations of man's alienation from biological genesis,
of the effort to impose man's will and control upon the natural form of
reproduction. Thomson notes patterns in these celebrations, including
the need for ritual male rebirth to include a 'trial of endurance'
accompanied by real physical pain, but he is at a loss to understand why
this final act should have been preceded by a 'period of seclusion which
may last for months.'[13] Thomson simply fails to see that this is an
elaborated couvade, a ritualized gestation and labour; man, pregnant
'for months' with manliness, is preparing to give a second birth to
himself. Similarly, in his discussion of the 'stranger' in ancient society,
Thomson notes that in some instances strangers could be initiated into
the Mysteries after a probation period. This period included what
Thomson calls an 'obscure' stage of 'staying at home' following a ritual
'spilling of blood'.[14] From a woman's perspective, this doesn't seem
obscure at all, but looks like a representation of a final menstrual period

and ensuing pregnancy. Indeed, Thomson goes on to remark that the 'rite of initiation was called a *telete*', the same terminology as for marriage; 'marriage was constantly regarded as a mystery'.[15] The societies for the propagation of Mysteries, Thomson has told us, developed into guilds of actors, which retained 'to some extent the character of a mystery which *somehow* renews life'[16] (my italics). This 'mystery' is each man's experienced alienation from the act of reproductive labour by which women renew life. The societies are men's attempt to control and appropriate the renewal of life in a collective cultural mediation of their own dualism.

To be sure, the physiology of biological reproduction was not understood in the polis, but both Hippocrates and Aristotle thought that it was, and it is erroneous to deduce that because they were wrong they somehow really knew that they were only guessing – the position which Evelyn Reed takes. The mystery lies elsewhere; the persistence of couvade and the anxiety of men to emulate the actual process of reproduction is explicable when it is understood that the 'mystery' was their real exclusion from the regenerative labour of parturition.[17] Their response is much more than 'womb envy'. This is the individual psychic reflection of a fundamental contradiction in male thought and experience, for which the whole sex must work out a cultural mediation.

Thomson, who is sensitively aware of the historical fact that these new and exclusively male rites were replacing older community rituals in which both sexes participated, still fails to see that they are mimetic usurpations of the objective forms of the process of reproduction, that their base is in this process, and that the attempt to relate them directly to modalities of economic production simply does not work. These are rituals of generic struggle, which can be explained only in their differentiation from class struggle, not by subsumption by that struggle. Kinship, Thomson insists, was 'a fetter on the new economic and social realities', and this was what Aeschylus understood:

> he regarded the subordination of women, quite correctly, as an indispensable condition of democracy. Just as Aristophanes and Plato perceived that the abolition of property would involve the emancipation of women, so Aeschylus perceived that the subjection of women was a necessary consequence of the development of private property.[18]

This string of pronouncements is, to say the least, problematic. Like Engels's pronouncement that an increase of wealth makes the man's position in the family more important than the woman's, it is derived from the ideological illogicalities of male supremacy rather than the real world of history. It is not the certainty of property but the uncertainty of paternity which is the key. Plato, as has been noted, was interested in extending the uncertainty of paternity to maternity, throwing in a Spartan fixation with improving blood-lines for good measure. It is not at all clear why the subjection of a large number of people is not in fact inimical to democracy, rather than necessary to it. Thomson may be accepting uncritically an Arendt-style belief that for civil society to develop a participatory politics, someone must stay home and mind the kids and feed the family. This, from the male perspective, may be desirable, but it does not have the status of a logical or cultural necessity, and Thomson in fact does not make even this kind of practical argument. He appears to be more attuned to the Hegelian notion that women make politics impossible, but this is related in Thomson's case to a view that politics and 'blood' do not mix, are necessarily violent. Hegel chided women for not being violent enough, for having an unheroic and irrational objection to the slaughter of their children. In terms of social practice, there is no absolute need to leave property to one's 'own' offspring, no immediately evident reason why private property must be in male hands, no clear reason why property need be individually heritable at all. Many of the Athenians' neighbours, the people they called barbarian, appear to have got along quite well with public ownership of property and without monogamous marriage.

That the defeat of kinship as the organizing determinant of social life had recently taken place in Athens is clear; that class struggle was endemic in antiquity is also clear; that both of these developments were determined in a clear-cut way by new modes of production and consequent class struggles is a highly problematic claim.

The reasons for the historical defeat of matrilinear kin determinants remain as obscure in Thomson's work as they do in Engels's reflexive economism. The opacity emerges from the theoretical model. Economic determinism cannot account for generic struggle, and the evidence of myth and cult suggests strongly that the dynamic historical forces which led human society from kinship to polity were contradictions within the social relations of reproduction, material contradictions emerging from the formal dialectics of reproductive process itself. The theory of a historical evolution from a 'natural' division of labour to a 'social' division of labour loses explanatory force if it simply throws out the significance of reproductive labour, genetic continuity and forms of social relations of reproduction. It is as misleading as Arendt's failure to differentiate between production and reproduction within the domestic sphere; both are distortions of the categorical and empirical realities of two distinct but related processes. It is in the 'best' tradition of male-stream thought, for Aristotle made little distinction between slaves and women. The failure to reckon with the logical and human significance of the biological continuity established by female reproductive labour and male appropriation of children limits Aristotle, Marx and Thomson alike in their understanding of the dynamics of social change. At the same time, such onesidedness perpetuates the dogma of male supremacy.

The efforts of the men of the polis to emulate reproduction in cultic activity, together with the persisting view of marriage itself as having mystical properties accessible only to religious consciousness and ritual imitation, indicate that the discovery of paternity was perceived in the first instance in terms of magic. No doubt property and politics are more satisfactory and practical objectifications of male reproductive consciousness, but magic persists until property becomes dynamically reproductive in the capitalist era. The fact of male preoccupation with and appropriation of magic has been widely appreciated; its genderic implications remain unanalysed. It is taken for granted that men in primitive societies looked after the magic while women looked after more immediate bodily needs. We saw this in Lévi-Strauss's work; by the time of the Athenian polis, Arendt argues that politics and the public realm had been developed to give a more sophisticated and rational forum in which men – some men – could escape both the labours of necessity and the irrationalities of the shaman, in showing forth their political personae and individual distinction. Thomson's work shows that Arendt's view is a little too sanguine, that magic indeed played its part in the Athenian version of the ideology of male supremacy. Yet that ideology is far more than a mere psychological yearning: it is a deeper epistemological need to mediate the contradictions of male reproductive consciousness, a need which unites men in the brotherhood of man and divides them from genetic continuity and paternal certainty. Magic itself requires cult, and cult is a cultural affair. Lévi-Strauss, it will be recalled, saw the oppositions of totemic societies as those of flesh and dream, the former female and the latter male.[19] If indeed flesh was perceived in totemic society as a biological determinant, it is quite clear from the Greek drama that 'blood' had taken the place of flesh as the symbol of biological life and of genealogical integrity. Why this should happen is a very important question, because with flesh and blood, as with sexuality and parturition, we find a dialectical opposition in the genderically determined experience of these two natural raw materials. In brute terms, flesh and blood are universals; in human terms, the experience of *having* flesh and blood is universal, while the experience of *losing* blood is genderically differentiated. For men, bleeding is symptomatic only of injury or death. For women, the loss of blood is, as well, symptomatic of the power to give life, while the 'loss' of menstrual bleeding signifies a new life. Blood is a pervasive symbol in the patriarchal myths of classical antiquity, while flesh is negated as surely when Thyestis eats his children as it was when Eve ate the apple from the Tree of Life and left the Hebrew patriarchs preoccupied with death and genealogy.

Blood has a double significance: it symbolizes kinship and birth while at the same time it signifies individual death. This, the signification of both birth and death, is not antagonistic when it is perceived in terms of natural, cyclical time, but it becomes antagonistic when placed on the continuum of rectilinear time. In Greek drama there are few natural deaths; death itself is the drama, a situation which Thomson also finds in the transitional cults or mysteries developed between simple cults of life process (birth, seeding, harvest and so forth) and the patriarchal mysteries. What happens is that the cyclical relation of birth and death are replaced by cancelling of death's significance by the magic of *re*birth. The Orphic and Dionysian cults are structurally similar to the Passion of Christ, they are of death and *re*birth, a drama in which the shedding of *male* blood in an agony of flesh is a tragic triumph in which fleshly man dies and spiritual man is born. This is the first flowering of men's need to define their second nature, a birth uncontaminated with uncertainty, with flesh, with women. As a bonus, men also appear to have developed forms of second nature which aspired to the crown of immortality, which transcends and mediates the opposition of cyclical time and historical time in an ideological way which must be symbolized for social use.

The cults were advanced and sophisticated rituals soon to flower into the powerful splendour of formal Attic drama. More primitive societies developed simpler rituals of menstrual taboo and blood sacrifice.[20] Early menstrual taboos suggest strongly that women's ability to bleed without injury is regarded as her own magic; quite a black magic, too, clearly contributing to the occult threat which femininity poses to masculinity. The discovery of physiological paternity is the discovery that the seed has the power, the innate potency, to stop the bleeding. Creation myths, whether classical, canonical, romantic or psychoanalytical, are metaphorical representations of the dialectic of blood and seed, of womb and phallus, her magic and his magic, black magic and white magic. That 'spirit' can conquer the inevitability of death has always been recognized: that it also mediates men's alienation from genetic continuity has not been much discussed. The historical events underlying these myths may have been, as Engels says, peaceful, but the cults and the drama suggest that the triumph of father over mother was anything but that. The birth goddesses became 'Furies' before their final defeat at the hands of the lustful and rapacious sons of Zeus.

It may be the case that the emergence of a symbolism of blood and death to replace the totemism of flesh and life develops in part from a belief that the suspended menstrual flow is utilized in the manufacture of the child. Aristotle evidently believed this to be the case.[21] Existentially, blood, which is the harbinger of new life for women, is the harbinger of violent death for men. We have already seen in Thomson's work that a harmless, ritualized shedding of blood occurred before man's rebirth. Aeschylus is more radical: he deals with blood in a way which mediates by reversal the dialectical tensions between the biological, life-giving continuity of flesh-and-blood relationships and the murderous, death-dealing spilling of blood. Femininity, the source of life, becomes the source of death, and must then be punished by death for this unnaturalness. This paves the way for the triumph of legal, man-made, second-nature bonds over natural, man-negating first-nature process.

In the Homeric version of the myth, it was not the sexual indiscretions of Helen and Clytemnestra in which the woes of the House of Atreus were rooted; the real catalyst was the propensity of blood brothers to seduce each other's wives. This exacerbation of the uncertainty of paternity is no doubt particularly reprehensible in a male dynastic household. The accepted Marxist interpretation of *The Oresteian Trilogy* is that Aeschylus is dramatizing the sexual revolution. Engels's objection to Bachofen's interpretation – 'new but undoubtedly correct'[22] – is that Bachofen finds the basis for these mammoth struggles in changed religious consciousness. Engels, as has been noted, does later concede some spiritual power to missionaries himself, but in his discussion of the Oresteian drama he maintains that these changes must be rooted in the material conditions of men, and the material condition of Athens was the rise of a money economy and the state, which challenged the Gentile social organization, and 'the customary appointment of members of certain families' to high office, a practice which came to be perceived by these families as a right.[23] Engels does not tell us how his interpretation of these events enriches interpretation of the *Oresteia*, or why Aeschylus viewed political economy through the lens of sexuality. Thomson, who does address this question, says that the dramatist's reason for expressing the class struggle in terms of sexual relations was to demonstrate the incompatibility of female equality with democracy and private property. This position makes no sense if the danger posed to patrilinear succession of title, property and right by the uncertainty of paternity is ignored.

Engels has simply telescoped too long a period; as far as the struggle within the polis in Aeschylus' time was concerned, it was a struggle of democrats with an aristocracy and a conception of hereditary office already patriarchal, already hundreds of years old. Aeschylus is not attacking hereditary succession on the grounds of its vulnerability to the uncertainty of paternity and the vagaries of male sexual lust. He is attacking femininity, on the grounds that it is irrational and essentially bloodthirsty, and he is telling his audience that the benefits of agnate heredity and wider male co-operation require a stronger and *political* defence apparatus. They cannot be left to individual male enterprise or the workings of the family. Families need women, and why would women agree to the odd-ball proposition that uncertain paternity constituted a better ground for hereditary right than certain motherhood? On that one, men must work together, difficult though this might prove to be.

Engels knew that the uncertainty of paternity was a problem for early patriarchal society, but he did not see it as a ground of historical transformation in the social relations of reproduction.[24] He has no conception of generic struggle on the tragic scale which Aeschylus understood so clearly. Women, Engels says, could at one time have intercourse with several men 'without offending morality'. Engels clearly feels that women did not like this situation, though it did not disappear entirely without trace in 'the limited surrender which was the *price women had to pay for the right to monogamy*[25] (my italics). Women, we are to understand, traded property rights and even their children in a desperate attempt to avoid sexual variety. Engels's whole position — that the greatest revolution in all history took place without struggle; that is to say, had a non-dialectical form — is based on a facile and prudish assumption that women would accept these social changes mildly and without protest as a welcome relief from the unpleasant duty of copulation.

In the older forms of the Oresteian myth, Thyestes ate his own children after they had been cooked by his brother Atreus. Atreus performed this piece of culinary callousness in revenge for Thyestes' sexual dalliance with his wife. Revenge, we are told, was the law only of the female Furies, but they were not operating here; this was a quarrel between brothers, and it was brotherhood and its sexual distrusts which set off the idiocy of the Trojan war. Genetic continuity, it seems, only exacerbates such nastiness, for Aegisthus, son of Thyestes, who became the lover of Clytemnestra, committed against his cousin Agamemnon the same offence, which brought about the hideous revenge drama between the fathers of the two men. Cyclical time, indeed, but bringing forth only blood and death without renewal; but note the way in which female sexuality is separated from reproduction once the children are eaten or sacrificed.

In Aeschylus' version, all this earlier nastiness does not appear. Agamemnon's sacrifice of his own daughter is done in the name of piety, military expediency and sexual honour, and his wife Clytemnestra's first offence is to protest against the right of her husband to dispose of their child in any way that he wishes. Her second offence is to decline to stay celibate during the long years of her husband's absence at the Trojan wars, whose direct cause, we are to understand, was Clytemnestra's own flesh and blood, her sister Helen. Clytemnestra's third offence is to show considerable political know-how, and to take over the administration of the state in a reasonably competent way. Her fourth offence is to murder Agamemnon, who had left with a flourish of infanticide and comes back brandishing his concubine Cassandra, having lost the lives of almost a whole generation of men. Clytemnestra perceives this combination of unnatural cruelty and political irresponsibility as anti-social foolishness which ought to be stopped. She becomes an agent of death, pouring Agamemnon's royal blood into his bath water. It is for this *legal* offence, for her husband is no kin, that Clytemnestra becomes the victim of matricide, a 'natural' revenge by her natural son, Orestes, for the 'unnatural' act of cleaving a legal bond with an axe. The naturalness of family relations and the constraint of legal bonds get a little mixed up in all of this, but it is none the less the legal bond which finally asserts supremacy.

In the trial of Clytemnestra, her divine ancestry is never mentioned, though great play is made on the parentage of Athene, who has the great good fortune to have had no mother, but to have been born from Zeus the god acting alone. To be sure, the twin sisters, Helen and Clytemnestra, have a curious enough maternal heritage, for it will be recalled that they are the daughters by Zeus out of Leda the swan, but while Helen is often called 'daughter of Zeus', this courtesy title is rarely extended to Clytemnestra. Apollo, a sort of Norman Mailer of the polis, boasts all throughout the trial of his divine parentage and that of Athene, but Clytemnestra has clearly been excommunicated. Her divinity is never mentioned, perhaps because she has very clearly been deprived of immortality, but more likely because of her keen appreciation of the need to integrate public and private life, an integration absent from the consciousness of her husband and children. She is tried as a woman who has offended against the canons of male supremacy, for the trial is as much a trial of the dead mother as her living son. In fact, Orestes claims that she committed two murders: his father and her husband, a double jeopardy indeed!

The conventional notion that the theme of the play is the impossibility of justice based on revenge, which is a particular attribute of matriarchal kinship forms, needs qualifying; the vengeful ones are men, and none more so than Apollo and Orestes, the big winners. Thomson sees all this as class struggle, with the Areopagites representing the winning of a democratic extension of political power. It is therefore rather tiresome that they promptly demonstrate themselves as ineffective, for they record a tie vote which the androgynous Athene must break. Thomson tends to play down the sexual dimension in his anxiety to show the advantage of political relations over kin relations. For example, he tells us correctly that Apollo fails to convince the jury that Zeus always demands 'justice' for a father's death, for the excellent reason that the Areopagites see this as contradicted by the fact that Zeus' own behaviour in castrating Cronus was hardly that of a loving son. Apollo, Thomson says, 'now goes further and declares that the child is more closely related to the father than the mother'.[26] This is evasive; Apollo *negates* the maternal relationship;

> The mother is no parent of that which is called her child, but only nurse of the new-planted seed that grows. The parent is he who mounts. A stranger she preserves a stranger's seed, if no god interfere.[27]

Apollo goes on to point to Pallas Athene herself as the magically glorious living evidence of the reality of a motherless child.

The play may well represent the triumph of polity over family, but the genderic struggle is not a metaphoric struggle which is really a representation of class war and economic struggle. Eight hundred years after the Trojan wars, genderic antagonisms have clearly been fierce enough and prolonged enough to have left their historical mark. Male supremacy has been established, but Aeschylus is not saying that this is simply fact; he is moving to the realm of exculpatory ideology in the claim that male supremacy is not only factual but is just. To make this ethico-political claim, the whole order of reproductive process is inverted: sexuality and death take precedence over parturition and birth. It is the moment of sexuality, the adulteration of Helen's privately reserved reproductive incubator, which sets the whole thing off. It is Clytemnestra's offence in acting as a woman who loves her daughter, while she also acts sexually and politically like a man, which makes the genderic tension unbearable. Clytemnestra becomes the agent of death, while the son born of her reproductive labour transforms his birth relationship to a death relationship, murdering his certain parent for the dubious sexual honour of his uncertain father. It is only *after* this male supremacy over natural relationships has been established that the public realm of rational/legal politics can be developed. These rest absolutely and resolutely on the negation of femininity, in the symbolic person of motherless Athene, and the banishment of the Furies to the perpetual privacy of an Eternal Maternity Unit under the earth.

Aristotle tells us that Aeschylus was prosecuted for revealing in public the sacred secrets of the Mysteries. We do not know where Aeschylus did this, or if the offending work is among those surviving, but if the 'mysteries' consisted of the mimetic pregnancies of ancient couvades Aeschylus may well have derided them. Aeschylus knows quite well that it is easier to transform destiny than biology, and the need for men specifically to assert destiny over alienating biological process is what the play is about. Athene seems remarkably unimpressed by Apollo's petulant prosecution, and she never once addresses him directly; she is not interested in his problematic magic. She makes her dicastery decision entirely on the grounds that she herself had no mother. This may be a consoling notion for male supremacists, but it is a curious ground for a rational and just politics. Male supremacy is established on the motherless basis of a new political brotherhood, predicated on the equality of death and a high and rational ethic of giving one's life for one's polity. Having offered, by rebirth, a second nature and a second public realm for it to live in, polity can rationally demand a death. These unified men, with Athene to lead them, will fight outsiders but not one another. They will keep under firm control the tamed women, once again 'kindly ones' because their Fury has been interred, by means of the legal bond of repressive marriage which, if men are rational and true political brothers, will successfully mediate male uncertainties within the biological bond of kinship.

'Fraternity' thus released itself from kinship, and took on new social forms in clubby Athens. If one might be mildly poetic about it, the male understanding of blood – death and discontinuity – triumphs over the female understanding of blood – life and integration. The most powerful service club of all becomes men's death machine, the Army, a potent and magical force which has continued to exert its fraternalizing/fratricidal dialectic for a very long time. There are other historical consequences; the classical world contributes to male-stream thought's tremendous preoccupation with death. Birth was not, and will not become, a worthy subject for male philosophy. It is negated so that man may make himself, control the conditions of his self-made second nature and house his divided self in an uneasy separation of the public and private realms.

Death and birth are, of course, universals but the act of killing is a universal possibility, while the act of giving birth is generically particularized. There is an objective ground for the preoccupation with death, for anyone may kill or be killed. Men are not passive unto death as they are passive unto birth. Many centuries later, Thomas Hobbes will proclaim the fact that all may kill or be killed as the only real human equalizer.[28] There is, however, no rational ground for the symbolization of woman as the *agent* of death. This is an ideological inversion of the reality of women as real, live agents of birth.

Thus, there is no need to ask, as Thomson does, why the outcome of the trial turns on the social relations of the sexes; it does so because that is what the play is about, and a marvellous historic vision it reveals. The question to be asked is why Thomson asks the question, and the answer is that the struggles of the ancient world cannot be understood within the one-sidedness of economic determinism and relations of production.

The custodianship of magic is not, as Lévi-Strauss thinks, an innate masculine attribute. It is the first historical attempt to mediate the contradictions within the male process of reproduction. The brotherhood of man, so fiercely achieved, so fragile, so contradicted by reality, none the less has a material base. It is the relationship of those freed from necessary social labour, forced to make choices, compelled to mediate in thought and action the natural 'injustice' of paternity. Aeschylus shows us the historic struggle to transform male mediation of the ambiguities within the relations of reproduction from an exercise in magic and mystery to an affirmation of rational control buttressed by the concept of law. Rational polity succeeds primitive magic as mediator of the 'Mysteries' of the creation of life, and a much more adequate mediator it is, for it mediates the contradictions both within and between the social relations of production and reproduction. It does not lose its magic: it supplements it with the versatility of second-nature ideology. Indeed, it will come to refine its magic, until eventually women and men will harken to Herald Angels singing of One born that man no more may die:

Born to raise the sons of earth
Born to give them second birth.

What women thought of this magic we did not know for a long time, for their opinions reverberated in the fastnesses of the private realm, hidden from history and denied significance.

Historically, men have used freedom, the highest human value, to institutionalize the inequalities which have hitherto been the condition of freedom. It is not claimed that inequality or freedom are derived exclusively from reproductive relations; the relations of production do create inequalities within the brotherhood. A true universality is, however, the human goal of socialism, and, unless the generic restrictions on freedom are analysed and acted upon, nothing can be expected but a phoney 'universality' which excludes any foundation for a workable theory and practice of equality. To lump liberty, equality and fraternity together is to make a categorical error. Fraternity is the ideologically formulated condition of an actual liberty, the brotherhood of fathers who are forced to be free. It is universal only in male terms, and absolutely precludes a truly universal freedom and equality, for its condition is the suppression of women.

Marxism and Feminism[29]

A study of the dialectical interaction of the social relations of production and reproduction may well give a more illuminating account of the relation of the public and private realms, and of individual and social existence, than notions of a natural hierarchy of values, the flight to metaphysics, the doctrine of harmony of interests or the salutory compulsions of an Invisible Hand. It may also be more illuminating than a historical materialism, in which 'material' is conceived solely in economist terms, and 'labour' is exclusively productive labour.

Capitalism, in its historic development, has increasingly integrated politics and economics, while transforming sexual and kinship relations to property relations. The difference between pre-capitalist property and property in capital is, as Marx clearly sees, that capital has generative and accumulative qualities which, in his words, respond to the ancient invocation to increase, multiply and replenish the earth.[30] Capital, like the Leviathan of legend and the Sovereignty of Hobbes, is capable of self-regeneration. It improves on Plato's mystic brotherhood, for it has the capacity to reproduce and multiply itself without recourse to sexuality and without any need for females. This may seem to be merely metaphorical, if not downright fanciful, except that historically it can be demonstrated that the uncertainty of paternity is *no longer a problem* with the advent of the capitalist mode of production. The uncertainty of paternity can be, of course, a distinct advantage to the philandering male, but paternity suits quite unrelated to hereditary titles or property disposition are a modern phenomenon related to female economic dependence. The most obvious political effect of the solution of the problem of paternity by the development of wealth which has learnt to breed is the disappearance of absolute hereditary monarchy, patriarchy's most compelling political symbolization of potency plus continuity. Primogeniture, which reckons that the first child of a certified virgin is more likely to know its father than subsequent children, follows the absolute monarch into a realm where, one hopes, the Furies welcomed them with a few sarcastic barbs.

The final solution of the problem of patriarchy is elaborated by John Locke in his first 'Treatise of government', while the legitimacy of property as a self-generating 'principle of continuity' is celebrated in his second. To be sure, property, whether entailed or disposable by testamentary disposition, favours the production of a male heir in a male dominant society; early entrepreneurs appear to have derived almost as much pleasurable satisfaction in writing the familial '& Sons' after their name as they did from the legal and more lucrative joys of writing 'Limited'. The hereditary principle is, however, inimical to capitalism in concrete ways, and men seem, on the whole, to have been more ready to entrust a fool with a crown than with the management of capital assets. One rarely analysed trouble with hereditary rule unguarded by Salic law was that it would on occasion throw up females, whether foolish whores like Mary of Scotland or wise virgins like Elizabeth of England.

The uncertainty and generally unsatisfactory nature of male succession was clear enough to Oliver Cromwell. Addressing the first Puritan Parliament in January 1655, Cromwell quoted Ecclesiastes in his argument against heredity: 'who knoweth whether he may beget a fool or a wise man?'[31] Yet Cromwell still named his own foolish Richard as his successor. No alternative 'principle of continuity' to that of heredity was yet present to political consciousness, for capitalism was ill-developed and parliamentary government unstable. C. B. Macpherson has remarked that Hobbes, given his historical milieu, could not yet see the possibility of a class of property owners achieving a sufficient degree of cohesion to act in a united and stable way.[32] Hobbes therefore clung to the notion of self-perpetuating sovereignty rendered necessary by the atomism and competitive particularity of autonomous individuals. Clearly, and more immediately, Cromwell was faced with a similar limitation in comprehending the political potential of the new ruling class which had produced him.[33]

Capitalism is, however, something more than a new mode of production creating a new ruling class. It is a new principle of continuity, capable of apparently infinite self-regeneration. This fetishistic property of capital, the apparently magical ability to generate *things*, dehumanizes both reproductive and productive relations ever more radically, generalizing market relations and contracting the private realm incessantly. True potency appears only in the marketplace, while generic antagonisms flare where men and women become rivals in the labour market. Capitalism slowly erodes male supremacy, but it does not immediately transcend it, for the dialectics of reproduction do not change until corporate technology attacks and transforms the objective process of reproduction. It does this finally with reluctance, not to liberate women, but to attempt to adjust the balance of world population and production in an enterprise with strong racist overtones.

The impact of capitalism on reproductive consciousness, on reproductive praxis as opposed to abstract family structure, hovered only on the edge of Marx's understanding. None the less, Marx's theory still offers the most promising basis for the critique of male-stream thought, which is the necessary starting point of feminist theory. Making history is something more than the definition of issues and the attempt to solve immediately pressing problems. It is, in the Marxist phrase, praxis, a unity of theory and practice. This is one reason why the development of specifically feminist theory is an urgent task. Yet neither intellectual nor material history can stop and start all over again for women. It is not simply a matter of 'catching up' either. Unlike men, women have had no objective basis for a separation of genetic continuity from human history. Now, we do have such a challenge to meet, for the separation of sexuality and reproduction which nature decreed for men technology has now decreed for women. This constitutes a material change in that combination of consciousness and experience which is the process of reproduction.

In this book, which is an anticipation and exploration rather than a promulgation of feminist theory, the process and relations of reproduction have been isolated with a sort of calculated naiveté, designed to rescue biological reproductive process and its material base from historical obscurity and ascribed unimportance. This artificial isolation must be abandoned where praxis overtakes analysis, as it must. Feminism cannot root out economic determinism with the equally blunt trowel of biological determinism. Human oppression emerges from both productive and reproductive dialectics, and Marx's analysis of the former perhaps offers the most promising starting point for a feminist praxis, which must then proceed to extend dialectical materialism to give a synthesized account of both poles of human necessity.

Marx's model is material, historical and dialectical, and an approach to the theoretical comprehension of the material base of the antagonisms within the social relations of reproduction must be all of these things. Further, since Marx, political theory, the dialogue of men with man, has been a puny affair and, indeed, Marx himself has been accused of subsuming politics in political economy. In western society and most particularly in the United States, political theory has acquired rude labels — speculative, normative, traditionalist and so forth — and has shown itself as somewhat cowed in the face of attack by the atheoretical and ahistorical empiricism of a dominant quantitative approach to social science.

Genderic inequality can of course be described and, in limited areas, quantified. Feminist scholars are engaged in doing both of these things, often usefully but increasingly repetitively. Such activity cannot *change* genderic inequality, and therefore shows the distinct tendency to the collapse into utopianism, polemic or mere statistics, which tendency is a direct consequence of an inadequate theoretical ground.

On the other hand, Marxism by itself cannot provide the grounds for feminist theory, not only because of Marx's own historically specific Victorianism with regard to sexual matters, but for other quite concrete reasons. First, the experience of women in communist revolutions and their aftermaths has been discouraging, especially in the Soviet Union.[34] Second, developments in the social sciences since Marx's time have furnished data which orthodox Marxism has had difficulty in interpreting, the prime case being, of course, the findings of psychoanalysis. Wilhelm Reich has addressed himself to both of these considerations, and argues vigorously and persuasively that psyches honed by the oppressive patriarchalism of Czarist Russia could not respond to a transformation of the merely external conditions of family life or the merely polemical declaration that the family was now defunct.[35] There can be no doubt that psychoanalysis offers important data in the realm of generic identity, and that the initial anti-Freudian polemic with which Betty Friedan launched the current American feminist movement is due for the more thoughtful reconsiderations which Juliet Mitchell in particular has offered.[36] A developed feminist theory cannot blithely neglect the question of the psychic dimensions of generic culture with the vulgar aplomb displayed by economic positivism.

The appeal of Marx to feminism also emerges from the fact that feminist praxis must be, in some sense, revolutionary, and Marx is the revolutionary theorist *par excellence*. The revolutionary implications of feminism create discomfort and discord within the movement: we have observed Millett's struggle with the ambiguities of a doctrine of women as less aggressive than men, and a theory of the need for revolution. The whole question of violence is a difficult one for feminism, but as far as women are concerned, even a modest reformism is perceived as revolutionary, and even the mildest critique of the family incites contempt and angry resistance in both communist and capitalist states. The common ground of both liberalism and socialism, the assertion of human freedom, shrinks and trembles at the logical implications of women's humanity.

Finally, the relation of women to capitalism creates serious problems. Pious defences of the family frequently mask concern for bourgeois property relations and the male job market, as well as for institutionalized and ideological male supremacy. Charles I of England, with an uncharacteristic degree of perspicacity, once proclaimed that where there were no bishops there would be no king. The revolutionary class of Charles's time, now in our time in its days of reactionary senility, has not yet said outright: 'No husbands, no capitalists.' It is, however, this unpleasant truth which contributes to such things as media attempts to mock and denigrate or, more recently, ignore the women's movement. It is also the realistic ground of corporate attempts to turn token women into pseudo-men. That there does exist real misogyny, superstitious dread of femininity as such, is no doubt a psychic truth. That unpaid female domestic labour creates a lucrative bonus for state capitalism and for men of all classes is an economic truth. Just as important, and less often proclaimed, is the fact that the liberation of women presents an equal threat to state socialism. Stalin in the late 1920s did not, as Wilhelm Reich suggests, simply throw up his hands in despair over the moral chaos of liberated sexuality which did not know how to conduct itself. He was faced with the disintegration of the five year plan, and the return of women to the private realm mitigated burgeoning unemployment.

In capitalist economies, domestic productivity has been judged as busily and endlessly creating use values: characterized as not engaged in commodity production, it is therefore conceived of as outside the market matrix, ironically enough now understood as a 'private realm', the realm of private enterprise. Here, certain men can be private in public, while politics orchestrates the conditions of a 'private' enterprise which reproduces capitalism. The definition of women's work as non-work leads to a definition of women as 'consumers' who are not producers, a definition which contradicts Marx's correct contention that production and consumption are dialectically composed.

The appropriated products of the socially necessary labours of reproduction, nurture and women's endless production of individual use values constitute a bonus not only to the capitalist mode of production but to individual men, two opposed economic classes but one homogeneous generic entity. To be sure, the calculation of wages traditionally includes the costs of subsistence, reproduction, nurture and so forth, and capitalism since Marx's time has permitted this figure to rise, relatively if not absolutely. This cost is calculated as a portion of the labour of commodity production, but generic homogeneity ensures that is not paid directly to the domestic labourer, the woman at home who 'doesn't work'. When women are themselves engaged in wage labour, they are paid lower wages irrespective of their rate of creation of surplus value, their concomitant domestic labours, the number of their economic dependants or the absence in any particular private realm of a male breadwinner. For that matter, the presence of male breadloser is no help either. Women are *not paid* the 'subsistence component' of wages, which is the main technical reason for wage differentials. It is a technical wrinkle that accords comfortably with the general deprecation of women and their works which is central to the ideology and practice of male supremacy. The productive work of women and the genetic dialectics of male reproductive consciousness both work to sustain capitalism, and it is very doubtful that capitalism can be replaced by a rational economy by class struggle alone. As long as it continues to lug through history the irrational fetishes of private property and appropriative paternity, capitalism as a mode of production can be transformed only by a combination of class and generic forces.

Questions about the status of women and the value of wage labour have constituted a lively forum of debate among Marxist feminists and progressive Marxists of all kinds.[37] The rigidly orthodox have tended, like Bebel and Lenin, to insist upon the strategic priority of class struggle, with the implicit promise that the classless society will liberate women. Others have attempted to distinguish between 'productive' and 'socially necessary' labour. None the less, the contention that domestic labour produces only use values has been subjected to some criticism, and discussion of the nature of domestic labour under advanced capitalism has been the subject of much speculation, though protagonists do not believe this work to be speculative. Indeed, the whole debate among Marxist feminists (where emphasis is on the Marxist) is infused with a yearning to make the oppression of women 'concrete', to confirm its historical actuality, as it were, by plugging it into productive labour and the creation of surplus value. However, the debate so far has been conducted ideally rather than materially, for it has been largely an attempt to manipulate categories rather than develop a genuinely feminist praxis. The 'problematic' of domestic labour, to use the terminology of the New Left, is probed by adding neo-Marxist terminology – conjuncture, surplus repression, valorization, for example – to the older categories of class analysis. Household activities are abstracted from the private realm to see if they can be bent to the forms of market relations. This abstraction constitutes an idealism which does not know itself as ideal. The reason it remains ideal is because it analyses women and their work in terms of alienated women workers, rather than women as integrative women. There is absolutely no conception of the need to understand the value of the product of reproductive labour, the child, as anything other than a potential source of labour power. To be sure, the reproduction of labour power by working families does take place, but it does not take the place of the value of the human being as human being, as objective species continuity. The orthodox will no doubt regard the assertion of individual human value as sentimental liberalism, but they might pause to consider the relation of the theoretical negation of the personal in class analysis and the very concrete negation of individuals in Communist Party dictatorships. The related notion that history has two concrete substructures in the continuity of the species as well as in modes of production cannot be analysed in genetically sterile categories, and is therefore not considered as significant.

A commendable attempt to move from theory to practice has been that created by the Wages for Housework movement,[38] but this has more recently been damped down by its lack of popular appeal and its difficulties in persuading either men, capitalists or the state to pay the bills. If husbands and 'providers' in general have to do this, what emerges is a further generalization of market relations, with each husband set up as a petty employer of labour which reproduces comfort and use value but does not *create* value. The idea of the state paying would constitute yet another advance in the transfer payments with which capitalist welfare states feed women enough money to ensure their survival in humiliating dependence. Capitalism believes that the existing wage formula looks after the problem. Meanwhile, it reluctantly opens up token pathways in corporate structures to a few reliable women: women, that is, who support the capitalist system but want a larger share of its wealth and status.

All of this confusion presents a momentous strategic problem to the feminist movement, but feminism meanwhile poses a dual threat to the capitalist mode of production. It seeks to intrude pure use value into the exchange value matrix, the 'GNP', and to demand compensation for domestic labour, the effect of which can only be to raise the subsistence component of wages absolutely and to reduce the real wages of male producers. On the other hand, it seeks to make female productive labourers truly competitive in market terms, to be able to earn equal pay for work of equal value. The effect is to place women, both as reproducers and producers, into opposition with both capitalist and proletarian males, and extend the penetration of the market mechanism into the one area of society which has, however feebly, resisted it, for children are not yet commodities. In fact, it might well be the case that

Marx's most spectacularly erroneous prophecy – the progressive immiseration of the working class – is at least in part due to the historical tendency of women to insist on the survival and the value of the products of their reproductive labour, their children. It has been the subsistence relations of the private realm which have provoked the development of the welfare state.

The threats which feminism poses to capitalism are, however, inseparable from the challenge which feminism throws down to the ruling sex. Women's position is a position in real history and in the real world. The Marxist attempt, in the dreary tradition of male-stream thought, to limit that position to the domestic realm not only fails as economic analysis, but fails even more miserably as historical materialism. Feminism insists that 'value' is not an exclusively economic category, but an ethical, affective and genetic one. It further insists that feminism presents and represents a fundamentally different experience of the relation of people and nature than that posed by male dualism. It insists, further, that the principle of integration can form the basis for a political praxis which is rational, humane and far more progressive than any generically one-sided praxis, including Marxism, can ever be. Women are competing with men not only in the workplace, but in making history.

In the workplace, the question of women as serious competitors no doubt explains the traditional reluctance of the trade union movement to take up the cudgels on behalf of women workers. A further aspect of this situation is the difficulties which women, with their double labour loads in the home and in the workplace, have had in finding time to participate in union politics, even where they have the good and rather rare fortune to work in unionized situations. There have been recent and encouraging signs that unions have become aware of the importance of women's struggles. Here in Canada, both the United Auto Workers and the United Steel Workers have given high-level support to women strikers, and public service unions have increasingly become aware of the potential of women in supporting union objectives. None the less, the vast majority of women workers are not employed in Union shops, and the major economic category in which women invariably figure in the greatest numbers is that of the unemployed. Orthodox Marxism murmurs here about industrial reserve armies, yet the hard fact remains that equal competition in the job market by women cannot be analysed properly in terms of such economic categories. Proletarian males are subject to the aspirations and practices of male-supremacist society, and no amount of theoretical waffling can obscure this fact. No doubt it is subjectively true that men feel superior to women, but that is not the major consideration here. It is objectively, historically true that there is a social structure of male supremacy, a structure of separation and alienation of public and private which long predates capitalism, and which has its roots in the dialectics of reproductive rather than in the dialectics of labour process.

It is for these reasons that feminist praxis is revolutionary in an economic sense which transcends the realities of class struggle. It is also revolutionary in a political sense. Politics as experienced in the contemporary world is the culmination of centuries of man's preoccupation not only with overcoming nature but also with the metaphysical premise of a 'natural' dichotomy of ruler and ruled, a dualism articulated in antiquity and still holding ideological sway. It is not claimed here that these dichotomies have been discovered to be wholly generic, or to proclaim a hollow conceptual victory for Yin and Yang over Eros and Thanatos, or master and slave, or mind and body, or universal and particular. It is claimed that the insistent dualism of man's thought has a material, generic component which has been inadequately analysed. Political and social institutions objectify specifically masculine needs and mediations, as well as representing the interests of a ruling class. To insist upon the participation of fecund women in the conduct of communal life is to do more than seek strategies of female emancipation: it is to drag the process of reproduction, its objective contradictions and its historical mediations, from the dark corners of historiography and the hidden premises of political philosophy to its true status as a necessarily social and humanly valuable activity. It is also to claim for procreativity the capacity to transcend its natural roots and to 'make history' in a significant way. This is revolutionary in both theory and practice.

Such conclusions cannot be drawn from Marx's understanding of materialist dialectics. For Marx, despite his compelling humanism, generic relations and the social position of women remain only as quantitative indicators of how near prehistory, represented by class struggle, is drawing to a real universal history of a truly human classless society. The relations of reproduction are incapable, in their own right, of initiating qualitative social change. Marx does not display any historical sense of reproductive process at all, for he simply appropriates the natural dynamic of reproduction and arbitrarily awards it to economic history. Hegel had proclaimed nature impotent. Marx, attuned to the post-Hegelian developments in evolutionary theory and the brilliant synthesis of these in the work of Darwin, asserts that nature, too, has a history. While it is by no means clear exactly what Marx means by this, it is clear that he does not see reproductive process in these terms: thus, for example, 'the natural division of labour' yields any dynamic property it ever had to the social division of labour, and itself remains as some kind of natural residue in a primitive 'economic unit', the family, existing uneasily in the interstices of substructure and superstructure, while changing its form historically.

What Hegel and Marx understood is that all human interaction with nature is *process*.[39] The two philosophers give us a clearer view of the question of continuity. The 'need' for continuity is not merely a psychological need, a yearning for certainty or a permanent infatuation with the imaginary comforts of womb and tomb. The odd idea that wombs are blessed places of peace and quiescence is the high point and ultimate fallacy of romantic naturalism, another ideological inversion of birth and death. Nor is the need for continuity only a practical sociological need, though it is this too. Again, it is not exclusively the need of a ruling class to perpetuate the *status quo* and the protection of class interests, though it is this too. Beneath these historic grapplings with the need for continuity and its cultural objectifications lies the fact that process itself is inseparable from separability. Process is dialectical, an active series of negations and mediations. What both Hegel and Marx miss is the mediation of cyclical and historical time by human reproductive labour, and the fact that paternal appropriation of children is an attempt to resist alienation from the dialectics of natural and historical time, which are mediated by reproductive labour.

Marx is in fact ambiguous on the subject of nature. In the use of the term *Naturwüchsig* (growing naturally) in *The German Ideology*, Pascal has noted a lack of consistency:

> He uses it (p. 20) to distinguish the economic development of pre-capitalist times, where the division of labour is determined by 'natural pre-dispositions', e.g., physical strength needs, accidents,

etc. On pp. 47 and 51 similarly, where 'natural' capital is attached to the labour and inherited environment of a guildsman, as opposed to the capital of the modern capitalist, which is movable and can be assessed in terms of money. But elsewhere (pp. 22, 63) 'natural' society is one in which there is a cleavage between the particular and the common interest, hence where men have no control over themselves or society. To this 'natural' society he opposes communist society with its planning.[40]

Marx's ambiguity arises from a one-sidedness in his logic of necessity, for there are two necessary processes in the experiential matrix of human nature which are both dialectically structured, but which are not identical. These are, of course, the necessities to produce and reproduce. Marx's one-sidedness is the source, too, of the ambiguity in his use of the word 'reproduction'. In the production/ consumption relationship, Marx maintains, people 'reproduce' themselves, fuel their own life process. The facts that all animals must eat to stay alive, and that human animals must additionally produce their own subsistence, are rescued by Marx from their status as crude empirical truisms and restored to their proper significance as *a priori* of social life. Marx's problem, like that of Hegel and the state-of-nature theorists of the Enlightenment, is to move from the individual to the social, from the particular to the general. Hegel treats the problem with the philosophical parable of master and slave as a sort of Platonic 'noble lie'. In this primordial drama of adult male versus adult male, the prior birth and nurture of the protagonists in an already patriarchal society is presumed. Process as such enters human subjectivity in the self-conscious challenge to otherness, and to the power of death as the Great Negation. The annulment of the slave's capacity for self-determination in the fear of death, and the refusal of the master to recognize him as a potent force, is in turn negated in the labour by which the slave remakes his cathexis with the natural world. This is a very elaborate second birth indeed, in which the fear of death, an emotion, is the true parent of biological and conscious life.

Marx wants to historicize the parable without proposing any mythical alienations of man from nature. His strategy is to negate, to deny in theory, the historicism of reproductive process, and this is a negation which is never in turn negated, never transcends its historical non-being. It must, of course, remain a negation only in theory, for the *fact* of reproduction persists in human experience, and there would be no history without it. Marx therefore makes a categorical shift. There is no qualitative transformation possible in reproductive process, there is simply empirical variation in reproductive relations, in the forms of family, imposed by the stage of the historical process of change taking place in modes of production. The necessary sociability, the continuity and creativity of reproductive process, are arbitrarily transferred to productive process, and man starts off on the task of producing history and producing himself with a force mysteriously appropriated from reproductive process. This theoretical, indeed magical, appropriation of labour power freezes reproductive process in a floe of impotence, and leaves the social relations of reproduction to tag along behind modes of production as best they may.

Idealism's metaphysical banishment of reproduction to the heavens stands opposed to materialism's metatheoretical banishment of the dialectics of reproduction to a prehistorical but eternal sexual division of labour.

The first of these, idealism, then appropriates the creative function and dialectical form of male reproductive consciousness, and awards these to mental processes, to 'pure' thought. Materialism appropriates the formal structure of reproduction for production, so that productive process now includes among its products people and history. All history may indeed be class struggle, but that struggle does not produce its protagonists: it reproduces them; they are born. The necessity of birth is a substructure of human history, but it is not the same as, nor a product of, the necessity to produce the lives with which the process of biological reproduction has peopled history.

In the third of the 1844 Manuscripts Marx introduces the question of sexual relations in the context of his critique of crude communism, which, he says, wishes to destroy everything indiscriminately in a passion to generalize private property.[41] Marriage is 'incontestably a form of private property' expressed in 'an animal form' and contrasted to the idea (the 'open secret' of crude communism) of women as common property, of universal prostitution. Both bourgeois property relations and unreflective communism, according to this young and passionate Marx, crave for universal access to all women. He seems to see however, that this broad castigation needs some further explanation, and development of an alternative, materialist view of genderic relations. He proceeds in an attempt to strip the 'open secret' – a simple and primitive lust and resentful envy – of its secrecy. The passage must be quoted in full:

> In the relationship with *woman*, as the prey and handmaid of communal lust, is expressed an infinite degradation in which man exists for himself; for the secret of this relationship finds its *unequivocal*, incontestable, *open* and revealed expression in the relation of man to woman and in the way in which the *direct* and *natural* species relationship is conceived. The immediate, natural and necessary relation of human being is also the *relation* of *man* to *woman*. In this *natural* species relationship man's relation to nature is directly his relation to man, and his relation to man is directly his relation to nature, his own *natural* function. Thus, in this relation is *sensually revealed*, reduced to an observable *fact*, the extent to which human nature has become nature for man and to which nature has become human nature for him [original italics].[42]

The almost indecent haste in which a relation of man to woman becomes a relation of man to man is perhaps exacerbated in translation, for English, unlike German, does not provide separate words for masculine man (*man*) and mankind (*mensche*). We do not wish to become bogged down in the contentious linguistic issue of whether either the English collective 'man' or the German *mensche* in fact really means 'everyone'. Giving Marx the broadest possible latitude in this respect we may interpet him as saying: the immediate natural and necessary human relationship is that of men and women. In this relationship people are conscious of their own sexual needs and their need, therefore, of other human beings. Sexual need confirms them as both natural and social beings, and the degree to which they can create humane conditions for the expression of this relationship is an indicator of how far they have progressed from mere animality. Such an interpretation proclaims an important truth, that sexual relations are necessary and necessarily social. They are not, however, perceived as dialectical, there is no genderic struggle, and there are not yet any products, namely, children, who are merely implied in the term 'species relationship'. Marx, like Hegel before him, has in mind the moment of sexuality rather than the reproductive process as a whole. In fact, he later goes on to deny to birth any real human significance on the existential grounds that any man who owes his existence to another is a 'dependent being' and thus precluded from free expression of his humanity: 'But I live completely by another person's favour when I owe to him [*sic*] not only the continuance of my life but also *its creation*; when he is its *source*' [original italics].[43]

Marx rejects a hankering after creation myths, but he does appear to share Sophocles' notion that the male is 'true parent of' the child, without recognizing that this is an ideological formulation. He also argues, in the same passage, that popular consciousness cannot reject the notion of creation, because the fact that 'nature and mán exist on their own account' posits an existence which 'contradicts all the tangible facts of practical life'. To be sure, in the Manuscripts Marx has not yet parted from Hegelian ways, but it is still surprising that he seems quite unperturbed by the positing of a 'material' view of a fundamental life process which 'contradicts all the facts of practical life'. Marx, quite traditionally, is interested here in the historical constitution of man's second, self-made nature. To this end, he quite specifically negates reproductive continuity, which he sees as infinite regress lurking as progress. If, like Aristotle, he argues, you say that man is produced by the coitus of two human beings, you lapse into infinite progression (who engendered my grandfather and his father and so forth) and do not keep in mind 'the *circular movement* which is perceptible in that progression, according to which man, in the act of generation reproduces himself: thus *man* always remains the subject'[44] [original italics]. Marx sees the essentially social character of reproduction and appears to be aware of the temporal contradictions within the process, and it would probably be unfair to read him as implying that, as man always remains the subject, woman becomes mere object of man's sexual desire. He certainly does not consider the actuality of man as alienated subject, nor does he fully understand that paternity is radically subjective, in that it is present to consciousness as idea to be objectified only by appropriation of the child. He does not see that alienation from time and nature is mediated in reproductive labour, but only by women, for he does not deal with the fact that the production of children needs reproductive labour as well as sexual activity. A stubborn insistence that biological continuity *is* continuity, he says, can only lead to the question of who created man in the first place, a 'perverted' and 'abstract' question which posits non-existence.

The young Marx, still engaged in 'hating all gods', the passion which had informed his doctoral dissertation, and still clearly under the influence of Feuerbach's anthropological determinism, simply takes refuge in polemic at this point. It is, none the less, a significant polemic, for it is shot through with an unarticulated awareness that it might just be the case that paternity is an abstraction, that there just might be problems for male reproductive consciousness in the relation of thinking and existing:

> If you ask a question about the creation of nature and man you abstract from nature and man. You suppose them *non-existent* and you want me to demonstrate that they *exist*. I reply: give up your abstraction and at the same time you abandon your question. Or else, if you want to maintain your abstraction, be consistent, and if you think of man and nature as non-existent think of yourself too as non-existent, for you are also man and nature. Do not think, do not ask me any question, for as soon as you think and ask questions your *abstraction* from the existence of nature and man becomes meaningless. Or are you such an egoist that you conceive everything as non-existent and yet want to exist yourself? [original italics.][45]

Socialist man, on the contrary, takes his proofs of his man-made existence from real experience, even though his existence contradicts his now denatalized autonomy. Marx is overly excited because the question that he raises is not the one which needs to be asked at all. We must ask Marx what is wrong with biological reproduction as a basis of real continuity. Of course people 'make themselves' in their interaction with the world and other people, but why can socialist man not be created until birth has been deprived of the capacity to create continuity? Marx could have posited a dynamic dialectic between biological time and historical time without lapsing into the trap of an infinitely regressive and crude causality. He did not do so, and could not do so, first, because of his male perspective and, second, because he did not anticipate the possiblity of *rational* control of reproduction.

This is not the mere aberration of a young thinker. The transfer of reproductive power and sociability to productive relations remains constant. In *The German Ideology*, Marx is less confused, but he still insists on the hegemony of productive labour in the formation of human historical consciousness, a position from which he never retreats.[46] In the version of *The German Ideology* he seems at first sight to be presenting us with the remarkable spectacle of people eating and producing and needing before they are born at all – 'life involves *before everything else* eating and drinking' (my italics) – while the second determination of life process emerges from the fact that needs produce more needs: 'and this production of new needs is the first historical act.' Only as the 'third circumstance which from the very first enters into historical development' does reproduction appear, a process described as men making other men.[47] Marx backtracks a little from the 'before everything else' which I italicized above: these are not to be seen as stages of development, he says, but as aspects of development which exist simultaneously, and production and reproduction appear as a double relationship, on the one hand natural, on the other social. But it is a tenuous concession, for immediately and momentously Marx proceeds to negate by neglect the actual sociability and historicism of reproductive process: 'It follows from this [the double relation, natural and social, of production and reproduction] that a certain mode of production ... is always combined with a certain mode of cooperation.'[48] It also follows, in history and in logic, that reproduction also involves a certain mode of co-operation, but Marx does not say so. The co-operation of men as appropriators of children, and of women as bearers and nurturers of children, slips out of history. Only production thereafter has the capacity to make history and inform consciousness. Production also, by an unexplained alchemy, determines the forms of the social relations of reproduction.

In *Capital*, Marx has made up his mind on the question of what constitutes a natural economy, and he has also abandoned the radically liberal individualism which produced the youthful diatribe against the indignity of having to depend for one's life on the sexual activity of others. In his discussion of commodity fetishism, he defines 'the particular and natural form of labour' as that in which the personal interdependence of the members of the economic unit is present to consciousness in its true social form.[49] For an example of this directly associated labour form, Marx tells us, we do not need to go back to 'that spontaneously developed form which we find on the threshold of the history of all civilized races'. We still have examples of this 'spontaneous' form close to hand, for we can find it 'in the *patriarchal* industries of a peasant family' (my italics). Like Hegel, Marx presumably feels that the patriarchal family had developed 'spontaneously' before the dawn of dialectical history, that is, without a struggle. This is no doubt due to the fact that it is natural. Male-stream thought in general seems to live contentedly with the vague notions that women's 'special relation' to nature unfits her for activity outside of the private realm, while patriarchy derives its power from its naturalness, but manages to switch it to the public realm. This is, of course, because male-stream thought has not analysed the sense in which patriarchy is a resistance to experienced alienation from nature, a historical move from the idea of paternity to the concreteness of patriarchy. Marx, indeed, considers alienation from nature to be specific to capitalism. Not without a touch of nostalgia, he argues that the family, both ancient and modern, 'possesses a spontaneously developed system of division of labour'.[50] As we saw, the discovery of the ancient matriarchate did not sully, for Marx or Engels, the naturalness and spontaneity of patriarchy.

One of the reasons for Marx's position, apart from the uncriticized dominance of the dogma of male supremacy which was specific to his epoch, is that he is preoccupied with the notion of universality. The notion of integration, which Hegel had yearned for but found only in the Absolute Idea, is for Marx a worldly possibility. Real history will start with human equality and rational, co-operative sociability. Sociability and co-operation are the preconditions of classless society. Marx perceives 'universality' concretely, as the annulment of alienation and the restoration of a unity of men with nature, with their products and with other men. This socialist universality is the goal of history and the condition of human freedom, but Marx has to uncover practical and material universals in which this goal can be grounded: he needs to find true universals, experiences common to all. In this quest for a concrete universal, he finds, correctly enough, hunger and sexuality. However, he perceives the latter as immediate, while the former requires the mediation of production. He translates *male* experience of the separation of sexuality and reproduction into *a priori* universal truth. Thus the labour of reproduction is excluded from the analysis, and children seem to appear spontaneously or perhaps magically. Reproductive labour, thus sterilized, does not produce value, does not produce needs and therefore does not make history nor make men.

Birth as such is contingent, immediate and uninteresting, a 'subordinate' relationship.

De Beauvoir, as we saw in Chapter 1, suggested that Hegel's dialectic of master and slave was suggestive of generic relationships in an unacknowledged way. Marx's notion of the origins of class struggle is much more so:

> Every self-alienation of man, from himself and from nature, appears in the relation which he postulates between other men and himself and nature. ... in the real practical world this self-alienation can only be expressed in the real, practical relation of man to his fellow men. The medium through which alienation occurs is itself a *practical* one. Through alienated labour, therefore, man not only produces his relation to the object and to the process of production as to alien and hostile men; he also produces the relation of other men to his production and his product, and the relation between himself and other men. Just as he creates his own production as a vitiation, a punishment, and his own product as a loss, as a product which does not belong to him, so he creates the domination of the non-producer over production and its product. As he alienates his own activity, so he bestows upon the stranger an activity which is not his own [original italic].[51]

Marx never perceives the alienation of the seed as a material alienation which sets up an opposition between men and children, men and women and man and other men. The act of appropriation by the non-labourer of both product and 'means of production', of the actual child and the mother's reproductive labour power, remains for Marx a natural relationship. As far as reproductive process is concerned, Marx's thinking is bourgeois by his own definition of bourgeois thought:

> Man's reflections on the forms of social life and consequently also his analysis of these forms, take a course exactly opposite to that of their actual historical development. ... the characters ... have already acquired the stability of natural self-understood forms of social life, before man seeks to decipher not their historical character (for in his eyes they are immutable) but their meaning.[52]

Marx does not transcend the ideological fetishism of paterfamilias

Victorian style, but, unlike other thinkers who are also entrapped in the ideology of male supremacy, Marxist theory permits us to understand its own limitations. His view is historically specific in a sense which goes beyond male supremacy, and goes to the heart of the necessary relation of production and reproduction. Marx is able to see the economic realm as the sole progenitor of consciousness precisely because of capital's capacity to *disguise itself as progenitor*, but he believes this to be appearance only, a source of telling metaphors. The reproductive capacity of capital does more than provide metaphors, though it does this abundantly in Marx's own work. The generation of species being, the womb of history, the bursting of slim similitudes of assorted umbilical cords, the struggle of history to give birth to new social forms, the assorted 'embodiments' of process: all these are ubiquitous images in Marx's writing. Further, the transformed significance of the word 'proletariat' from its Latin meaning (he who has no wealth but his children) to its signification of he who has no wealth but his labour, is not one of these arbitrary and mistaken mistranslations which annoyed Arendt. All transformations in word meanings must have a social signification, if they are not to remain the arid neologisms of lesser writers. Marx is able to use the word in this sense precisely because capitalism has itself transformed the meaning of 'continuity'; it does itself increase and multiply and replenish the earth, and it does so 'continuously'.

Capitalism does not, as Marx and Engels say in *The Communist Manifesto*, rip from the family its 'sentimental veil'. It creates that veil. Prior to the bourgeois era, there is no 'sentimental' veil shrouding family relations, and children, for example, barely appear on the stage of history until the appearance of bourgeois family. Marx, a devotee of Shakespeare, evidently did not find it remarkable that the very few children who appear in the illustrious canon do so mainly to be immediately and symbolically murdered, that Lady Macbeth and Cleopatra and Gertrude are hardly more loving mums than was Medea, or that domestic love is 'the generation of vipers'.[53] Marx, like Shakespeare, knows that the marketplace permits the exchangeability of everything, and he quotes approvingly Shakespeare's definition of money as the 'equation of the incompatible'.[54] He is less perceptive than Shakespeare on the corrupting exchangeability of political power and sexual potency. There is little sentimentalization of family in either classical or Renaissance drama; the corruption of powerful families is a theme for political thought. It is the bourgeoisie which sentimentalizes the family, particularly in its peculiar and specific literary creation, the novel. Here, the much vaunted privacy of the domestic realm is publicized as never before, very often in a sentimental way.

The contractual and exchange dimension of family life is indeed peculiar to bourgeois relations, which try to ameliorate the dark struggle between public and private market interests with a sentimental ideology of connubial bliss. The suppression of women is of course much older. Capitalism transforms the relation of public and private, the arena of generic struggle, putting appetitive men into a shrunken domestic realm where they are supposed to discover that their 'private' needs are now identical with the needs of private enterprise. Women, conversely, are forced into the expanded 'private' realm of the factory, so that they too may feel that the happy harmony of their private interests with that of their masters, at home and at work, can be met by unpaid domestic toil and miserably paid wage-labour. The bourgeois attempt to define the economic realm as 'private' relates only to individual, private ownership, and turns its face from the real sociability of labour. This is precisely the contradiction of particular and universal within capitalism which Marx believes ensures its eventual self-destruction. The once-hidden contradiction, the real 'open secret' of male-dominated bourgeois society, is that women are admitted to the sociability of labour while ideological rhetoric and real social conditions continue to privatize them as individual servants to class socialized masters *at all class levels.* Thus, women in capitalist society find themselves in dialectical struggle with the masters of private industry and the masters of the private realm, both groups working out whatever version of the potency principle their objective conditions allow. Women are disadvantaged in this struggle by their dual responsibilities to *necessita*, to reproduction and production, which leave little energy for struggle. This is why women's struggle is taken up in the first instance by middle-class women. Our brothers on the Left would have us believe that this fact somehow renders suffragism, for example, less authentic, somehow fraudulent. No feminist underrates the difficulties of unifying working-class women and women of that analytically ambiguous contemporary 'middle' class, but such a unification is impossible from the basis of a one-sided theory of history structured upon economist fallacies of universality. Such theories simply cannot address the objective lives of men and women coping with fundamental change in the material process of reproduction.

The crucial conceptual and historical role of division of labour in Marxist theory has something in common with Machiavelli's equally important conceptual notion of *vertu*. The division of labour has its origins in a 'natural' division of labour, just as *vertu* has its origins in a 'natural' property of Florentine manhood. Just as *vertu* must somehow be abstracted from nature to reappear in politics, division of labour must somehow be extracted from nature to reappear in economic history. This remains a theoretical shift only, for the natural dialectics of reproductive labour cannot be annulled any more than the process of reproduction can be dispensed with, and as, similarly, no mode of production can transcend the dialectics of the actual process of labour. The division of labour in practice has more to do with the social than the natural, and Marx and Engels's flirtation with 'natural' (sexual) division of labour does nothing more than justify the superiority of male labour. It is neither logically nor historically significant for the brilliant insight into the historical process by which division of labour becomes division of labourers and non-labourers. Likewise, the division of labour in reproductive relations is not a division between labourers, but a division of labourer and non-labourer. As such, it is generic struggle. The gap between natural and social division of labour *appears* to widen only in so far as the actual generic struggle is neutralized: a historical process of female privation which is not essential to production and which is unconcerned with class distinction, but which is essential to male supremacy. The relation of production and reproduction becomes a hierarchical relationship.

The separation of public and private is perceived by Marx as having economic roots, and the development of a separate domestic economy 'is made only the more necessary by the further development of private property'.[55] Here, Marx does not seem to mean 'private property' in the sense of the ownership of means of production, for he is talking of a period prior to the formation of towns. The abolition of individual economy is impossible, he adds, without machinery and the removal of the antagonism between town and country; lacking these, a communal economy would rest on 'a purely theoretical foundation. ... that the abolition of individual economy is inseparable from the abolition of the family is self-evident.'[56] Unfortunately, this latter statement itself rests on 'a purely theoretical foundation', as the experience in developed communist countries has demonstrated. The theory in question is, of course, the theory of the capacity of modes of production to account for all social forms and social change, which, by definition, must include changes in forms of family. Marx himself renders the material process of reproduction and biological continuity abstract, and the 'embodiment' of productive process as the material substructure of history rests upon the disembodiment of reproduction. We are left with a mission to abolish the social division of labour which must leave the 'natural' division of labour intact, for even the discovery of Morgan's work did not suggest to Marx and Engels a historical struggle to confirm the recognition of male participation in reproductive process. They were content with a notion which excluded women from the developing social division of labour without generic struggle.

Marxism offers one important clarification of the question of continuity. Marx shows us that continuity is specifically a 'need' of a ruling class anxious to perpetuate itself in power; that is to say, continuity is both the principle and practice of class regeneration, political activity to create the ideological conditions for the maintenance of the *status quo*. This limited view of politics as ideological enterprise accounts in part for the curious attenuation of political discussion in this most political of thinkers, though Marx planned to turn to politics had he lived longer. Subsequent Marxists have been largely content with the master's epigrammatic dismissal of the state as the executive committee of the ruling class, and Marxist work on the state is, like that on the family, fairly rudimentary. Yet Marx's other laconic comment – that the political realm is the battleground of opposing ideologies – is of equal importance. Marx did not recognize male supremacy as an ideology with an objective material base in the relations of reproduction. Marxist sociology, tending to study work relations and to neglect family and political relations, attenuates a theory of consciousness which already has problems in accounting for individual as opposed to class consciousness. Ideologies, including that of male supremacy, are developed by political thought in its interpretation of the relation of public and private, and the symbolic and social representation of principles of continuity. These values are then enforced by the family. Certainly, political ideologies serve dominant class interests, but they are eagerly accepted by men who have no property but their uncertain children. They serve the ruling class, but they also serve the brotherhood of man.

Marx's remarks are inadequate characterizations of politics, largely because his historical model is ultimately non-dialectical. The relationship between substructure and superstructure is crudely reflexive. A materialist philosophy grounded on the dialectics of necessity must take into account *all* necessity, and a philosophy of history must presuppose the survival of the whole race of men and women. Politics is not a superstructural phenomenon, it is a practical *mediation* of the contradictions within and between the relations of production and reproduction.

The premise of Marx's observations on ideological continuity is that specifically human reality is historical. Marxism makes claims in which the universality of historical experience is particularized in class praxis, and which then fetishizes class interests as the sole motor of history. This class fetishism is matched historically with a generic claim, in which the practical feminine experience of continuity confirmed by labour is inverted to a patriarchal claim on species continuity originating in thought and objectified by an act of appropriation of children, a 'naming' rather than a laborious reproduction of one's child. Prior to the development of capitalism, the male version of species continuity must be symbolized – in so far as it contradicts one of the tangible facts of practical life, the discontinuity of male regenerative experience. Symbols of continuity must function publicly, proclaiming their entitlement to the fealty of all men, and are therefore political, even where they fall upwards into the ideal formulations of second nature, or downwards into the prehistory of fictitious 'social contracts'. They place upon men a duty to obey them, which men readily do, for they perform the epistemological mediation of the contradictions of male reproductive consciousness.

Such symbolizations appeal to two basic principles. On the one hand, they appeal materially to biology; on the other, they appeal metaphysically to eternity. The former favour organic analogy, modes of 'incorporation' which range from the notion of a binding constitutional law, through the organic version of patriarchal monarchy defended by James VI of Scotland, to the elaborate analogies of Social Darwinism and the romantic ancestral memories of vitalist supermen.

The second appeal, to eternity in God or nature, is expressed in the west in footnotes to Plato's ideological reproduction of the true, the good and the beautiful. The symbolism here is religious and spiritual, because it demands a form of duty predicted on the non-observable; the symbols include great chains of being, ancestor cults, doctrines of divine right and Hegel's mystic state. Such symbols, organic or eternal, are metaphors of continuity, and, while they certainly encapsulate caste- and class-based determinants, they are also manifest syntheses of man's fractured sense of continuity. They are dedicated to the transcendence of contingent first nature by a second nature, which is freed from biology to formulate the mediations of the contradictions within male participation in actual generation. Symbols of continuity create heroes, who take historically specific forms, ranging from earthy and heavenly patriarchs to assorted warriors against Fate in general. The political hero combines the ideal and the practical, at first in the ideal crudity of the philosopher king, then in the practical crudity of divine Caesar, and finally in the synthetic rationality of the absolute monarch, bolstered by divine approval and hereditary legitimacy. In less exalted terms, perhaps the contradictions of symbolic continuity are nowhere more visible than in the chivalric ideal of the Christian knight, who paused to swear fealty to the Virgin Mother before he rode off to slaughter her immaculate Son's sons, in the name of obedience to his bloodthirsty lords, spiritual and temporal.

The differences between representations of continuity in the pre-modern and modern world lies in the peculiar properties of capital itself. Capital does not merely symbolize continuity, it objectifies continuity, and comes complete with visible 'self-made men' who are the new heroes. Symbolism represents regeneration, capitalism objectifies regeneration. Symbols of continuity can never quite struggle free from their biological roots, and a hereditary procession remains visible in their social forms. Capital appears to be objectively self-generating. If social forms were indeed engendered exclusively by modes of production, capitalism would abolish the distinction between public and private, for it knows no generic particularism. Arendt maintains that this is precisely what has happened, but in fact the breakdown is partial, changing the economic relations within the private realm but continuing to guard the superiority of even the most impoverished and pathetic males.

Marx knows that capitalism objectifies the relations of production, but he does not comprehend the generic significance of the objectification of continuity, which is itself an essential precondition of a materialist philosophy of history. The continuity of the reproduction of the species is the actual and logical premise of the survival of that species, which distinguishes itself from other species by making history and conserving a historical consciousness. The theoretical comprehension of the reality of process is possible only under conditions in which an objective and dynamic continuity permits the comprehension of history as well as genetic continuity as objects materially present to consciousness.

De Beauvoir has remarked that the history of man is in a real sense an antiphysis:

> The theory of historical materialism has brought to light some most important truths. Humanity is not an animal species, it is a historical reality. Human society is an antiphysis – in a sense it is against nature; it does not passively submit to the presence of nature but rather takes over the control of nature on its own behalf. This arrogation is not an inward, subjective operation; it is accomplished objectively in practical action.[57]

The bringing to light of history as antiphysis is not so much the achievement of historical materialism, or even of the elated experimentalism of Bacon and founders of modern science. In creating socially recognized paternity, men outwitted nature long ago. Marx aspires to the restoration of a human metabolism with nature, which is to be a humane mediation of the dialectical opposition of man and nature of which women will be passive beneficiaries. What might seem the obvious theoretical route to such an achievement, namely, the positing of a dialectical relation of historical and biological continuity, eludes Marx's theoretical understanding. He turns to productive continuity, basically concerned with the 'reproduction' of the individual life, and proclaims it as the necessarily *social* base of co-operative endeavour. By means of some fancy theoretical footwork, reproduction, which is impossible in individual terms, remains particular and ahistorical. In the dialectical sense of particularity as the opposition to universality, both Marx and Hegel give individuality a normative evaluation. For Hegel, the principle of particularity is woman the ethical cripple; for Marx, the bourgeois property owner who is scheduled for burial. This emerges from the fact that at the centre of the prodigious insight that human reality is process lurks the negation of an actual social process, whose product is none other than the individual. Socialism must do better. One understands the puzzlement of Madame Cao, a Vietnamese freedom fighter, in conversation with a Western feminist socialist:

> Alice Wolfson explained the lack of leadership in the woman's liberation movement in terms of American individualism and the feeling that collectivity was an important and necessary stage. 'Madame Cao thought for a moment and then said, "yes, but the collectivity which destroys the potential of the individual is not good collectivity. It is necessary to reach a compromise." '[58]

A compromise is impossible in any theory where the individual is constituted abstractly without ever getting born, and the alienation of second nature from first nature is perceived as infinite.

6 Alienation and integration

Whether one regards the sort of analysis which has been presented in this book as useful or not depends a great deal on what sort of questions one thinks have to be answered before radical social change can take place. There are some presuppositions working here which would not and should not necessarily go unchallenged. What is being proposed is the development of metatheory from a feminist perspective, with the assumption that theory of this kind is essential to the dialectical tasks of understanding and changing the world.[1] Yet women have been properly suspicious of metatheory, of systems of thought and the huge edifices of ideology and political practice which they have generated. The whole question of the relation of systematic political theory and actual political systems is a quite abstruse one. How far does Locke's thought colour the contemporary forms of American politics? Would Locke have been comfortable in Vietnam, or Marx in Afghanistan? These questions are in one sense as silly as the question of whether Jesus of Nazareth would have enjoyed life in the Vatican. They are silly in that they infer a notion of history which is static and idealist. The works of any political theorist arise in a social context, are read in that or another context, and stay as fixed points in a history which moves and shifts and has its being in a changing world. None the less, I have tried to show that one fixed component of all these efforts has been that collection of historical mediations of male reproductive consciousness which I have characterized as the potency principle.

Political philosophy has developed historically as a conscious attempt to spell out the principles on which the 'good society' might be developed; the 'good society' being defined, or course, as the 'best for man'. The challenge to men has been to ground these principles in something other than mere opinion. The most persistent ground proposed has been some kind of assessment of the nature of human nature. Almost as popular a pastime for theorists as proclaiming what human nature is, has been the ethical endeavour to say what it ought to be. Unsatisfactory and ideological though the second option is, it at least has the merit of assuming the possibility, and even the desirability, of social change. The great divide in political praxis, the divide between conservatism and innovation, rests upon perceptions of human nature as either immovable or versatile, as fixed or as historical. Marx's great contribution to political thought, indirect though it may be, was to move the debate from one about what men are or ought to be to one about what men do. Thus, since Marx, the principles of the good society have been challenged to ground themselves in history rather than in human nature; or, more correctly, in history understood as the working out of the dialectical relation of man's world and the natural world.

This development does not take us much further forward unless we can now say something about the 'nature' of history: hence Marx's search for 'laws' of history. It also does not take women much further forward if all definitions of history and its 'laws' assume that process to be man-made. Marxism is a philosophy of history which gives an account of the grounds of historical process in human action in response to necessity. Yet this action, according to Marx, is not arbitrarily determined, nor is it totally free. It has its ground in biological necessity and its movement in social action to meet necessity in a creative way. Thus the making of history is the history of the struggle to make history. The ground of the struggle is nothing other than that persistent dualism which permeates all male-stream thought. The value of the work of Hegel and Marx is that neither see dualism as something to be sighed over, prayed over, preyed on or passively acccepted. Dualism, separation, estrangement, alienation are for dialectics a logic and a challenge, a challenge to understand the nature of dialectical process and to utilize its dynamism for a more scientific participation in the job of making history.

Dialectics rests on the notion of a whole string of oppositions that had seemed intransigent to previous thought, thought which had understood them as static dichotomies rather than as challenges to mediative thought and action. One can make lists: individual/social; mind/body; theory/practice; life/death; faith/reason; subject/object and so forth. It is not the case, of course, that no attempts had been made to mediate these perceived oppositions. Soul, for example, was proposed as mediator of mind and body; the church proposed institutional mediation of the battle of faith and reason. Politics, from antiquity onwards, was given the task of mediating the division of the social and the individual, and the good society was precisely that society which could bring ethical rules to the violently conflicting interests of selves and community. As we saw, Lévi-Strauss observed that what all these phrases attempt to do is give substance to the abstract form of dualism which is expressed, in the philosophical vocabulary, as the opposition of universal and particular. Lévi-Strauss attempted to give concreteness to the abstract form in terms of an opposition of nature and culture, which persist in Lévi-Strauss's work as abstract categories because he finds structure more entrancing than concrete content. Embedded in all this theorizing about the opposition of universal — all that we or any other entities have in common — versus particular — that which is uniquely individual — is an attempt to find a formula for a social structure which would somehow conserve the value of the universal, the public good, the commonwealth, the brotherhood of man, while effecting some kind of moral improvement on the particular, the selfish, the egotistical, the uncaring individual. Not often made explicit, but certainly present in the formulations of dualism which men have attempted, is the fact that one important aspect of universality is its function of providing *continuity over time* to human affairs, a function which death-haunted particularity cannot perform.

Also less than explicit is the centrality of the male/female dualism. It is not true that male-stream thought has neglected this dualism; on the contrary, it has been more concerned with it than contemporary exegetes are willing to allow, especially in these days when the ideology and practice of male supremacy were still in the formative stage. Generally, however, male/female opposition is still considered to be of a different character to other dualisms, as indeed it is. The categorical differences, however, have not been described analytically but normatively: quite simply, male is superior to female. One reason for this lies in the notion that male/female differentiation is, as it were, a subclass. It is, for example, a subclass of the nature/culture dichotomy, for women all belong with nature and therefore do not have to fight the good fights of mediation. In the mind/body puzzle, women are all body; in the faith/reason confrontation they do better with forms of faith given them as a gift by men to protect them from the ardours of thinking. Dualism, which urges men on to intensively creative acts of mediation in thought, in art, in religion and in politics, appears to pass passive women by. In fact, of course they are struggling to resolve their own mode of alienation in the restricted arena of the private realm.

It has not been, and is not now, my intention to deny either the historicity or the creativity of dualist perceptions of existence. What I have tried to do is to analyse dualism in terms of its material base. The only way to do this is to demonstrate that this material base is not static, brute, unchanging, ahistorical or inhuman. Thus, I have tried to show that the biological process of reproduction is a material substructure of history, and that this process is dialectically structured. I have also argued – and it does seem extraordinary that this should have to be argued – that there is an aspect of human understanding which might be called reproductive consciousness. I have further argued that this consciousness, unlike the productive consciousness which forms on the basis of economic class, is differentiated by gender. In making this kind of analysis, I have been concerned to give a materialist account of male supremacy as a historical phenomenon. I have not been concerned to excuse the violence and inhumanity of the phenomenon: to understand is not necessarily to forgive. What is far more important is the understanding that we have now reached a moment of history when the process of reproduction has been materially transformed. We must therefore remodel our theories of history and politics in a way which can do two things: first, give a theoretical account of that change; thereafter, build upon this model the principles of a good society which will be made in history by women and by men. Before this can be done, feminism must develop theory, method and strategy, and we must pursue this development from a fresh perspective, namely, the 'standpoint of women', women working from within women's reality. The question of feminist perspective raises directly the question of a feminist consciousness. The need to 'raise' consciousness has been appreciated by the women's liberation movement from the start. This is a crucial first step: whether feminist strategy is perceived as reformist, revolutionary or conservative, it is clear that nothing much will be gained without an awareness among women of the fact of oppression. There has been no confidence among women that a powerful and dialectical force called history will somehow enforce change in the relations of reproduction and in reproductive consciousness. The potency principle is in good shape. Confidence of the inevitability of transformation of class consciousness has clearly not become universal among proletarians either, hence the proliferation on the Old/New Left of various vanguard theories. Ordinary people will have to be *led* into true humanity, for their consciousnesses appear to remain callously indifferent to the dialectics of history. Feminists tend to be distrustful of vanguards, not only on the grounds that they are likely to be self-appointed and male, but on the practical grounds that they have not proven to be effective in highly technologized societies, and have recently shown a disturbing tendency to obliterate 'objects of reproduction', real people, in acts of random terrorism.

One major difficulty in understanding the dynamics of historical dialectics has always been in understanding how collective consciousness can be transformed, with the associated question of the transformation of individual consciousness. In the light of the findings of psychoanalysis, it is no longer even a question of how consciousness is transformed, but of when. It may at least be argued that in the contemporary understanding of the development of personality in childhood, a radical change in reproductive social relations is one possible route to a transformation of consciousness. Oddly, while the Left has struggled valiantly to transform consciousness on the assembly-lines of socialized, universal (in its materialist sense) capitalist production, the Right has far more clearly understood that the family is the key location of formation of consciousness. Thus, while the Left tries to recruit women in the workplace, the Right fights for the 'protection' of foetuses and fathers. Both recognize, but do not analyse, the fact that change in male/female relations is now inevitable. Such change is inevitable because of objective transformations in the dialectics of reproductive process, and this cannot be dealt with on one front, whether family, politics or industry. It is a *world-historical* event.

Consciousness among adult women may be raised in particular instances, but universal change in feminine consciousness will emerge from the alteration in women's relationship with life process, a change which clearly will not be confined to women. None the less, women are necessarily the progressive force in the transformation of reproductive relations, in so far as men are the jealous beneficiaries and creators of forms and fantasies of the separation of public and private, now due to be challenged effectively. Consciousness-raising as a pedagogical enterprise tends to a negative formulation, in that it attempts to explain to women that they are not what they in fact are. There is some let-down when transformed consciousness faces unchanged social realities. One emotional result is resentment and envy, which springs from a promise that what women might be is pseudo-man, that women ought to be like men, to have the same chances, privileges, etc. This is because consciousness-raising operates on the individual level, it has only begun to reach towards the universal. It is on the level of the particular that women who have access to contraceptive technology have become like individual men, free from the necessity of reproductive labour. The next step, which men took many aeons ago, is to mediate collectively and from the ground of *women's* historical experience, the separation of sexuality from parturition. In terms of reproduction, women are still the owners of the reproductive labour *power* which creates synthetic value and confirms the integration of nature and history. We now have to decide how to objectify and demystify this opposition of alienation and integration, of particular and universal, in the real world. In other words, we must proceed from individual consciousness-raising to the political expression of a transformed, universal, feminine consciousness.

The first wave of women's liberation set great store by sexual freedom. This development was greeted with considerable enthusiasm by many male radicals. Moments of tedium in revolutionary activity could be whiled away in pleasurable erotic dalliance, while a pool of female labour still remained to type up the minutes of class struggle. Women soon discovered that the emphasis on sexual liberation did little to create a feminist consciousness, or a true feminist sociability. This emphasis in fact increased the personal sense of sexuality as commodity, of women as sex-objects. The second wave of the movement was therefore a self-conscious seeking of new modes of social interaction among women. For women with reservations about a total commitment to class struggle, the question of political tactics has swirled round the problem of penetration of the public realm, the seizing of political power. The fact that the definition of politics as power relations is related both to the mediation of social classes and to the mediation of public and private life under the aegis of the potency principle has not yet been seen with sufficient clarity, so that the need for individual escape from the prison of the private realm has taken precedence over the need to destroy collectively the artificial barriers between public and private. Only some have escaped: large numbers are left within, or left to run between their doubled-up workplaces at home and in the capitalist or communist economic infrastructure.

The isolation of the moment of sexuality from reproductive process in general is as old as male dominance, and is, indeed, a material base of that dominance. Men value the moment of sexuality for more than the immediacy of sexual gratification and the pleasures of copulation. It has symbolic value in social terms; it confirms an inclusion in genetic continuity and access to the double freedoms which the idea of paternity translates historically into forms of male dominant society. Male sexuality is thus experienced as the heart of the doctrine of potency, the potency which claims power over a natural ambiguity, obscuring the reality that men's inclusion in reproductive process is at the same time his exclusion from that process. Millett's dilemma, in attempting to divorce patriarchy from biology by awarding the development of patriarchy to cultural determinants, springs from this fundamental contradiction. She recognizes very clearly that the symbolic manifestations of cultural potency are pervasively phallic. For men, sexuality is the basis of a free appropriative right, a power over women and children and a power over time itself. It is also the basis of the radical uncertainty of that right, of a fundamental alienation from natural process, and of a lack of immediate recognition as progenitor. It is, further, a power sustained in its contradiction by violence, sometimes overt, sometimes covert, in part personal, in part political. The social relations of reproduction are relations of dominance precisely because at the heart of the doctrine of potency lies the intransigent impotency of uncertainty, an impotency which colours and continuously brutalizes the social and political relations in which it is expressed.

For women, the historical, technological, separation of sexuality from parturition is an objective equalization with men, but not an identity with men. It permits women in the first instance to turn a 'masculine' perspective on sexuality, a perspective that embraces freedom while it obscures the fact that the voluntarism which is a mere anatomical destiny for men is a historical destiny for women. Freud did not consider his epigram, anatomy is destiny, with due care, for his whole analysis omits to note that anatomy destines *men* to the attempt to resist genetic alienation. Historically, women have been perceived precisely as those for whom 'destiny' holds no promise, no tragedy, no existential drama, no dialectical tension, no challenging dualism. The access to a destiny, with its concomitant compulsion to create a second nature which can cope with it, is now presented to women by historical action, the creation of a technology, and women must mediate this separation historically. For men, mediation is historical, but the alienation is natural. Men are necessarily rooted in biology, and their physiology is their fate.

Too enthusiastic an embracing of the male perspective on sexuality as a no-strings-attached libidinal adventure at the individual level may bring some transitory satisfactions, but does very little for the universal, for the establishment of sisterhood or the transformation of public life. The high value which men have given to the moment of sexuality obscures the alienated relation of sexuality to reproductive process in general. Sexual gratification is contingent in its natural form for all people, an alienation only for men consciously pursuing physiological paternity. The history of the social relations of reproduction is precisely the history of male attempts to impose order on contingency and to anneal alienation, and part and parcel of these efforts has been the ascription of inertia to the post-coital process of reproduction. In taking over a perspective of human fulfilment in terms of sexual freedom, women take over a perspective of sexuality which has said not merely that free sexual gratification is importantly desirable, which it is, but that free sexuality is *more important* in human terms than unfree reproduction. This is potentially divisive. Sexually liberated women have been known to turn upon their domesticated sisters a cold eye of contempt, to dismiss maternal consciousness as false consciousness, a passive submission to a massive male-chauvinist conspiracy to enslave them, a denial of an authentic humanity.

To point this out does not imply a reactionary argument in defence of conventional motherhood, for it is not suggested that men have been right all the time in privatizing women, nor even that they have been right for the wrong reasons. Women who shrug off those who are 'only housewives' are unreconstructed elitists, whose 'sisterhood' is as oppressive as that of the brotherhood: *someone else* must look to the socially necessary labours of reproduction and nurture and be despised for doing so. A new class division appears between those who breed and those who do not.

The understanding of the historical relation of public and private as the social condition of generic struggle does not lead to the destruction of one or both. A good argument can be made for the position that privacy and seclusion are human needs, not primordially nor in the romantic sense of the existentially solitary wanderer, but in the sense of a historically created need, the other side, as it were, of the coin of sociability, the need to be by oneself, or with those who 'share one's life' in a personal, affective way. Marx never argues for the abolition of property as such, and castigates the primitive communism which did so: he argues the specific need to abolish private ownership of the means of production, and sees that marriage is an instance of this, though he believes this to be a property of specifically bourgeois marriage. What is argued here is not that reproduction be abolished, now a real possibility, or that intimacy be abolished. What is argued is that proprietary rights to appropriate women and children must be abolished, not merely because they are unjust, but because they are incompatible with the newly transformed material base of reproduction. Socialist men and women will presumably continue to produce and reproduce, make love and make places for themselves to live their biological lives; and the fruits of human labour, people and goods, will continue to create new human needs and values. What will be abolished are the artificial, magical and symbolic barriers erected between public and private, between production and reproduction, between women and men; barriers built and heretofore violently maintained in the interests of a ruling class and a ruling sex. This is only possible given the premise that the mediation of the dialectics of production and reproduction are subject to rational human control.

The awareness of such a possibility cannot come simply from educational modes of 'consciousness-raising', but only from objectively based transformations of consciousness in the lived dialectics of people and nature. At our moment in history, what is being materially presented to human consciousness is a clear view of the inhuman pretensions and alien oppressiveness of the forms of the social relations of reproduction generated by generations of male supremacists, whose perspective on these relations is, and always has been fraught with the radical ambivalence which is its root and its product.[2] The female perspective is still perhaps a little stunned by its discovery of its significance *qua* perspective. This transformed consciousness cannot rest on its mere promise or on its real perplexities; women now must seek to understand our own possibility and our own freedom, 'projecting', as de Beauvoir would say, a creatable future.

The task of demonstrating that a feminist perspective grounded in female experience does exist has been a major objective of this enquiry, with the further objective of advancing the assertion of such a perspective from polemic to analytic and critical utility. The elaboration of feminist perspective, freed from the brute contingency of biological compulsion, faces difficulties formally similar to those which confronted men in their comprehension of the dialectics of reproduction and the problematics of its freedoms so many centuries ago. In other words, women are necessarily about to embark upon the elaboration of their second nature. Like men, we have first to speculate upon the nature of this nature, and like men we have to establish the values which are to be strengthened and the strategies to be developed. Unlike men, we must advance upon this speculative, normative and practical enterprise within a historically specific ambience in which the ways in which we speak and think are crippled by centuries of human hobbling through history on one leg of dialectical reality, supported by the problematic crutch of the potency principle. Further, man's hostile relation to nature has left us with the task of reintegrating with a world weary from that battle, a natural world which cries out to the daughters of time in a voice choked with technological sewage, cries out over a wasteland strewn with the garbage of the brotherhood's machines of war. It is from behind their barricades of radioactive productivity and in the chattering language of electronics that men now pour derision on feminist speculation and women's first efforts to make history. This inevitable ambuscade must simply be endured, for the ideological struggle is in any case but a pale shadow of the practical struggle which is its corollary, and which is currently developing. To be ambushed is a distinct advance on being merely privatized, for it moves generic struggle from the petty realm of private tensions between individuals to the realm of public confrontation. The ambush tends and is intended to make women defensive, but only for a short while. The very fact of public struggle is currently transforming this defensiveness, as women gleefully recognize the element of *angst* in male contempt which defeats its putative potency, and begin to learn the value of their own unified potentiality. It is becoming increasingly clear that the struggle of feminism is not the struggle for women's liberation, or for some abstract humanism, but a historical force whose task is the regeneration and reintegration of historical and natural worlds.

There is a further similarity between the two historical enterprises, in which at one time men and now women strive to mediate their reproductive consciousness. This similarity arises from a structural resemblance between the historical base of women's reproductive liberation and the natural base of men's reproductive liberation. Men could not do without biological continuity and kinship relations, despite their efforts to develop asexual modes of continuity and autoregenerative social and intellectual chimeras. Reproductive process cannot be abolished, but neither can historical process. Women cannot abolish the real history of patriarchal praxis in the attempt to elaborate a theoretical understanding of their own. This creates terminological and conceptual problems: women are accused of distorting the meanings of words and phrases and ideas, when we are in fact attempting to clarify the generic bias of such concepts.

The accusations need not deter us, even where they enrage us. The new and radical is always fair game for the old and conservative, but historical process remains process because of these vital contradictions. To be sure, Plato plunders the dynamics of reproduction for metaphysics, and pilfers the vocabulary of reproduction for eternity. Marx appropriates the dialectics of reproduction for production, while he raids its vocabulary in his still metaphorical conception of history. These incursions are but a part of the otherwise impressive contributions of both thinkers, but the effort to demonstrate their significance, which is an effort to analyse a distortion, looks like a distortion itself, while the effort to evoke context looks like an arbitrary wrench from context.

The emphasis on the little which is said about reproduction gives the impression of too much weight placed on too narrow a base, when in fact the narrowness of the base is the problem. However, women must be especially sensitive to the danger which accrues to babies when the bath water gets murky. The distortions wrought in political theory by the operations of the potency principle do not mean that the forms in which political questions have been raised in the past are not only passé but, as liberal bureaucrats like to say, 'unacceptable', Questions of political obligation, for example, or the implementation of democracy, or the boundaries, rights and obligations of political communities remain important to any non-anarchic politics. Further, the analysis of male-dominated history has occasionally provoked women to the view that men in general are hopeless cases, to be exiled to sperm concentration camps as quickly as possible. These visions are part of what is probably a necessary stage of feminist utopianism. History cannot be destroyed and, as a political principle, apartheid, whether racial or generic, is oppressive and ultimately unworkable. We must deal with a world of objects, and among such objects we find real live men, their institutions and their ideologies. The struggle for women is not to destroy these, but to transcend them, to build upon them the conditions and realities of their own transformation. The struggle will be bitter, but, as women's struggle, it is not a struggle 'to the death' but a struggle 'for life'.

Thus, while I have speculated upon the fruitfulness of a feminist perspective on theoretical traditions, I have none the less attempted to root this preliminary speculation on a material base within the process of reproduction itself, but at the same time deal with selected and limited male interpretations of that process. In this endeavour, I have developed the rudiments of a possible theory of socio-historical evolution, and a number of concepts with which to proceed to the large task of concretizing feminist perspective as social science. As I have been concerned with theory, it is primarily the theoretical tradition which has engaged my attention, but, even so, one thing is already clear. Feminist scholarship cannot engage in the disciplinary fragmentation which currently pervades social science, nor can it afford the ahistorical indulgences of here-and-now empiricism. A feminist social science, responding to the cultural pervasiveness of male supremacy, must be a unified social science, a unification which also transcends the partiality of 'political economy'.

When one asks what such a unified social science would be like, we are not yet ready to give answers in terms of refined hypothesis and established methodology. We can repeat the contention that feminist social science will rest on a theory of society which is both like and unlike traditional social theories. The sense in which such a theory would be like all traditional theories is that it must respond to real problems which history is currently presenting to the human makers of history. The sense in which it would be unlike all traditional theories arises from the fact that these problems now command the praxis of women as well as men; indeed, of women in opposition to man in general, though not necessarily to individual men. Men in relation to genderic struggle are a little bit like intellectuals in relation to class struggle, as Karl Marx (perhaps intellectually defensive in this instance!) saw that relation. Men who recognize feminism as the progressive force in history may join the struggle, and there is no doubt that some women will join the forces of the reactionary male-supremacist bourgeoisie. However, intellectuals in class struggle have been known to fall prey to destructive vanguardism, and men in feminism will have to be watched rather carefully for similar tendencies.

The establishment and growth of feminism as the progressive force in history constitutes a world turned upside down. After many centuries in which men have developed the rationales and practice of the oppression of women, man and women alike are called upon to analyse the conditions of the emancipation of women. This is not a call which is necessarily answered with alacrity, but as it emerges from an objective trans-formation in the material process of reproduction it cannot ulti-mately be muffled. The process of reproduction stands in dialectical relation to the process of production as the material substructure of history.

Simone de Beauvoir's paradoxical achievement, in writing a history of women grounded axiomatically on the proposition that women have no history, is paradoxical because of an inadequate theoretical comprehension of the living process and material substructure of history. As Juliet Mitchell has observed, de Beauvoir attempts a precarious balance between idealist form and material content mediated by a psychology of desire: an ontological desire for freedom on the one hand, a material craving for property on the other.[3] De Beauvoir has subsequently recognized in part the difficulties of her position:

I should take a more materialist position today. ... I should base the notion of woman as other and the Manichean argument it entails not on an idealist and *a priori* struggle of consciousnesses, but on the facts of supply and demand.[4]

De Beauvoir here moves from duelling ideological dualisms to a more material position, but the 'facts' of supply and demand cannot of themselves give an exhaustive account of male supremacy. De Beauvoir does not appear to have transcended her conviction that biological reproduction is immaterial; the fact that reproduction is indubitably concerned with 'matter' in a physical sense is consistently submerged in the prejudice that it 'does not matter' in a historical sense.

De Beauvoir's more recent position casts the two traditions of materialism and idealism into opposing and contrasted forms, and demands that an existential choice be made: either one or the other. This is a regression from her earlier position, whose defect was not the attempt to mediate the ontological and the actual, but a limited understanding of the actual. In the last two chapters I have attempted to show that both traditions, materialist and idealist, treat reproduction in an ideological way, and it is argued that this can happen precisely because paternity is ideal while maternity is material.

Feminist theory does not therefore, have a choice between idealism and the materialism, but must give an account of the way in which both develop and are historically and intellectually necessary to each other. There is no ground for a correct understanding of human reproduction in a theory which is one-sided, either in generic or philosophical terms. Substantial contemporary 'bodies' of thought, whatever their ontological concerns, attempt a reunion of the natural and the human in a material way. Thus, we have a substantial intellectual movement, bearing the name if not always the perception of Marx, based on the necessity of subsistence. We have another body of thought, exemplified in the followers of Freud, resting upon the imperatives of human sexuality. We have a further body of thought, existentialism, resolutely anticipating the absurd necessity of death. We have no philosophy of birth. Existentialism and its phenomenological parent have come close to a unification of body and thought with the everyday world, in a search for a philosophy and a method which transcends the dualism of subject and object, of general and particular. Merleau-Ponty, for example, insists on the mediative power of the 'lived body', while Herbert Marcuse attempts to unite the notion of social surplus with the individual psyche in a theory of the surplus repression of natural body function in the interests of a bourgeois maximization of private profit through public oppression. These are valuable insights. The difficulty lies in the unchallenged postulate that 'man makes himself', with whatever degree of voluntarism, and the failure to see the relation between the authentic and rather soulful man who makes himself and his vulgar cousin, the 'self-made man' of bourgeois heroics. The proposition that man makes himself is not untrue; it is merely one-sided, still theorizing on a second nature for man abrupted from his first. In a sense, it is still affixed to Locke's *tabula rasa* view of maturation, with the important qualification that the hand that writes now writes upon itself. In existentialism particularly, the effect of this is to transform a right to privacy to a *pathos* of isolation, thus removing it effectively from the possibility of political praxis. The relation of isolation to bourgeois alienation is understood, but the failure of the proletariat to fulfil its historic role leads to a depressed sense of loneliness among middle-class intellectuals, and alienation comes to be understood as neurosis. The body as such has only what Heidegger calls facticity, it is 'thrown' in preternatural solitude into a world it did not make. It therefore has no intrinsic value, and is imbued with a 'fallenness', intransigent and perhaps not unrelated to that of Adam. Whatever men's perceptions of their spiritual and ethical tumbles through history have been, they have refused to relate them explicitly and openly to the very real 'fall' from reproductive process at the moment of alienation of their seed.

What is neglected in thought about people who never get born is the fact that a value is always produced by all human labour, productive and reproductive. The attempt to root unique human value in the labourless birth of man's second nature is doomed: this doom echoes through literature, but appears more ominously in a male-dominated history which consistently opposes the ideological declaration of human worth to the passionate pageantry of killing. The notion that the individual has value is not a wishy-washy humanist stand taken in the teeth of evidence to the contrary. Human value exists concretely as all value exists, as the product of human labour. It is a value subject to intense internal contradiction when it is, as it has previously been, a product of the physical labour of women and the mental labour of men. Only now can these contradictions be mediated, for only by human control can the process of reproduction be rendered rational in a shared praxis of a man and a woman. This does not mean that women will not have to labour to produce human value: it does mean that men no longer will be permitted to appropriate that value. Appropriation is inappropriate between freely co-operating equals, but equality itself is meaningless between the non-differentiated. Truly human value is the value of the child produced by labour, rational intention, shared purpose, equal responsibility and mutual joy.

Feminist theory cannot solve all the problems of philosophy. Doubtless in due course a feminist philosophy will arise to deal with the contradictions in human experience which have been noted here in a preliminary way. The development of feminist theory, however, does not need to wait for women's liberation. There is both theoretical and practical work to be done and to be done now. This much, however, may be said: feminist philosophy will be a philosophy of birth and regeneration, not in a simple-minded or metaphorical way, but in an arduous re-examination of traditional philosophy and a vigorous critique of the pervasive oppressiveness of the potency principle as it lurches monolithically to Nirvana.

All of these considerations demand a new approach to the study of history and politics. It may well be the case that male supremacy has been a historical necessity, in a sense related to the historical necessity of capitalism in the task of raising productivity. Male supremacy has ensured the participation of fathers in the nurture of the new race, not necessarily in terms of actually doing the work, but in terms at least of reluctant responsibility. No non-utopian claims can be made that either capitalism or patriarchalism, the liberal state and the privatized family, are about to burst asunder, unless the material base of both is comprehended in adequate theoretical terms. Capitalism embodies surplus value, in a way which has the deceptive but satisfying aura of auto-regeneration, while it abolishes scarcity. At the same time, it continues to create increasingly artificial needs, wreaking havoc upon the environment provided by a nature perceived as man's natural enemy. Uncontrolled reproduction creates a quite different surplus: surplus population, further assaulting nature's providence. The comforting thought that technology will overcome a real imbalance between people and resources in the course of accelarating capital accumulation is a pious hope. The real impact of capitalism on the relations of reproduction is uneven, and, in the chill vocabulary of Vietnam, people can always be 'wasted'.

The study of history and politics, exciting though it is, must not be alienated from political practice. It is not the purpose of this paper to make detailed strategic pronouncements. Indeed, the basic argument is that such pronouncements cannot be made until an adequate theoretical basis is developed, and we have done no more than indicate the dimensions of this task. Some practical considerations do and must emerge, however, for women cannot sit back and wait while Minerva's owl folds her wings, hooting throatily on network television of man's latest disposition of women's destiny. Further, the feminist revolution is not something which is going to happen or which might happen; it is something which is already happening, and already eliciting a response from the institutions of male ruling classes. We do well to recall the modes of historical development of major revolutions in the past, few though they have been. The bourgeoisie did not leap, full-dressed in the costume of rugged individualism and capitalist appropriation, into all-out war on the feudal aristocracy. They spent centuries in the painful development of an understanding of the potentiality of the division of labour, in the superstructural struggles for reform, in the ideological sweat of justificatory parturition and in the mastery of a new mode of production. They also had to invent, elaborate and refine their new science, which they called political economy. Feminism has to do all these things and more, and it has to do them in different countries with different antagonists and enormously variant superstructures. It also has to do them in the teeth of the opposition of vested interests and in the ambience of man's antiphysis, his notion of himself as a warrior against a nature which he is beginning to suspect might foil his quest for glory on earth by dropping dead into a murky grave of destructive half-lives. The fact that one is making history on a cosmic scale does not necessarily help one in mundane decisions about what to do next. Marx once remarked that men could only tackle the problems which history presented to them, and that is a truth which prevails, except that women are now active protagonists on the stage of historical dialectics.

What, then, are the problems which history now presents, and how does a historical theory help to define them and work out strategies for change? In very general terms, the problem is to move from the war against nature and against life to policies of integration with nature and with life. It is not at all surprising that feminism finds allies among pacifists, among conservationists and among the neo-Luddites who resist the technology-for-technology's-sake thrust of capitalism. It is not surprising that feminism finds opposition among those with a narrow faith in class war, and friends among those who see that resistance to capitalism and imperialism must come to terms with the reality of feminist revolution. It was predictable that feminism would elicit a new and panic-stricken 'defence' of the family as the 'fundamental unit of society'. Capitalism cares not one whit for the forms of the social relations of reproduction, provided they continue to reproduce labour power, fulfil the 'ethical' function of educating children in the stability of existing class structure, and provide a cheap labour pool of women and children which can be utilized to threaten uppish unionized male workers. Male supremacy, on the other hand, cares a great deal about the family, and we are currently witness to the revival of a particularly crude fundamentalism, the new conservatism which is breaking its neck to make up for its failure to understand the necessary relation of production to reproduction.

Thus, feminism has in the first instance to resist the forces in society which are mounting a huge campaign of quite vicious repression of early feminism's hard-won gains: the vote, for example, is attacked obliquely in the anti-ERA campaign in the USA; all modes of contraception, and particularly abortion, are subject to highly organized and well-funded resistance everywhere – religious fundamentalism is revived to find itself in bed with the Catholic church, a coitus which would be hilarious if it did not pose a very real threat. Domestic violence may be increasing, or may simply be emerging from the obscuration of the private realm, but, in either case, it continues to be blandly swept back into the hidey-holes of life with father by the neglect of the putative forces of law and order. All of these developments require organized resistance. They are the womb issues of the struggle at its current stage of development. Central to all of them is the struggle for women's economic independence, against women's assigned role as the guardian of the new morality of mindless consumerism, for women's struggle for dignity within the social relations of production. There is plenty to do.

In fact, in the hurly-burly of issue-orientated politics, it too often seems that there is too much to do, and the reality of 'burning out' is an authentic problem for women activists. There is a sense in which the activities of the opposition help here, though the process is slow. The refusal of the economic ruling classes to give up the advantages of cheap women's labour cannot ultimately be hidden beneath the tailored skirts of token women executives, any more than the reluctance to give up the power and comfort of domestic hegemony can be drowned out by the sweet voices of female neo-conservatives singing hymns of praise to Man and his fatigue. The transformation of feminine consciousness is not only underway, but is spreading more rapidly in resistance to these excesses. As the strength of the opposition reveals itself, the factional fights of the women's liberation movement are fading in a new synthesis of women who are committed to the cause of women, very widely defined, rather than to the effort to fit feminism into some kind of male-generated model of history and politics which not only divides women from women, but drives wedges between women and those still few men who have seen where the progressivist cause is at.

The time has come when feminism begins to know itself as a universal process, uniting women in a way which transcends nationality, race, class, sexual orientation and marital status. In Canada, feminists are busy translating the basic documents of French and Belgian theorists. American women are getting thrown out of the citadels of Islamic patriarchal nationalism. In Africa, western women are offering help in resistance to the horrors of genital mutilation, and understanding why such help is suspect. In communist states, women are beginning to question the assumptions of bureaucratic vanguardism. In Ireland, while heroes throw bombs, Protestant women throw packages of contraceptives to their Catholic sisters. To be sure, none of these developments are enormous. International co-operation is constantly assailed with charges of cultural imperialism and female nosiness. The organization of good intentions without money or power does tend to frustrate and disappoint. Yet such developments are symptomatic of the movement of a new phase of history, which is not going to go away and bury itself once more in the isolation of private mud-huts or suburban wastelands. Feminism is going universal.

Beyond this, there are major issues to be resolved, some soon, some late. Immediate questions in the capitalist democracies relate to political strategy vis-à-vis existing political structures. It simply does not do to sniff at the chauvinist corruptions of political process while that process is taking away hard-won gains. The lived conditions of women are intolerable *now*, and what can be done *now* is a practical question of an often quite localized nature. It would be absurd to suggest that for example, American feminists give up the ERA struggle and wait until the political system dies of its own internal corruption. It would be equally absurd to suggest that women workers everywhere give up the struggle for recognition in trade unions until unions cleanse themselves of economism or sexism or left revisionism or power-intoxication – or whatever it is one thinks is wrong with unions. On a more personal level, it would be foolish to insist that women give up reasonably satisfactory marriages or 'relationships' with individual men simply because man in general is an unfeeling chauvinist pig. It is only within the actual conditions of our lives, the reality which we in part inherit, but in a great measure create within the limits of our social being, that we can work at all.

Having noted these local and urgent imperatives, it is still important to begin to specify the universal norms, values and strategies of progressive feminism. The barriers erected by man and his history come closer and rear larger as the possibility of storming them is transformed to the actuality of the attack. Access to universality is much more easily accomplished on the theoretical level than on the practical level, but it is never to be accomplished on the one without the other. Clearly, the unmediated divisions with which the brotherhood has not been able to deal in its own historic quest for universality stand in the way of feminist universalism. This is clearly so of class, but the brotherhood has had lots of difficulty with nationality, ethnicity and race as well. These are, of course, genetic factors, and the brotherhood's genetic fragility has not been able to surmount them nor mediate them all. Race is a case in point: the legal mediation of the uncertainty of paternity in its most successful form has involved the bestowing on particular men the right of paternity vis-à-vis the fruits of the womb of particular women. It is not the easiest legal fiction to maintain where the fruit of the womb has too long a nose or too dark a skin, and racial mistrust and envy and hatred may well have originated in such considerations, which also lend fuel to the impetus to privatize women. It has always been difficult to link racism to capitalism for, like patriarchy, it is much older than capitalism.[5] Women are reluctant heiresses to these bitter divisions and their political and psychological power. One understands that women of different classes and races distrust each other, for race and class are evidently intrinsic to the social construction of male-supremacist reality, and only the development of shared values and concrete co-operation in the pursuit of clearly defined political and economic objectives can transcend these centuries of exploitation of people by men.

But where to start? The implications of the analysis of reproductive process offered here point clearly in one imperative direction. I have spoken rather glibly of 'the rational control of reproduction' and 'contraceptive technology', but it is clear that this technology is in a very primitive and often still quite lethal stage of development. There is some ground for thinking that the ruling classes would not be unhappy if it remained so, but information on decision-making in this area is hard to come by. One unanswered and uninvestigated question is why contraceptive technology was developed in the first place, and who made the resource allocations necessary for such development. To be sure, technology has an inner 'self-regenerative' dynamic of a very scary nature, and the briefest investigation of, say, the nuclear power industry or of 'sophisticated' arms development suggests that the brotherhood have gone quite mad and lost control of their creations in some cosmic sorcerers' apprenticeship. We must not believe, though, that because capitalism has preferred the thing relations of the marketplace to govern human relations of exchange, individual capitalists are thoughtless fatties with more money than brains. Indeed, sometimes one wonders if *only* capitalists have understood Marx! The men of the ruling classes do make decisions about resource allocation, and this is a truly private realm which is difficult to penetrate. It is the realm in which the decision to allocate resources for contraceptive technology was made, and perhaps where the decision to limit this development has also been made.

There were no doubt sound reasons for such a decision and, as I have noted before, it is unlikely that the liberation of women was a burning priority. More likely, concern about the capacity of high technology to keep the population of the world employed, worry about political instability in the Third World and among the unemployed in the bastions of capitalist production, and the loss of control of capital itself in the energy 'crisis' were among the curious reversal of capitalism's long dedication to pro-natalism. There is a thread which connects reproductive technology with laws relating to abortion and to homosexual practice; tentative and ambivalent as these are, they are basically policies which tend to reduce birth rates. An imperfect reproductive technology then becomes doubly effective, as it prevents babies being born and kills off women in their childbearing years. This is no paranoid fancy of conspiracy theory, for as policy it makes sound economic sense where the supply of labour power exceeds the demand. Yet it is, after all, speculation, and is likely to remain so until some bureaucrat somewhere can't resist the temptation to write a minute of memorandum which will ultimately be sold for its market value to the sensational press.

It is not, however, even necessary to indulge in speculation to see that women have a vital interest in the development of a safe and effective contraceptive technology. Feminism might do well to consolidate what power women have – productive power, consumer power, voting power and the formidable force of sisterhood – around this absolutely basic issue. The consolidation of rational control over reproductive process is the precondition of liberation, and it is urgent.

There are other questions which can be raised and not yet answered, but the practice which can produce answers and develop strategies can proceed in a more orderly way if the questions are clearly enunciated. One such question relates to violence; will violence be the only possible way to overthrow the economic power of capitalist patriarchy? In terms of class warfare, there is no real alternative to violence, and many feminists sincerely believe that power and wealth will not be wrested from their present owners without violent struggle. This is a depressing belief, for those who own power and money do so by virtue of their control of the instruments of violent destruction, and an arms race with the brotherhood is not an encouraging prospect. Women have neither access to nor technical training in the art of war; Venus was disarmed many moons ago. No doubt such skills can be acquired, and armed women have played a part in revolutionary activity when the brotherhood have needed them.

The problem is not, of course, a technical one at all, but an ethical one. Feminist critique of male supremacy has generally argued that precisely one of the things which is most radically wrong with *homo dominandi* is the contradiction between his idea of himself as rational man and his practice of solving problems by resort to violent means, means which now have the potential to wind up his historic struggle against nature in the total destruction of the natural. Further, the resort to violence as a justified means to a moral end, which will stop when the end is gained, has proven to be the greatest of fallacies. The psychology of doing violence to the biological and natural world is engrained in the social relations of reproduction in the first place, and men appear to find forms of violence 'natural' and often effective. Would women be different? We cannot say, but in any case feminism's commitment to the principle of integration makes the whole question of violence a very difficult one.

Are there, then, other means of social change other than violence? We need not linger with pious hopes about moral regeneration and the changing of 'attitudes'; attitudes are the product of social reality and, as Marx famously noted, consciousness does not make the world but the world makes consciousness. So the question is the quite large one of how that world can be changed. There is no slickly packaged action-module to make this happen, and none is offered here. What does emerge from the study of the dialectics of reproduction, however, is the clear vindication that heretofore in history the effort of changing social reality has been directed at the public realm. The private realm has had to adapt itself as best it may. Yet dialectical analysis shows that the material roots of the private realm are dynamic, that the private realm has not only the capacity to transform the social relations which mediate its internal contradictions, but has, at this moment in history, an irreversible imperative to do so.

Implicit in a historical analysis of the private realm is an indication that women have a large army of allies in their quest for liberation. These are their children. Knowledge of the development of personality in early life alters the whole question of the understanding of consciousness. The actual change in reproductive relationships alters radically the conditions of child rearing. We already have had in the United States the spectacle of large numbers of young men refusing to take for granted a military destiny. True, the motivations of the young men in question were no doubt of enormous complexity, but the ability of the army to symbolize masculinity has clearly been eroded. Likewise, and without violence, the authority of the Catholic church in reproductive relationships is fading quite peacefully, as millions of Catholics quietly disobey the papal encyclical forbidding contraception.

The recurrent masculine dread that women hold a potential political weapon in the withholding of sexual access to their persons belongs in the same conceptual category as the myth of the general strike. It is ultimately anarchic in its divorce from rational co-operation, to say nothing of the prejudiced postulate that women can quite easily forego sexual satisfaction. The real weapon which women hold is the one which they have always potentially held: maternity itself. This is not the abstract maternity of Mariolatry, but the working face of maternity in the nurture and socialization of children. That its potentiality as a weapon has been perceived not only by Mao but by Adolf Hitler is no reason to turn from it in terror. Hitler's view of Aryan motherhood was grounded absolutely in male dominance and an irrational genetic vision. With the liberation of women, children will be different. *How* they will be different is a question which does not have to wait quietly on history, but is subject to the practical and theoretical activities of transformed feminist consciousness.

Feminist praxis has already perceived that the private is political. Such issues as day care, abortion, the rewards for domestic labour, family violence, the legal disadvantages of women: all of these issues emerge from the lived experience of women, but their coherence does not come from the fact that they are *women's* issues. It comes from their social situation in the private realm, which is why they have such trouble making an impact in a public realm which has historically defined them as non-political. In practice, given the historical-material upheaval in the substructure of the social relations of reproduction, the private realm is where the new action is. Feminists have perhaps occasionally entertained the thought that we must get these impediments cleared up before we can step into the public realm on equal terms. The truth is that the struggle around these issues, as it expands and intensifies, will transform the relation of public and private in a radical way: it is not a preliminary skirmish, but a beginning of a massive political movement.

This is because the struggle is a conscious struggle to transform a social reality which in turn will transform consciousness. Female reproductive consciousness, in the course of this struggle, transcends the isolation of women in their domestic prisons; women grasp the reality of a universal consciousness, the sisterhood of which we already have primitive but profound adumbrations. But it also transforms the consciousness of the products of reproduction, the children. Perhaps the opposition have understood this more quickly and more thoroughly than those of us engaged in struggle, but feminism is not of course the destroyer of the family; feminism liberates and transcends the social relations of reproduction, a transformed dialectic of necessity which is the condition and the locus and the promise of the next historical stage in human liberation.

Changing the mode of production cannot, all by itself, transform all social relations. Social relations are the ground of the development of consciousness of ourselves and our world. They are rooted in necessity, the dialectically related necessity to produce and reproduce. Consciousness is formed, to be sure within the relations of production, but it is an ongoing process, a phylogenetic and ontogenetic process which is intricately and often confusingly woven in the locations of the process of consciousness formation: in the family, in the schools, in the workplace, in political practice. We do not need a utopian blueprint of the future; indeed, we cannot have one, because the future is not the product of mind but the product of praxis, the unity of theory and action. What we must have is the continuation of the struggle to transform and reintegrate public and private, and in doing so to transcend the alienation of one from the other.

The old and now outworn Baconian call to overcome nature and torture her secrets from her fell on the ears of a ruling sex whose rule was contingent upon an ability to overcome the natural alienation of the idea of paternity, and to impose upon the natural a pattern of oppression which confirmed them as universal victors over natural process and cyclical time. In an age in which the taming of nature threatens to become the annihilation of the natural world, the psychology of conquest does more than oppress women; it threatens the foundations of life process itself. This psychology will not yield to the rational arguments of the classroom or the therapy of the couch. It may well yield to a change in the objective base of the potency principle. A feminist theory need not fly to the melodrama of romantic vitalism, but it will be a theory which celebrates once more the unity of cyclical time with historical time in the conscious and rational reproduction of the species. It will be theory of the celebration of life in life rather than death in life. The reintegration of men in general in the harmony of people and nature, without an act of wilful appropriation by individual members of the brotherhood, but by a co-operative decision between voluntarily reproducing adults, changes the social relations of reproduction in a radical way. Under these circumstances, the notion of a 'love child' need no longer be a euphemism for stigmatic illegitimacy.

Further, the unity of the individual and the species with nature becomes a relation of co-operation, to which neither nature nor time appear hostile. The harmonization of people with nature, and the accompanying transformation of consciousness, presents a possibility of a challenge to the rape of nature in the name of corporate profit. This is not utopian; unlike, for example, Herbert Marcuse's sensuous Valhalla, it does not depend on the reactivation of slumbering ancestral memories, nor on the exoneration of the 'hostile father' of a primal hoard.[6] Marcuse wants a future society naturalized and made playfully gentle by a maternal superego, which a mature civilization will dredge from its phylogenetic infancy to abolish the surplus repression created by the patriarchal reality principle. Marcuse, however, retains Freud's error in rooting repression in individual sexuality, rather than in the social relations of reproduction. His thought therefore remains utopian in that it has no social dynamic, and nothing to say about the reproduction of this polymorphously perverse and fondly irrational race of men.

Finally, the integration of women on equal terms into the productive process is a necessary but not sufficient condition of liberation. Liberation also depends on the reintegration of men on equal terms into reproductive process. Perhaps one might have the temerity to rephrase one of Marx's more celebrated pronouncements. In a rational human society, people will be producers in the morning, child carers in the afternoon, and critical critics in the evening. Only then can men and women abandon a long preoccupation with sleeping together in favour of being awake together.

Notes

1 The dialectics of reproduction

1 Simone de Beauvoir, *The Second Sex* (New York, 1953). Shulamith Firestone, *The Dialectic of Sex: The Case for Feminist Revolution* (New York, 1971). These views are discussed in detail in Ch. 2, *passim*.

2 Karl Marx and Frederick Engels, *Manifesto of the Communist Party*, in *Selected Works* (Moscow, 1969) pp. 134–6.

3 Hegel struggled with the problem of reproduction in his early work. The significant passages here are the fragment 'On love', in his *Early Theological Writings* (Chicago, 1948), pp. 303–4. I have also been fortunate in having access to the manuscript of an unpublished translation of the *System der Sittlichkeit* by T. M. Knox and H. S. Harris. I am grateful to Professor Harris for his permission to quote from this work and to read in manuscript his invaluable 'Introductory essay to Hegel's *The System of Ethical Life*'.

4 'Prehistorical' is used in the sense in which Hegel used the word 'anthropological', a sense now misleading. For Hegel, 'anthropological' means the preconscious, pre-rational, therefore prehistorical, forms of human spirit.

5 For Hegel's conception of death rather than birth as the 'lord and master' of family life, see his *The Phenomenology of Mind* (New York and Evanston, 1967), pp. 471–2.

6 This is a recurrent theme in Hegel's work, given its most austere expression in the *Philosophy of Right* (London, Oxford and New York, 1967).

7 A feminist critique of the Hegelian system might well be an exciting task. For our limited purpose here, we make no claims to a critique of the system: we have not, for example, dealt with the long discussion of

reproduction in *The Philosophy of Nature*. For a more detailed but still tentative discussion of Hegel, see my *Man, Physiology and Fate: Hegel* (GROW Paper No. 13, Ontario Institute for Studies in Education, 1977).

8 Hegel, 'On love', in his *Early Theological Writings*, pp. 303–4, et seq.

9 Ibid., p. 307.

10 Ibid., p. 305.

11 Ibid., p. 307.

12 Ibid.

13 'Since possession and property make up an important part of men's lives, even lovers cannot refrain from reflection on this aspect of their relations' (ibid.).

14 Hegel already sees the significance of productive labour in the 1804 lectures. (*The System of Ethical Life* (New York, forthcoming), pp. 437, 438). The more developed treatment of the status of labour as mediator with, and transformer of, the world comes in the famous parable of lordship and bondage in *The Phenomenology*, B.IV.A.

15 Hegel, *System*, pp. 429–31. See also Harris, 'Introductory essay' (see note 3 above), pp. 34–5.

16 Ultimately, male/female relations become essentially spiritual:

> Just as the individual divine man [the historical Christ] has an implied father and only an actual mother, in like manner the universal divine man, the spiritual communion, has as its father its own proper action and knowledge, while its mother is eternal Love, which it merely feels, but does not behold in its consciousness as an actual immediate object (Hegel, *The Phenomenology*, p. 784).

17 Karl Marx, *Capital* (New York, 1906), Vol. 1, Pt III, Ch. VII, Section I.

18 Ibid., p. 198.

19 For a discussion of the need to conserve the past as a condition of the humanity of a proletarian solidarity, see Christian Lenhardt, 'Anamnestic solidarity: the proletariat and its manes', *Telos*, No. 25, Fall 1975, pp. 133–54.

20 Sigmund Freud, *Totem and Taboo* (New York, 1918), pp. 182–207.

21 It is thus not surprising that Freud tells us that, in his account of the evolution from primal horde to totemic society, he is 'at a loss to indicate the place of the great maternal deities who perhaps everywhere preceded the paternal deities' (ibid., p. 192).

22 Ibid., p. 186.

23 Marx, *Capital*, p. 199.

24 For a recent description of this battle, see Jean Donnison, *Midwives and Medical Men* (London, 1977).

25 Josephine Iorio, in *Principles of Obstetrics and Gynecology for Nurses* (St Louis, 1971), divides the process into antepartal, intrapartal and postpartal stages.

26 M. Edward Davis and Reva Rubin (eds) *Dr. Lee's Obstetrics for Nurses* (eighteenth edition, Philadelphia and London, 1966), not only give short shift to fathers, but even manages to plug some male-supremacist assumptions: '[woman's] sexual life in general is more intense and plays a greater role in her existence' (p. 30). Obviously, there is room for romantic poetry in textbooks. Davis and Rubin give one third of a column to fathers, under the rather forbidding rubric of 'sperm transport' (p. 46). Perhaps the nineteenth edition will be better, for this is a 'classic' work.

27 The current movement to restore even limited midwifery in the United States carries these overtones. Dr George A. Slater – 'The problem', in *The Midwife in the United States: A Macy Conference* (New York, 1968) – deplores the poor showing of the USA in infant mortality statistics (24.8 in the USA, 14.12 in Sweden: p. 3). He calls for a new professional category, and 'we must think how to train *him*' (p. 10) and 'what kind of job would *he* do?' (p. 11) [my italics].

28 Karl Marx and Frederick Engels, *The German Ideology*, (New York, 1947), p. 18.

29 Aristotle, *De Generatione Animalium* (Oxford, 1912). See especially II.737a.25 and I.724b, 725a, 725b. For a discussion on Aristotle's reproductive biology and its genderic prejudice, see Harold Cherniss, *Aristotle's Criticism of Pre-Socratic Philosophy* (New York, 1964), pp. 269–88.

30 See Plato's *Symposium* (New York, 1956), S. 192a and Ch. 4 below.

31 Quoted by Patrick Gardner from Vico's *Scienza Nova*, in *Theories of History* (Chicago, 1959), p. 14.

32 My colleague, Dr Dorothy Smith, has properly cautioned me against the assertion that patriarchy, as opposed to paternity, is a universal phenomenon. Most familiar of the studies of non-patriarchal societies is, of course, Margaret Mead's affectionate portrait of the Arapesh (Margaret Mead, *Sex and Temperament in Three Primitive Societies* (New York, 1963)). What does seem to be the case is that what are known as 'great civilizations' are patriarchal (Mogul, Inca, Greek, Roman and so forth). Patriarchy is associated fairly consistently with class differentiation, imperialism and some form of racism, and may therefore have been, in the Marxist sense, historically necessary. The difficulty with historically necessary movements is inertia and an incapacity to recognize the end of their usefulness. This is the reason why human history is always the history of struggle.

33 The selection of wolves in this analogy is prompted by Farley Mowatt's sensitive but anthropomorphic observations in *Never Cry Wolf* (Toronto, 1963).

34 The Marxist notion of surplus value as the value appropriated cannot readily be adapted to reproductive labour. Surpluses in terms of reproductive product have quite often tended to be eliminated rather than appropriated. In very early societies, this appears to have been done without regard for gender, though in developed patriarchal societies girls appear to have been considered more dispensable, and the myths of these societies are concerned to demonstrate the perfidy of destroying male children: Isaac, Romulus, Remus and Oedipus are among the more noted victors over child sacrifice and exposure. There are no reliable statistics relating to child exposure in Greece, but there are many references to child destruction, practical or ritual, in ancient writings. Both Jane Harrison and Philip Slater argue that infanticide was an important component in the fantasy 'life of the ancients'. See Philip E. Slater, *The Glory of Hera* (Boston, 1971), pp. 214–16; Jane Ellen Harrison, *Prolegomena to the Study of Greek Religion* (New York, 1957), pp. 482–8. Harrison quotes Plutarch, Clement and Arnobius in support of the contention that infanticide was practised well into the fifth century. It is a contentious and grey area, floating uneasily between economic, religious and psychoanalytic interpretations.

35 This is a term which Marx scorned in its usage in relation to productive activity. Karl Marx, *The Poverty of Philosophy* (New York, 1963), pp. 43–50.

36 For a discussion of Claude Lévi-Strauss's misunderstanding of this point, see Ch. 3 below.

2   Sorry, we forgot your birthday

1 Simone de Beauvoir, *The Second Sex* (New York, 1952).

2 Shulamith Firestone, *The Dialectic of Sex: The Case for Feminist Revolution* (New York, 1971), p. 7.

3 Ibid.

4 De Beauvoir, *The Second Sex*, p. 26.

5 Ibid., p. 59.

6 G. W. F. Hegel, *The Phenomenology of Mind* (New York and Evanston, 1967), pp. 229–40.

7 The slave does not remain immured in animality, and Beauvoir's analogy must stop at half point. Hegel's bondsman 'By serving ... cancels in every

particular his dependence on the attachment to natural existence, and by his work removes this existence away' (*The Phenomenology*, p. 238). Presumably, reproductive labour and the 'serving' of infants confirm an 'attachment to natural existence', both for Hegel and de Beauvoir (*The Second Sex*, p. 59).

8 De Beauvoir, ibid.
9 Ibid., pp. 59–60.
10 Hegel, *Janenser Realphilosophie* quoted by George Armstrong Kelly, *Idealism, Politics and History* (Cambridge, 1969), p. 98.
11 G. W. F. Hegel, 'On love', in his *Early Theological Writings* (Chicago, 1948), p. 303.
12 De Beauvoir, *The Second Sex*, Pt VII, Ch. XXV, pp. 636–73.
13 Jean-Paul Sartre, *Search for a Method* (New York, 1968), p. 89.
14 'Women are not the same as other oppressed groups. Unlike the working class, who have no need for the capitalist under socialism, the liberation of women does not mean that men will be eliminated. Sex and class are not the same' (Sheila Rowbotham, *Women's Consciousness, Man's World* (Harmondsworth, 1973), p. 117).
15 Ibid., p. 124.
16 Ibid., p. 117.
17 Ibid.
18 Firestone, *The Dialectic of Sex*, pp. 12, 13. Thus, Engels's 'Historical materialism is that view of the course of history which seeks the *ultimate* cause and the great moving power of all historical events in the economic development of society' (Firestone's italics, ibid., p. 4), becomes 'Historical materialism ... seeks the ultimate cause ... in the dialectic of sex' (no italics, ibid., p. 12).
19 Frederick Engels, *The Origin of the Family, Private Property and the State* (New York, 1972), p. 46.
20 Firestone, *The Dialectic of Sex*, p. 198.
21 Ibid., pp. 174–5.
22 Ibid., p. 75.
23 Ibid., p. 8.
24 Ibid., p. 11.
25 Kate Millett, *Sexual Politics* (New York, 1971).
26 Ibid., p. 4.
27 Ibid., p. 25.
28 Ibid., pp. 23, 24.
29 Ibid., pp. 220–3.
30 Ibid., p. 43.
31 Ibid., p. 45.

32　Ibid., p. 54.

33　Ibid., pp. 107–8.

34　Ibid., p. 121.

35　Engels's working man is heroic, considering the conditions in which he lives. Engels is occasionally sentimental, as in his Jack and Mary story (Frederick Engels, *The Conditions of the Working Class in England* (London, 1969), pp. 173–4). He has, as all feminist commentators note, a Victorian stuffiness about women. His notion of the adverse effect of wage labour on women is illuminating: 'works up to the hour of confinement, incapacity as housekeepers, neglect of home and children, indifference, actual dislike of family life, and demoralization' (ibid., p. 226). However, neither he nor Marx was ever naive about corruption. 'In Willenhall, Commissioner Horne asserts, and supplies ample proof of his assertion, that there exists no moral sense among the workers' (ibid., p. 229). 'The capitalist mode of production produces thus ... the deterioration of human labour-power by robbing it of its normal, moral and physical, conditions of development and function' (Karl Marx, *Capital* (New York, 1906), Vol. 1, Bk I, Ch. X, Section V, p. 292). Shaw's position is put most uncompromisingly in *Major Barbara* (Harmondsworth, 1960).

36　Millett, *Sexual Politics*, pp. 362–3.

37　Ibid., p. 74.

38　Ibid., p. 39.

39　August Bebel, *Women and Socialism* (New York, 1910).

40　The question of women's rights has always been marginal to European working class struggles, and the declaration of acceptance of the principle of full suffrage for women did not come until the 1907 Stuttgart meeting of the International. The fight here was led by Clara Zetkin. For a recent account of these events and factual analysis of the generic struggle in Czechoslovakia, see Hilda Scott, *Does Socialism Liberate Women?* (Boston, 1975).

41　Evelyn Reed, *Woman's Evolution: From Matriarchal Clan to Patriarchal Family* (New York, 1975).

42　Ibid., p. 35.

43　Ibid., p. 49.

44　Ibid.

45　Ibid., p. 137.

46　These are arbitrary choices, but these women's work has been important and exciting for me, as has the work of theorists whom I know well: Lorenne Clark, Angela Miles, Dorothy Smith.

47　Angela Miles's doctoral dissertation analyses the relation of developing theory and feminist activism. Angela Miles, 'The politics of feminist radicalism: a study in integrative feminism' (unpublished, University of Toronto, 1979).

3 The public and private realms

1 For a careful and scholarly study of the longevity of patriarchy, most specifically as a rationalization of political obligation, see Gordon J. Schochet, *Patriarchalism in Political Thought* (New York, 1975).

2 For a discussion of the mythical structure of metatheory see Northrop Frye, 'New directions from old', in Henry A. Murray (ed.) *Myth and Mythmaking* (Boston, 1968), pp. 115–32.

3 The tutor tells the young couple that they may have a chance to found a 'Paradise on earth' but only if 'you ... can set an example which you have not received' (Jean-Jacques Rousseau, *Emile* (London, 1911), p. 440). The exemplary intentions which are to be embodied in Emile governed Rousseau's selection of a name for the boy. The Aemilius were a Roman patrician family of such worth and integrity that they became symbols of probity, and gave the English and French languages the words 'emulate' and 'emulation'.

4 It also enticed from Mary Wollstonecraft her ovarian work, *A Vindication of the Rights of Women* (New York, 1967).

5 Ibid., p. 324: 'she alone can win the father's love for his children and convince them that they are indeed his own'.

6 George Armstrong Kelly, *Idealism, Politics and History* (Cambridge, 1969), p. 11.

7 Ibid., pp. 290–1.

8 Most widely known, of course, is August Bebel's *Women Under Socialism* (New York, 1971). For useful recent critiques of the early Marxist literature, see especially Hilda Scott, *Does Socialism Liberate Women?* (Boston, 1975) and Alena Heitlinger *Women and State Socialism: Sex Inequality in the Soviet Union and Czechoslovakia* (Montreal, 1979).

9 It is intended to deal with Arendt's most ambitious work, *The Human Condition* (New York, 1959).

10 Ibid., p. 301. In the first of her footnotes Arendt observes that it is 'illuminating' in the analysis of human thought to discover which of the two biblical versions of creation is favoured. Jesus of Nazareth preferred Genesis 1:27 ('male and female created he them'), while Paul liked the Adam's rib version. Arendt claims that activists like Jesus favour the first version, while salvationists prefer the second, so that the 'difference indicates much more than a different attitude to the role of women'. The

implication, which Arendt does not pursue, is that the equality version is kinder to women than the reversal of reproductive process in which Adam the patriarch produces woman out of his body. In fact, this is not necessarily the case. John Milton, for example, starts with the equality version in *Paradise Lost*, and then has Eve lose her primordial equality when God includes subservience to Adam in her punishment for the revolt in Paradise. If the two versions in Genesis mean anything at all, they probably indicate some confusion in the minds of the writers of the Old Testament, who were consciously engaged in elaborating a male mythology which must balance itself between the denigration of women and a reliance on biological continuity for the preservation of the genealogical purity of the Semitic peoples.

11 Ibid., p. 30.
12 Ibid., p. 31.
13 Ibid., pp. 30 ff.
14 Aristotle, *The Politics* (London, Oxford and New York, 1969), I.XII, No. 1, p. 32.
15 Ibid., No. 7, p. 35.
16 Aristotle, *De Generatione Animalium* (Oxford, 1912), II.737a.25: 'For the female is, as it were, a mutilated male, and the catamenia are semen, only not pure; for there is only one thing they have not in them, the principle of soul.' The notion of the mutilated female is very substantially pre-Freudian.

It may be noted that Aristotle lends some support to the contention made in Chapter 1 that the discovery of paternity is a historical event. It appears that the view of the 'ancients' that semen was waste matter had not been entirely dispelled, and Aristotle spends some time refuting it (I.724b, 725a, 725b). For a discussion on Aristotle's reproductive biology and its generic prejudice, see Harold Cherniss, *Aristotle's Criticism of Pre-Socratic Philosophy* (New York, 1971), pp. 269–88.

17 Arendt, *The Human Condition*, Ch. V *passim*.
18 Ibid., p. 29.
19 Ibid., p. 176.
20 Thucydides, *The Peloponnesian War* (Harmondsworth, 1954),Bk II, Ch. 4. See especially pp. 120–3.
21 Ibid., p. 122.
22 Arendt, *The Human Condition*, p. 176.
23 Thucydides, *The Peloponnesian War*, p. 123.
24 Victor Ehrenberg, *The Greek State* (London, 1972), p. 85.
25 For a discussion of Marx and necessity see T. B. Bottomore's Introduction to Karl Marx, *Early Writings* (New York, London, Toronto, 1963). See

also Istvan Meszaros, *Marx's Theory of Alienation* (London, 1970), pp. 180–6.

26 Arendt, *The Human Condition*, p. 115.

27 Ibid., p. 17.

28 Ibid., p. 25.

29 See Evelyn Reed, *Woman's Evolution*, p. 393. Ehrenberg believes not only that Mycenaenean society was tribal, but that women, both human and divine, played a decisive part in its development, roughly between 1600 and 1100 BC. However, by the time of the Trojan wars (about 1200) female prestige was on the wane, although legal wives and mothers enjoyed greater respect than their descendants in Socratic Athens. The tenth and ninth centuries are the dark age of antiquity, with not even the ferociously difficult Linear B surviving. Within this period, patriarchal social forms apparently vanquished matrilinear kinship, and the tribal forms of the eighth century were largely aristocratic 'clans'. By about 700 BC Hesiod was producing his pessimistic and mysogynist epics of lost heroism. Victor Ehrenberg, *From Solon to Socrates* (London, 1968), Ch. 1, 2, pp. 3–8. See also Engels, *The Origin of the Family, Private Property and the State* (New York, 1972), especially Chs 4 and 5; and André Bonnard, *Greek Civilization* Vol. 1 (London, 1957–61), *passim*.

30 Aristotle, *The Constitution of Athens* (New York, 1973), ix. 2.

31 Ehrenberg, *The Greek State*, p. 93.

32 Arendt, *The Human Condition*, p. 37.

33 Rowbotham, *Women, Resistance and Revolution* (Harmondsworth, 1972), pp. 103–4.

34 For an account of these events, see J. P. V. D. Baldson, *Roman Women: Their History and Habits* (London, 1962).

35 There is still in Ovid the dark strain of the equation of sexual orgasm and death: 'But as for me, let me go in the act of coming to Venus.' For a discussion of the relation of male sexuality to death, see H. R. Hays, *The Dangerous Sex: The Myth of Feminine Evil* (New York, 1964), p. 95. Hays's discussion of Ovid and Juvenal is the source of these remarks about the two poets. See also Phillip E. Slater *The Glory of Hera* (Boston, 1971), p. 103. The long history of the notion of orgasm as a form of death challenges psychoanalysis which relates this sombre theme to its objective base in the alienation of the seed, which Slater calls a 'trivial' reality.

36 St Augustine, *City of God* (New York, 1950), XV.I.

37 Theodor Mommsen, *The History of Rome* (New York, 1891), Vol. II, pp. 431–84. See also Samuel Dill, *Roman Society from Nero to Marcus Aurelius* (New York, 1956), especially Ch. 2, 'The world of the satirist', which draws widely on the contemporary material from the Domitian Age.

Juvenal's sixth satire, 'The legend of bad women', can be found in a rather more staid translation than that quoted here from Hays's book (above, note 35) in *The Satires of Juvenal*, (Ann Arbor, 1965). Compare lines 121–30. An exhaustive and useful commentary on the Latin text is included in Juvenal, *Dolvnii Iuvenalis Satvrae XIV* (Cambridge, 1955).

38 Keith Thomas, 'Women in the Civil War sects', in Trevor Aston (ed.), *Crisis in Europe 1560–1660* (New York, 1967), p. 366.

39 'occurent multae tibi Belided arque Eriphylae mane, Clytemnestram nullus non vicus habebit' Juvenal, *The Satires of Juvenal*, Bk. VI, pp. 655–6.

40 Thomas, 'Women in the Civil War sects', p. 348.

41 R. A. Knox, a historian of religion, has remarked that 'From the Montanist movement onwards, the history of enthusiasm is largely a history of female emancipation' (quoted ibid., p. 345).

42 Miles, 'The politics of feminist radicalism: a study in integrative feminism' (unpublished, University of Toronto, 1979), especially Ch. VII.

4 Creativity and procreativity

1 The phrase is Bonnard's, and what is strange is that such a perceptive historian should find Sappho's physiological concern strange – André Bonnard, *Greek Civilization* (London, 1962), p. 88. See also J. M. Edmonds (ed. and trans.), *Lyra Graeca* (London and New York, 1922), Vol. I, pp. 140–307.

2 Engels was scathing about Maine's 'tremendous discovery' which 'so far as it is correct was already in *The Communist Manifesto*' (Frederick Engels, *Origin of the Family, Private Property and the State* (New York, 1972) p. 142). Leacock's introduction to this edition deals with the arguments between the 'historical', 'functionalist' and 'comparative' schools (ibid., pp. 14–25).

3 Plato, *The Republic* (Harmondsworth, 1955), S. 457.

4 Plato, *The Laws* (Harmondsworth, 1970). See S. 70–8, 741, 781, 784.

5 De Beauvoir, *The Second Sex* (New York, 1953), p. 103. De Beauvoir is arguing that all forms of socialism favour women. Elsewhere (p. xxii) she refers to Plato's thanks to the gods for making him free and not a slave, and a man and not a woman.

6 Plato, *Timaeus*, in *The Dialogues of Plato* (London, 1970), S. 69, 70.

7 Ibid., S. 51.a.b.

8 Ibid., S. 81.b.

9 Ibid., S. 90.c. In *The Laws* (S. 944) Plato regrets that the most appropriate punishment for the cowardly soldier – to transform him into a woman – is

not possible: but he can be given 'the closest possible approximation to such a penalty: we can make him spend the rest of his days in utter safety, so that he lives with his ghastly disgrace as long as possible'.

10 Hannah Arendt, *The Human Condition* (New York, 1959), p. 201.

11 See Emil L. Fackenheim, *The Religious Dimension in Hegel's Thought* (Boston, 1967), especially p. 152, where Fackenheim comments:

> As far back as in Plato and Aristotle, the god even of pagan philosophy was so lacking in 'envy' as to disclose His nature – or some of it – to human thought. The Christian God who is love can do no less. As will be seen, He does far more. … His unity is self-complete and alive. Its self-complete life is a blessed play of Love, in which Son separates from Father only to be reunited as Spirit.

12 The translations consulted are those of Jowett and Rouse. Quotations are from the latter: Plato, *The Complete Texts of Great Dialogues of Plato* (New York, Toronto and London, 1970), pp. 214 ff. For Plato on the general inferiority of women, see also *Meno*, S. 81.b.c.; *Phaedo*, 81.d; 82.3 (both in the Rouse edition); and the myth of Er in *The Republic*, S. 609.b. ff. See also the discussion of Plato's misogyny in T. M. Robinson, *Plato's Psychology* (Toronto, 1970), pp. 87 ff.

13 Plato, *The Complete Texts*, p. 143 fn.

14 D. H. Lawrence, Henry Miller, Norman Mailer. Unlike Diotima, the women in these novels are 'smart' rather than wise; they know that only their sexuality counts for anything. They are also, unlike Diotima, tremendous in their endless sexual appetites.

15 Plato, *The Complete Texts*, p. 148.

16 Ibid., p. 150.

17 See, for example, *Protagoras*, S. 336–9, in ibid., where Socrates makes rules about the permissible length of speeches, and then applies them only to his adversary when he is losing the argument.

18 Plato, *The Laws*, S. 636–41. While a little alcohol oils male conceptual intercourse, it is absolutely forbidden before sexual intercourse: 'as a sower of seed a drunkard will be clumsy and inefficient, and he'll produce unbalanced children who are not to be trusted' (ibid., S. 775).

19 Claude Lévi-Strauss, *Totemism* (Boston, 1963), p. 53.

20 Ibid., p. 54.

21 Ibid., p. 100.

22 Victor Ehrenberg, *From Solon to Socrates* (London, 1964), p. 7. Aristotle also reports that some people of upper Libya still had 'wives in common': Aristotle, *The Politics*, London, Oxford, New York, 1969, II.iii.9.

23 I. M. Crombie, *Plato, The Midwife's Apprentice* (New York, 1964). See

also F. M. Cornford, 'The doctrine of Eros in Plato's Symposium', in his *The Unwritten Philosophy and Other Essays* (Cambridge, 1967), especially pp. 71 ff. There is some discussion of the ambiguities in Plato's conception of femininity by Viola Klein, *The Feminine Character: History of an Ideology* (London, 1971). Klein notes consistencies though, in the general history of male supremacy, 'whatever its origin' (p. 164), and quotes the male view that women have no desire for immortality without noticing that they do not need one.

24 Arthur O. Lovejoy, *The Great Chain of Being* (Cambridge, Massachusetts, 1964), pp. 55–7.

5 Production and reproduction

1 For Marx on Greek literature see Karl Marx and Frederick Engels, *Literature and Art: Selections From Their Writings* (New York, 1947), p. 19. Juliet Mitchell quotes from one of Marx's early works in which he speaks of 'the sanctification of the sexual instinct' as 'the spiritual essence of marriage' (Juliet Mitchell, *Woman's Estate* (New York, 1973), p. 110).

2 Barbara Ehrenreich and Deirdre English, *Witches, Nurses and Midwives: A History of Women Healers* (Old Westbury, New York, 1973).

3 Engels, *The Origin of the Family, Private Property and the State* (New York, 1972), pp. 119–20.

4 Ibid., p. 120.

5 Ibid.

6 Ibid., p. 145.

7 See note 2, Ch. 4 above.

8 George Thomson, *Aeschylus in Athens* (New York, 1967), p. 47. This fine book is regrettably out of print.

9 Ibid.

10 Ibid.

11 Plato, *The Republic* (Harmondsworth, 1955), Bk. X.

12 Robert Graves, *The Greek Myths* (Harmondsworth, 1955), p. 48 and *passim*.

13 Thomson, *Aeschylus in Athens*, pp. 97–9.

14 Ibid., p. 121. Evidently pigs' blood was favoured.

15 Ibid., p. 127.

16 Ibid., p. 103.

17 Mock pregnancy and parturition (couvade) are not exclusive to antiquity, but have been noted in a wide range of cultures. See Evelyn Reed,

Woman's Evolution: From Matriarchal Clan to Patriarchal Family (New York, 1975), pp. 343–6.

18 Thomson, *Aeschylus in Athens*, p. 288.

19 Claude Lévi-Strauss, *Totemism* (Boston, 1962), p. 53. See discussion in Ch. 4 above.

20 There is a large anthropological literature. Particularly interesting is Robert Briffault, on whom Reed leans extensively (Robert Briffault, *The Mothers: A Study of the Origins of Sentiments and Institutions*, (New York, Macmillan, 1952)). See also Ian Hogbin, *The Island of Menstruating Men: Religion in Wageo, New Guinea* (San Francisco, 1970).

21 Aristotle, *De Generatione Animalium* (Oxford, 1912), II.738a, 738b.

22 Engels, *The Origin of the Family*, pp. 76–9.

23 Ibid., p. 172.

24 'Far into the period of monogamy, with its certain or at least acknowledged paternity, the female line was still recognized (ibid., p. 77).

25 Ibid.

26 Thomson, *Aeschylus in Athens*, p. 282.

27 Aeschylus, *The Euminides*, pp. 658–61. This is David Grene and Richard Lattimore's translation (*Aeschylus I* (New York, 1967)). Philip Vellacott gives 'The mother is not the true parent of the child' (Aeschylus, *The Oresteian Trilogy* (Harmondsworth, 1956)).

28 Thomas Hobbes, *Leviathan* (Harmondsworth, 1968), Vol. 1, Ch. XIII, p. 183.

29 An earlier version of this section, entitled *Reproducing Marxist Man* appears in Lorenne M. G. Clark and Linda Lange (eds), *The Sexism of Social and Political Thought* (Toronto, 1979).

30 Karl Marx, *Capital* (New York, 1906), Vol. 1, p. 217.

31 Antonia Fraser, *Cromwell: The Great Protector* (New York, 1975), p. 664.

32 C. B. Macpherson, *The Political Theory of Possessive Individualism: Hobbes to Locke* (London, Oxford, New York, 1964), pp. 90–5.

33 Between Hobbes and Locke, Milton appeared to announce that marriage was no longer a political or civil affair, but was entirely spiritual. In Milton's four divorce pamphlets woman as mother gets very short shrift indeed. Those who have argued that Hobbes could not possibly have grasped the essential structure of market society at such an early date in its development should note that Milton was able to grasp quite clearly the still empirically indistinct enucleation of the family. As male creativity is able to express itself in a regenerative way in the continuous accumulation of capital it comes down from the heavens, as Marx notes. In Milton's work at least, sexuality and marriage are despatched to the spiritual realm where the sentence

imposed upon Eve operates with renewed vigour. In practice, the new phenomenon of woman as commodity as opposed to property appears on the scene. Milton's pamphlets are *The Doctrine and Discipline of Divorce* (1643–4); *The Judgement of Martin Bucer Concerning Divorce* (1644); *Tetrachordon* (1645); *Colasterion* (1645). They may be found in *The Complete Prose Works of John Milton*, Vol. II; edited with an Introduction by Ernest Sirluck (Oxford and Yale, n.d.). On the systematic use of marriage in the accumulation of landed property, see Christopher Hill and 'Clarissa Harlow and Her Times', in *Puritanism and Revolution* (London, 1968), Ch. XIV.

34 There is a fairly large literature on the subject: see, for example, V. S. Dunham, 'Sex: From Free Love to Puritanism', in A. Inkeles and K. Geiger (eds), *Soviet Society: A Book of Readings* (London, 1961); H. K. Geiger, *The Family in Soviet Russia* (Cambridge, Massachusetts, 1968); Isabel de Palencia, *Alexandra Kollontay, Ambassadress From Russia*, (New York and London, 1941); Wilhelm Reich, *The Sexual Revolution* (New York, 1971). See also Sheila Rowbotham, *Women, Resistance and Revolution*, (Harmondsworth, 1972), Chs 7 and 8; Katie Curtin, *Women in China* (New York and Toronto, 1975).

35 Reich, *The Sexual Revolution*, especially pp. 182–90.

36 Betty Friedan, *The Feminine Mystique* (New York, 1963), Ch. 5; Juliet Mitchell, *Woman's Estate* (New York, 1973), Ch. 9.

37 The 'domestic labour debate' has developed a fair literature. For recent update and bibliography see Paul Smith 'Domestic Labour and Marx's Theory of Value' in Annette Kuhn and AnnMarie Wolpe (eds), *Feminism and Materialism* (London, 1978). See also Zillah R. Eisenstein (ed.), *Capitalist Patriarchy and the Case for Socialist Feminism* (New York, 1979).

38 Selma James and M. Dalla Costa, *The Power of Women and the Subversion of the Community* (Bristol, 1973) is the major statement of this position.

39 It is important to stress that this is so only of *human* reality, that is to say, the reality which is subjectivized in a dialectic of sensory and mental experience mediated by human activity. The error which Engels perpetrates in *Anti-Dühring*, in extending the foundation of historical dialectic to all natural process, has created problems for Soviet natural science (Frederick Engels, *Herr Eugen Dühring's Revolution in Science* (New York, 1970), p. 42). Lenin goes on to criticize Mach 'because he did not understand or did not know the relation between relativism and dialectics', a relation which Lenin himself sees as emerging from 'matter organized in a definite way' (V. I. Lenin, *Materialism and Empirico-Criticism* (Moscow, 1970),

pp. 34, 217). Trotsky does not reach out beyond the ideology of Destutt de Tracy: 'Psychology is for us in the *final analysis* reducible to physiology, and the latter − to chemistry, mechanics and physics. ... The essence of Marxism ... analyzes history as one would examine a colossal laboratory record' (Leon Trotsky, 'Dialectical materialism and science' in Isaac Deutscher (ed.), *The Age of Permanent Revolution: A Trotsky Anthology* (New York, 1964), pp. 346–7). It is interesting to speculate as to whether Marx would have been more enraged by the charge of essentialism or the charge of reductionism.

40 Karl Marx and Frederick Engels, *The German Ideology* (New York, 1947), pp. 201–92 fn.

41 Cited in Erich Fromm (ed.), *Marx's Concept of Man* (New York, 1970), p. 125.

42 Ibid., p. 126.

43 Ibid., p. 138.

44 Ibid., p. 139.

45 Ibid., p. 129.

46 Marx and Engels, *The German Ideology*, Ch. 1.

47 Ibid., pp. 17–18.

48 Ibid., p. 18.

49 Marx, *Capital*, Vol. 1, Bk I, Ch. I, Section IV, p. 89.

50 Ibid., pp. 89–90.

51 'First manuscript', in Fromm (ed.), *Marx's Concept of Man*, p. 105 *et seq*.

52 Marx, *Capital*, Vol. 1, p. 87.

53 William Shakespeare, *Troilus and Cressida*, III.i.148.

54 'Thou visible God!/That solder'st close impossibilities/and makes them kiss!' (*Timon of Athens*, IV.iii), quoted in Karl Marx, *Grundrisse* (Harmondsworth, 1973), p. 163.

55 Marx and Engels, *The German Ideology*, p. 17 fn.

56 Ibid., p. 18 fn.

57 Simone de Beauvoir, *The Second Sex* (New York, 1953), p. 47.

58 Alice Wolfson's 'Budapest Journal' in *Off Our Backs*, 14 December 1970, quoted by Rowbotham, *Women, Resistance and Revolution*, p. 219.

6 Alienation and integration

1 The exploration of women's reality from 'the standpoint of women' informs the search for a feminist theory and method by many women

scholars. I am particularly indebted to the work of my colleague, Dr Dorothy Smith, for an understanding of the significance of standpoint in the production of social being. See Dorothy E. Smith, 'A sociology for women', in Julia A. Sherman and Evelyn Torbon Beck (eds), *The Prism of Sex* (Madison, Wisconsin, 1979).

2 'Our doubt is our passion and our passion is our doubt. The rest is the madness of art' (Henry James, quoted by John Le Carré, *The Naive and Sentimental Lover* (London, 1971), p. 57).

3 Mitchell, *Woman's Estate* (New York, 1973), pp. 81–2.

4 Quoted ibid., p. 81.

5 For a Marxist account of capitalism's ideological and political manipulation of population control, see Bonny Maas, *Population Target* (Toronto, 1976).

6 Herbert Marcuse, *Eros and Civilization* (New York, 1962), pp. 209–12.

Bibliography

Aeschylus, *Oresteia*, in David Grene and Richard Lattimore (ed. and trans.), *The Complete Greek Tragedies*, University of Chicago Press, 1957.

——, *The Oresteian Trilogy*, trans. Phillip Vellacott, Harmondsworth, Penguin, 1956.

Arendt, Hannah, *The Human Condition*, New York, Doubleday, 1959.

——, *On Revolution*, New York, Viking Press, 1965.

——, *On Violence*, New York, Harcourt Brace & World, 1969.

Aristotle, *The Politics*, ed. and trans. Ernest Barker, London, Oxford and New York, Oxford University Press, 1969.

——, *The Constitution of Athens*, critical and explanatory notes by John Edwin Sandys, New York, Arno Press, 1973.

——, *De Generatione Animalium*, trans. Arthur Platt, in *The Works of Aristotle*, eds J. A. Smith and W. D. Ross, Oxford, the Clarendon Press, 1912.

Bachofen, J. J., *Myth, Religion and Mother Right*, trans. Ralph Manheim, Princeton University Press, 1967 (n.d.).

Baldson, J. P. V. D., *Roman Women: Their History and Habits*, London, Bodley Head, 1962.

Beauvoir, Simone de, *The Second Sex*, trans. H. M. Parshley, New York, Bantam Books, 1953.

Bebel, August, *Women Under Socialism*, trans. Daniel de Leon, New York, Schocken Books, 1971 (1910).

Berlin, Isaiah, *Four Essays on Liberty*, Oxford University Press 1969.

Bonnard, André, *Greek Civilization*, 3 vols, vols 1 and 2 trans. Edward Sheils, vol. 3 trans. R. C. Knight, London, George Allen & Unwin, 1957–61.

Briffault, Robert, *The Mothers: A Study of the Origins of Sentiments and Institutions*, 3 vols, New York, Macmillan, 1952 (1927).

Carré, John Le, *The Naive and Sentimental Lover*, London, Hodder & Stoughton, 1971.

Cherniss, Harold, *Aristotle's Criticism of Pre-Socratic Philosophy*, New York, Octagon Books, 1971 (1935).

Clark, Lorenne M. G. and Lange, Linda (eds), *The Sexism of Social and Political Thought*, University of Toronto Press, 1979.

Cornford, F. M., *The Unwritten Philosophy and Other Essays*, Cambridge University Press, 1967.

Crombie, I. M., Plato, *The Midwife's Apprentice*, New York, Barnes & Noble, 1964.

Curtin, Katie, *Women in China*, New York and Toronto, Pathfinder Press, 1975.

Davis, M. Edward and Reva Rubin (eds), *Dr. Lee's Obstetrics for Nurses*, 18th edn, Philadelphia and London, W. B. Sanders, 1966.

Dill, Samuel, *Roman Society From Nero to Marcus Aurelius*, New York, Meridian Books, 1956 (1904).

Donnison, Jean, *Midwives and Medical Men*, London, Heinemann Educational Books, 1977.

Dunham, Vera S., 'Sex: from free love to Puritanism', in A. Inkeles and K. Geiger (eds), *Soviet Society: A Book of Readings*, London, Constable, 1961.

Edmonds, J. M. (ed. and trans.), *Lyra Graeca*, Vol. 1, London and New York, Arno Press, 1973 (1922),

Ehrenberg, Victor, *The Greek State*, London, Methuen, 1972 (1960).

——, *From Solon to Socrates*, London, Methuen, 1968.

Ehrenreich, Barbara and English, Deirdre, *Witches, Nurses and Midwives: A History of Women Healers*, Old Westbury, New York, Feminist Press, 1973.

Eisenstein, Zillah R. (ed.), *Capitalist Patriarchy and The Case for Socialist Feminism*, New York, Monthly Review Press, 1979.

Engels, Frederick, *The Condition of the Working Class in England*, London, Panther, 1969 (1845).

——, *Herr Eugen Düring's Revolution in Science (Anti-Dühring)*, trans. Emile Burns, New York, International Publishers, 1970 (1878).

——, *The Origin of the Family, Private Property and the State*, Introduction and Notes by Eleanor Burke Leacock, New York, International Publishers, 1972 (1884).

Fackenheim, Emil L., *The Religious Dimension of Hegel's Thought*, Boston, Beacon Press, 1967.

Firestone, Shulamith, *The Dialectic of Sex: The Case for Feminist Revolution*, New York, Bantam, 1971.

Fraser, Antonia, *Cromwell: The Great Protector*, New York, Knopf, 1975.

Freud, Sigmund, *Totem and Taboo*, trans. A. A. Brill, New York, Vintage Books, 1918 (1913).

Friedan, Betty, *The Feminine Mystique*, New York, Dell, 1963.

Fromm, Erich, *Marx's Concept of Man*, New York, Frederick Ungar, 1970.

Frye, Northrop, 'New directions from old', in Henry A. Murray (ed.) *Myth and Mythmaking*, Boston, Beacon Press, 1968.

Gardner, Patrick (ed.), *Theories of History*, Chicago, Free Press, 1959.

Gasset, José Ortega y, *The Revolt of the Masses*, New York, W. W. Norton, 1957 (1932).

Geiger, H. K., *The Family in Soviet Russia*, Cambridge, Massachusetts, Harvard University Press, 1968.

Graves, Robert, *The Greek Myths*, 2 vols, Harmondsworth, Penguin, 1955.

Grene, David and Lattimore, Richard (ed. and trans.), *The Complete Greek Tragedies*, University of Chicago Press, 1957.

Halle, Fannina W., *Women in Soviet Russia*, trans. Margaret M. Green, London, Routledge & Kegan Paul, 1933.

Harris, H. W., *Hegel's Development: Toward the Sunlight*, Oxford, Clarendon Press, 1972.

——, Introductory essay to Hegel's *The System of Ethical Life*, unpublished, 1975 (New York, SUNY Press, forthcoming).

Harrison, Jane E., *Prolegomena to the Study of Greek Religion*, New York, Meridian Books, 1957.

Havelock, Eric A., *The Liberal Temper in Greek Politics*, New Hampshire and London, Yale University Press, 1957.

Hays, H. R., *The Dangerous Sex: The Myth of Feminine Evil*, New York, C. P. Putnam's Sons, 1964.

Hegel, G. W. F., *Early Theological Writings*, ed. and trans. T. M. Knox, University of Chicago Press, 1948 (1802).

——, *The Phenomenology of Mind*, trans. J. B. Baillie, New York and Evanston, Harper Torchbooks, 1967 (1807).

——, *Philosophy of Right*, trans. T. M. Knox, London, Oxford and New York, Oxford University Press, 1967 (1821).

——, *The System of Ethical Life* (Hegel's 1802–3 lectures), trans. T. M. Knox and H. S. Harris, New York, SUNY Press, forthcoming.

Heitlinger, Alena, *Women and State Socialism: Sex Inequality in the Soviet Union and Czechoslovakia*, Montreal, McGill/Queens University Press, 1979.

Hill, Christopher, 'Clarissa Harlow and her times', in *Puritanism and Revolution*, London, Panther Press, 1968 (1958).

Hobbes, Thomas, *Leviathan*, Harmondsworth, Penguin, 1968 (1651).

Hogbin, Ian, *The Island of Menstruating Men: Religion in Wageo, New Guinea*, San Francisco, Chandler Publishing Co., 1970.

Iorio, Josephine, *Principles of Obstetrics and Gynecology for Nurses*, St Louis, C. V. Mosby, 1971.

James, Selma and Dalla Costa, M., *The Power of Women and the Subversion of the Community*, Bristol, Falling Wall Press, 1973.

Juvenal, *Dolvnii Iuvenalis Satvrae XIV*, ed. with a commentary by J. D. Duff, Cambridge University Press, 1955.

——, *The Satires of Juvenal*, trans. Jerome Mazzaro, Ann Arbor, University of Michigan Press, 1965.

Kauffman, Walter, *Hegel: A Reinterpretation*, New York, Doubleday Anchor, 1966.

Kelly, George Armstrong, *Idealism, Politics and History*, Cambridge University Press, 1969.

——, 'Notes on Hegel's Lordship and Bondage', in Alasdair McIntyre (ed.), *Hegel: A Collection of Critical Essays*, New York, Doubleday Anchor, 1972.

Klein, Viola, *The Feminine Character: History of an Ideology*, London, Routledge & Kegan Paul, 1971 (1946).

Kuhn, Annette and Wolpe, AnnMarie (eds), *Feminism and Materialism*, London, Routledge & Kegan Paul, 1978.

Lenhardt, Christian, 'Anamnestic solidarity: the proletariat and its manes', *Telos*, No. 25, Fall 1975.

Lenin, V. I., *Materialism and Empirico-Criticism*, Moscow, Progress Publishers, 1970 (1908).

Lévi-Strauss, Claude, *Totemism*, Boston, Beacon Press, 1963.

Locke, John, *Two Treatises of Government*, ed. Peter Laslett, New York and Scarborough, Ontario, New American Library, 1965 (1690).

Lovejoy, Arthur O., *The Great Chain of Being*, Cambridge, Massachusetts, Harvard University Press, 1964 (1936).

Maas, Bonny, *Population Target*, Toronto, Women's Press, 1976.

Machiavelli, Niccolo, 'The Mandragola', in *The Chief Works and Others*, Vol. III, ed. and trans. by Allan Gilbert, Durham, North Carolina, Duke University Press, 1965.

——, *The Prince and the Discourses*, trans. Luigi Ricci, New York, Modern Library, 1950 (c. 1513, c. 1527).

Macpherson, C. B., *Democratic Theory: Essays in Retrieval*, Oxford Clarendon Press, 1973.

——, *The Political Theory of Possessive Individualism: Hobbes to Locke*, London, Oxford and New York, Oxford University Press, 1964.

——, *The Real World of Democracy*, Toronto, Canadian Broadcasting Co., 1965.

Mandel, Ernest, *Marxist Economic Theory*, London, Merlin Press, 1968 (1962).

Marcuse, Herbert, *Eros and Civilization*, New York, Vintage Books, 1962.

Marx, Karl, *Capital*, Vol. 1, trans. Samuel Moore and Edward Aveling, New York, Modern Library, 1906 (1867).

———, *Early Writings*, trans. T. B. Bottomore, New York, London and Toronto, McGraw-Hill, 1963 (1844).

———, *Grundrisse*, trans. Martin Nicolaus, Harmondsworth, Penguin, 1973 (1853).

———, *The Poverty of Philosophy*, New York, International Publishers, 1963 (1847).

Marx, Karl and Engels, Frederick, *The Communist Manifesto*, New York, Appleton-Century-Crofts, 1955 (1848).

———, *The German Ideology*, ed. R. Pascal, New York, International Publishers, 1947 (completed but not published 1846).

———, *Literature and Art: Selections From Their Works*, New York, International Publishers, 1947.

———, *Selected Works*, 3 vols, Moscow, Progress Publishers, 1969.

Mead, Margaret, *Sex and Temperament in Three Primitive Societies*, New York, William Morrow, 1963 (1935).

Meszaros, Istvan, *Marx's Theory of Alienation*, London, Merlin Press, 1970.

Miles, Angela, 'The politics of feminist radicalism: a study in integrative feminism', unpublished doctoral dissertation, University of Toronto, 1979.

Millett, Kate, *Sexual Politics*, New York, Avon Books, 1971 (1969).

Milton, John, *The Complete Prose Works of John Milton*, Vol. II, general ed. Don M. Wolfe, New Haven, Yale University Press, 1953.

———, *Paradise Lost and Selected Poetry and Prose*, ed. Northrop Frye, New York, Chicago, San Francisco, Toronto and London, Holt, Rhinehart & Winston, 1950 (1667).

Mitchell, Juliet, *Woman's Estate*, New York, Vintage Books, 1973.

Mommsen, Theodor, *The History of Rome*, Vol. II, trans. William P. Dickson, New York, Scribners, 1891.

Morris, Desmond, *The Naked Ape*, New York, McGraw-Hill, 1967.

Mowatt, Farley, *Never Cry Wolf*, Toronto, McClelland & Stewart, 1963.

Palencia, Isabel de, *Alexandra Kollontay, Ambassadress From Russia*, New York and London, Longman's Green, 1941.

Plato, *The Complete Texts of Great Dialogues of Plato*, trans. W. H. D. Rouse, New York, Toronto and London, New American Library, 1970 (1956).

———, *The Laws*, trans. Trevor J. Saunders, Harmondsworth, Penguin, 1970.

———, *The Republic*, trans. H. D. P. Lee, Harmondsworth, Penguin, 1955.

——, *Symposium*, trans. Benjamin Jowett, New York, Library of Liberal Arts, 1956.

——, *Timaeus*, in *The Dialogues of Plato*, Vol. III, trans. Benjamin Jowett, London, Sphere, 1970.

——, *The Works of Plato*, trans. Benjamin Jowett, New York, Modern Library, 1956 (1928).

Reed, Evelyn, *Problems of Women's Liberation: A Marxist Approach*, New York, Pathfinder Press, 1970.

——, *Woman's Evolution: From Matriarchal Clan to Patriarchal Family*, New York, Pathfinder Press, 1975.

Reich, Wilhelm, *The Sexual Revolution*, trans. Theodore P. Wolfe, New York, Octagon Books, 1971.

Robinson, T. M., *Plato's Psychology*, University of Toronto Press, 1970.

Rousseau, Jean-Jacques, *Emile*, trans. Barbara Foxley, London, Everyman's Library, 1911 (1776).

Rowbotham, Sheila, *Woman's Consciousness, Man's World*, Harmondsworth, Penguin, 1973.

——, *Women, Resistance and Revolution*, Harmondsworth, Penguin, 1972.

St Augustine, *City of God*, trans. Marcus Dodds, New York, Modern Library, 1950.

Sartre, Jean-Paul, *Search for a Method*, trans. Hazel E. Barnes, New York, Vintage Books, 1968.

Schochet, Gordon J., *Patriarchalism in Political Thought*, New York, Basic Books, 1975.

Scott, Hilda, *Does Socialism Liberate Women?*, Boston, Beacon Press, 1975.

Shakespeare, William, *The Arden Shakespeare*, gen. eds Harold F. Brooks and Harold Jenkins, London, Methuen, 1967.

Shaw, George Bernard, *Major Barbara*, Harmondsworth, Penguin, 1960 (1907).

Sirluck, Ernest (ed.), *The Complete Prose Works of John Milton*, Vol. II, Oxford and Yale University Press, n.d.

Slater, George A., 'The problem', in *The Midwife in the United States: A Macy Conference*, New York, 1968.

Slater, Philip E., *The Glory of Hera*, Boston, Beacon Press, 1971.

Smith, Dorothy E., 'A sociology for women', in Julia A. Sherman and Evelyn Torbon Beck (eds), *The Prism of Sex*, Madison, University of Wisconsin Press, 1979.

Taylor, E. A., *Plato*, London, Methuen, 1966 (1926).

Terray, Emmanuel, *Marxism and 'Primitive' Societies: Two Studies by Emmanuel Terray*, trans. Mary Klopper, New York and London, Modern Reader, 1972.

Thomas, Keith, 'Women in the Civil War sects', in Trevor Aston (ed.), *Crisis in Europe 1560–1660*, New York, Doubleday Anchor, 1967.

Thomson, George, *Aeschylus in Athens*, New York, Haskell House, 1967 (1940).

Thucydides, *History of the Peloponnesian War*, trans. Rex Warner, Harmondsworth, Penguin, 1954.

Trotsky, Leon, 'Dialectical materialism and science', in Isaac Deutscher (ed.), *The Age of Permanent Revolution: A Trotsky Anthology*, New York, Dell Publishing Co., 1964.

Weber, Max, *The Theory of Social and Economic Organization*, trans. A. M. Henderson and Talcott Parsons, New York, Free Press, 1964.

Wollstonecraft, Mary, *A Vindication of the Rights of Women*, New York, W. W. Norton, 1967 (1792).

Index